PSYCHE AND BRAIN

PSYCHE AND BRAIN

The Biology of Talking Cures

Fred M. Levin

Foreword by John Gedo

KARNAC

First published in 2003 by
International Universities Press, Inc., Guilford, USA

This second edition published in 2011 by
Karnac Books Ltd
118 Finchley Road, London NW3 5HT

British Library Cataloguing in Publication Data

A C.I.P. for this book is available from the British Library

ISBN 978 1 85575 877 3

Edited, designed and produced by The Studio Publishing Services Ltd
www.publishingservicesuk.co.uk
e-mail: studio@publishingservicesuk.co.uk

www.karnacbooks.com

CONTENTS

To my patients, without whom I would never have learned a thing.

And to the memories of

Niels A. Lassen
and
Dragomir Michael Vuckovich

ACKNOWLEDGEMENTS

This edition of *Psyche and Brain* is an entirely new edition, with many changes to make it more up to date and readily understandable.

Earlier versions of some chapters were published in the following journals, as detailed below, but appear here in greatly modified form with the permission of the copyright holder:

Annual of Psychoanalysis: Chapter Thirteen, Psychoanalysis and knowledge, Part 1—The problem of representation and alternative approaches (1995), *The Annual of Psychoanalysis*, 23: 95–115; Chapter Four Part 2-The special relationship between psychoanalytic transference, similarity judgment, and the priming of memory (1995), *The Annual of Psychoanalysis*, 23: 117–130, written with E. W. Kent; Chapters One and Three derive from Part 3-Some thoughts on a line of development of a philosophy of mind (1995), 23: 131–151; Chapter Eight, Subtle is the Lord: the relationship between consciousness, the unconscious, and the executive control network (ECN) of the brain (2000), *The Annual of Psychoanalysis*, written with C. Trevarthen.

Journal of the American Psychoanalytic Association: Chapter Seven, Comments of Mark Solms' paper (1997) 45(3): 732–739; Chapter Five, Integrating some mind and brain views of transference: The phenomena (1997), 45(4): 1121–1152.

Psychoanalytic Quarterly, Chapter Fourteen, Abstracts: Neuroscience Section. The amygdala, hippocampus, and psychoanalysis, (1997) *66*(3): 555–568; Chapter Eleven, Review of Priel and Schrieber's article on bifurcation theory (1995), *LXV*(4): 843–846.

Samiksa: Chapter Fifteen, The psychoanalytic treatment of neuro-psychiatric patients (1996), *50*: 21–29; Chapter Six, Some thoughts on attention (1997), *51*: 23–30.

Yale University Press: Chapter Two, Psychoanalysis and the brain, Chapter 42 in *Psychoanalysis: The Major Concepts*, Burness Moore and Bernard Fine (Eds.) (1995), pp. 537–552.

John Gedo, MD, is Professor Emeritus of Northwestern University Feinberg School of Medicine and former faculty member and training analyst of the Chicago Institute for Psychoanalysis.

Meyer Gunther, MD, is a professor at Northwestern University Feinberg School of Medicine, and faculty member and training analyst of the Chicago Institute for Psychoanalysis and the Minneapolis Institute for Psychoanalysis.

Masao Ito, MD, PhD, is the Head of the Brain Science Institute (RIKEN), Wako, Japan, and winner of The Japan Prize.

Ernest Kent, PhD, is the Leader of the Thomas Wheatly and Marilyn Nashman Solwy-Interactive Robotics Group, National Bureau of Standards, Washington, DC.

Fred Levin is board certified in psychiatry and in psychoanalysis. He is Associate Professor of Clinical Psychiatry in the Feinberg School of Medicine of Northwestern University, Chicago, Illinois, and on faculty of The Chicago Institute for Psychoanalysis, where he is also a training and supervising psychoanalyst. Since graduating with honors from Dartmouth College in anthropology, and Northwestern University Medical School, and being an exchange student in Japan studying Japanese culture and language (Waseda University/The Stanford Center), he has been interested in bridging mind and brain, something he began in earnest during his residency training in psychiatry under Dr Roy Grinker Sr at Michael Reese Hospital in Chicago. By researching, teaching, and the clinical practice of psychotherapy and psychoanalysis, as reported in his approximately 110 publications (articles and 5 books) and many lectures around the world, he has gradually increased his understanding of how our brain seems to create its various functions, something he reports on in his current book, and hopes you find as interesting and helpful as he does.

Colwyn Trevarthen, PhD, is Professor Emeritus and Former Chairman of the Department of Psychology at the University of Edinburgh.

FOREWORD

John E. Gedo

Although there is all-but-universal agreement that all mental functions are dependent concomitants of the operations of a neural substrate, perhaps the majority of contemporary psychoanalysts dismisses this basic correlation as pragmatically irrelevant (for a recent example, see Smith, 1997). Such skepticism about the uses of biology in psychoanalytic work is probably the natural consequence of the disillusioning realization, about a generation ago, that Freud's metapsychological edifice had been erected on the quicksand of invalid biological assumptions (Holt, 1989; Rubinstein, 1997).

Once burned, twice shy. Thenceforward, many of our theoreticians committed themselves to efforts to develop constructs allegedly devoid of biological premises (see G. Klein, 1976; Schafer, 1976; Gill, 1994); others continued to use the construct language proposed by Freud with the proviso that it was henceforth to be understood metaphorically rather than as a scientific framework for the apprehension of a natural domain (Smith, 1997). A third group of contributors has explicitly disavowed the Freudian ambition to make psychoanalysis a branch of natural science; these scholars would have us content ourselves with a hermeneutic approach to the understanding of mind (D. Stern, 1997).

All of the foregoing revisionist positions within psychoanalysis simply side-step the age-old mind–body problem that contemporary scientists often refer to, ruefully, as "the hard question." Another way to put this is that, explicitly and implicitly, they construct psychoanalytic theories on purely mentalist grounds. As epistemologists who have recently dealt with psychoanalysis have uniformly concluded, hypotheses formed on such a basis are impossible to test (Grünbaum, 1984; Rubinstein, 1997; Strenger, 1991). In other words, mentalist theories can neither be confirmed nor refuted: if psychoanalysis is no part of a natural science it is, like any branch of speculative philosophy, condemned to endless disputation. (In purely hermeneutic terms, even Jungian hypotheses are as plausible as any others).[1] As Levin puts this, "without a question about mechanism, we remain hopelessly mired in religious belief."

In this volume, Fred Levin reviews the prehistory of these epistemic controversies; he traces their origins to classical antiquity and the rival philosophies of Plato and Aristotle. In agreement with Rapaport (1974), Levin sees Freud as the heir of Aristotle and Immanuel Kant. (Rapaport credits the British empiricists with fully developing this scientific tradition in the course of the Enlightenment.) In post-Freudian psychoanalysis, this empirical viewpoint was perpetuated by Hartmann (1939, 1964), Holt (1989), and Rubinstein (1997), among others (see also Bucci, 1993; Modell, 1993; S. Palombo, 1998; Rosenblatt & Thickstun, 1977; Wilson & Gedo, 1993b).

Levin rightly regards the alternative (Platonic) tradition as a religious doctrine. Through his dualism—differentiating the realm of material objects from that of mind—Descartes made possible the coexistence of science and religion in the modern world. At the same time, the dualist viewpoint should preclude the use of scientific methods in the study of mental phenomena. Rubinstein (1997) has shown that mentalist theories have only been able to account for the observations of psychoanalysis by covertly making use of various natural science assumptions, such as that of unconscious wishes or exceptionless psychological determinism. In the absence of such inconsistencies, mentalist theories are respectable enough, albeit they do not qualify *qua* natural science: As Levin recounts, even certain eminent brain scientists have adhered to the Platonic position through Cartesian dualism.

From a different viewpoint, it must be admitted that empirical science itself constitutes a belief system (Polanyi & Prosch, 1975). In certain quarters, this realization has been used (and abused) to discredit scientific findings—witness the fundamentalist claims for what they call "creation science." The scientific system entails belief in the reliability and validity of a complex of methods to attain knowledge about the natural world. Such knowledge, labeled "scientific," has led to the almost limitless increase in man's mastery of his milieu. (It is, incidentally, quite amusing that the countless opponents of science, who decry "scientism," never hesitate to consume its products, be they fertility drugs, the internet, or cardiac surgery . . .)

Human physiology is indisputably part of the natural world, but until just a few years ago so little was known about the central nervous system that mental functions could not be understood in physiological terms. Freud (1895) abandoned his effort to construct a neuropsychology, thereafter resigning himself to use of a speculative metapsychology based upon biological assumptions that were ultimately discredited. Only twenty-five years ago, Rubinstein concluded that contemporary brain science would serve him no better to undergird a similar effort. He proposed (1974, 1976) that psychoanalysis should specify the kind of neurophysiological data needed to understand the information processing that constitutes the principal subject matter.

In the past generation, a number of contributors have embarked on this interdisciplinary effort. From the side of psychoanalysis, they have included Morton Reiser (1984), Alan Schore (1997), and Fred Levin (1991), to mention only authors who have contributed important monographs to this growing literature. Levin's *Mapping the Mind* convincingly showed that psychoanalysis must encompass not only the symbolic world of the human repertory but the pre- and protolinguistic developmental levels that precede it, are partially assimilated to it, and derivatives of which persist throughout the lifespan. Hence early phases of development (and adult modes of functioning that correspond to them) may be directly illuminated by relevant neurophysiological data. In particular, developmental neurophysiology should make possible the refutation of (adultomorphic) hypotheses about the putative development of mental functions. Levin is committed to the idea that psychoanalysis and neurobiology should operate on isomorphic principles—in other words, that the concepts of "neural control" and "adaptation" are equivalent.

In the 1991 book, Levin outlined several specific applications of these basic principles. Perhaps the most impressive of these was his exposition of the psychological significance of the developing relationship of the two cerebral hemispheres. Levin inferred that regressive disestablishment of these connections is what psychoanalysis has called "repression" and "disavowal," depending on which hemisphere is disconnected from the rest of the central nervous system. The discovery that the corpus callosum becomes fully functional around the age of 3½ thus illuminates the onset of the era in which dealing with "intrapsychic conflict" becomes the typical adaptive challenge for the child.

Levin has assumed that all psychological processes (*not* mental contents) are manifestations of potentially knowable neurophysiological activities. He has concluded that neuroscientific findings about the hierarchical arrangement of the developing brain make necessary the formulation of psychoanalytic theory as a hierarchical system of "self-in-the-world-potentials." This conception parallels my own theoretical work (Gedo, 1979, 1993a; Gedo & Goldberg, 1973).[2]

Although *Mapping the Mind* was favorably reviewed, the importance of its conclusions for the actual practice of psychoanalysis was largely overlooked. Let me give one example of the practical importance of the proper understanding of brain function for adequate psychoanalytic work that Levin highlighted in 1991: Because retrieving procedural memories may not involve participation of the cerebral cortex, they may be recoverable only through pump-priming that will activate the vestibulo-cerebellar system (for instance, by repeating certain postures or gestures). Such priming will activate various modules of the central nervous system so that learning will be facilitated. Levin concludes that psychoanalysis as a technical procedure must therefore use semiotic tools that have the power to reach as many brain modules as possible (for example, through the use of metaphorical language that activates various perceptual channels, musical or gestural semiosis, or the analyst's affectivity). The traditional techniques still used by many psychoanalysts fail to provide analysands with the optimal ambience for learning.

In the present volume, Levin continues to spell out "how best to conduct a clinical analysis in keeping with the apparent organizational features of the mind–brain." Because his own Introduction spells out the crucial message of each of his chapters, I should refrain from going into detail about his presentation. Suffice it to say that, in addition to a review of the principal conclusions of *Mapping the Mind*, the present volume contains essential data necessary to develop both a learning theory and a theory of therapeutic change for psychoanalysis. Perhaps the most exciting section of the book is Levin's extensive treatment of the hitherto poorly understood topics of attention and consciousness—partly in collaboration with outstanding research scientists from brain science, neuropsychology, and other cognate disciplines.

For a psychoanalyst trained in the tranquil 1950s, as I was, the recent history of the discipline seems like a good illustration of chaos theory (one of the new intellectual tools applicable to the field discussed by Levin): changes in our view of mental life are following each other in ever more dizzying succession, but this seeming disorder actually constitutes the emergence of a set of more complex, sophisticated, and empirically based hypotheses in counterpoint to a variety of arbitrary, Platonic conceptions their adherents cling to with religious fervor. If psychoanalysis in America is ever to regain public favor, it must choose the tradition of Aristotle, Freud, Rubinstein—and Fred Levin.

Chicago

Introduction

Psyche and Brain represents a report of my progress in updating psychoanalysis since completing *Mapping the Mind*. The original volume was the cutting edge, *ca* 1991; it showed how psychoanalysis and cognitive neuroscience inform each other, illuminating various matters of psychoanalytic interest in a useful way: transference, defense, interpretation, dreams, self cohesion, psychological development, learning, memory, and adaptation. The analysis of such variables draws on the insights of untold numbers of scholars upon whose shoulders we currently stand. We need to become more familiar with their work.

Understanding the psychobiology of talking cures can improve our understanding of much within psychoanalysis and is deeply relevant to our clinical work. The problem is that the pace of research has continuously increased, making it difficult for individual practitioners to stay informed. To make matters worse, questions always outnumber answers in any quest for new knowledge, so the holy grail of a mind–brain synthesis will ever remain out of reach. But if things never get any easier, how then, should we orient our self towards a perpetuity of insufficient knowledge? My suggestion is that we take solace in Freud's unique perspective when confronting daunting tasks. He says "if we cannot see things clearly . . . [it helps to] . . . strive to describe the unclarity (die Unklarheiten) more precisely" (Freud in Kiell, 1988, p. 533). My hope in writing this book has been to follow Freud's suggestion here and better describe the Unklarheiten.

Section I (Retrospect) begins with two orienting chapters. Chapter One traces knowledge acquisition by combining the viewpoints of psychoanalysis and of philosophy. Specifically, I map a line of development of philosophy of mind from Aristotle to Kant to Freud. Chapter Two covers additional history of mind–brain research, especially as this concerns psychological development, complementing and extending discussions of similar matters in my book *Mapping the Mind*. The work of Lichtenberg and others on motivational systems is discussed, as well as that of the late Michael Basch on disavowal. Basch's work greatly influenced clinical psychoanalysis; my approach in turn has been significantly influenced by my friendship with this analytic scholar with a most special human touch, and my respect for his intellect.

Section II (Psychoanalysis and gnosis) approaches how the mind–brain deals with the acquisition, transfer, modification, and utilization of information. Chapter Three suggests a tentative but credible explanation for mankind's sometimes limited capacity to jettison its tightly held beliefs and acquire new ones: namely, *sometimes our beliefs reflect critical psychic structure and function, rather than mere psychic content*. My point here is that when our beliefs are relatively indispensable, we cannot really question them, for doing so increases our fear of or invites actual mental collapse. To allow for real change in our belief systems, compensatory structures first have to be established that render our beliefs mere contents of the mind. Only then can any one begin to allow the degree of temporary suspension of belief required for cautious reconsideration (modification), in other words, for genuine learning and change in our thinking to occur.

Chapter Four, co-written with Ernest Kent, examines an original cybernetic model of mind–brain that also expands the concept of transference by connecting it to two critical areas: research in neuroscience (on memory priming), and in cognitive psychology (on similarity judgment). In other words, *there is reason to believe that psychoanalysis, neuroscience, and cognitive psychology are, by their attention to such variables as transference, priming, and similarity, attempting to fathom a single core phenomenon of common interest.* In a nutshell, this core phenomenon has a special connection with learning: how we continuously identify similarities between past and present experience so as to work through our feelings, relive experience, and transfer knowledge between various content domains.

The concept of transference is important enough to tackle within this monograph from a unique variety of perspectives. The goal in repeatedly returning to details of learning and memory in relation to transference is as follows: *clinicians need sufficient understanding of the specific mind–brain mechanisms of transference in order to optimally exploit it within the treatment situation.* This book not only shows you how: it makes efforts to explain the basis for various phenomena in terms of closely related theories from multiple disciplines.

Chapter Five reviews and integrates psychoanalytic and extra-analytic viewpoints on transference, including a discussion of what motivates the transference, and what makes it adaptive both personally and in an evolutionary sense. This moves us perceptually closer to a credible *psychoanalytic theory of learning*, credible because it respects interdisciplinary knowledge of mind–brain. *My goal is to explain how certain technical measures, employed within treatment, and empirically found to be useful, might actually work.* For example, *it is possible that spontaneity in general and free association in particular (as occurs in every clinical psychoanalysis) work by creating learning readiness ("windows") through their activation of specific varieties of working memory.* In other words, *the activation of working memory may be the sine qua non for learning to occur, and analysis facilitates this activation* by a variety of means which every clinician can learn.

Section III (Conscious and unconscious systems) begins with Chapter Six on attention. It introduces the reader to the research of Posner (on *executive control*), and of Shevrin (on the role of conscious process), and through some clinical cases begins a major theme of the book: determining the precise relationship between conscious and unconscious (nonconscious) systems.

The first part of Chapter Seven (along with Chapters Eight, Nine, and Ten) focuses on conscious and unconscious processing. Few topics within psychoanalysis are as deeply meaningful, or as potentially confusing and rewarding as these two, obviously inter-related systems. Building from an essay on consciousness by Mark Solms (1997) I explore the functions of consciousness in detail. According to Howard Shevrin (1997a, 1998a,b), *consciousness tags experience into various categories, differentiating the kinds of mental activity from each other* (such as current perceptions versus wishes, fears, imagining, dreaming, etc.). In this way the reality-conferring and memory-organizing functions of consciousness are highlighted. All the chapters exploring the complex relations between unconscious and conscious systems also help to clarify the role of maintaining and modifying data bases of mind–brain without which learning could not ever occur. Much that is clinically and theoretically useful flows from our attempts to depict with precision the mind–brain's exact machinery for learning. This also means taking into account the latest research of Gerald Edelman and colleagues.

Chapter Eight, co-authored with Colwyn Trevarthen, follows up on the observation of John Gedo (1994, 1996a,b) that patients with early and continuing emotional trauma tend to manifest in their psychoanalysis disturbances in their states of consciousness as a consequence of post traumatic stress disorder (PTSD). The possible reasons for such shifts in consciousness are then systematically reviewed, tying together aspects of the work of Gedo, Posner, Levin, Trevarthen, Shevrin, Opatow, and Edelman.

Chapters Nine and Ten, co-authored with Gedo, Ito, and Trevarthen, rework an important paper by Ito (1998) on the subject of conscious and unconscious process, a subject of great interest to psychoanalysts and neuroscientists alike. I am also grateful to Michael Posner and Howard Shevrin for reviewing these chapters before publication. It is exciting when brain scientists, psychologists, and analysts collaborate on mind–brain research, as is the case in most of the chapters of this monograph.

In Section IV (Psychoanalysis and chaos theory) Chapters Eleven and Twelve take up the subjects of development, learning, and psychopathology and attempt a synthesis of psychoanalysis and chaos theory. Chaos theory has attracted a significant cohort of polymath analysts with unusual creativity; this group is providing us with undeniably novel insights into mind–brain developmental processes. The reader will greatly appreciate how *healthy mind–brains are those with sufficient complexity and freedom of "movement". Psychoanalysis appears to reduce psychopathology by also adding com-*

plexity, which translates sometimes into adaptability. In a wonderful visual metaphor, Shevrin describes this as follows: *healthy minds learn to "flex", much like prize fighters learn to shift from one foot to another in order to better throw or to dodge punches.*

Section V (Clinical consequences) conveys more of the clinical importance to psychoanalysis of integrating psychobiological research and knowledge of brain. Chapter Thirteen deals with the limits of analyzing mind–brain with the outdated concept of internal representations, a terminology that sometimes cloaks our ignorance. Much better is thinking about expert systems, since the key to knowledge utilization is updating useful mind–brain databases that started during our infancy. From this orientation I present a personal set of *psychoanalytic operating principles* which now guide my clinical psychoanalytic work with patients, and the *cognitive neuroscientific observations* from which they derive. *Understanding the biology of mind–brain helps our learning to be more effective psychoanalysts and psychotherapists.* And what happens clinically as a consequence sometimes becomes a critical test of the truth value of any analytic efforts, both clinical work and theorizing.

Chapter Fourteen presents a summary of aspects of learning, attention, and memory research on the amygdalar/hippocampal systems, and integrates this research with psychoanalytic perspectives. The work of Posner on visual attention operationalizes our understanding of consciousness. His detailed studies with Rothbart, Raichle, and others are summarized, including, most recently, Posner's attention to the time course during early childhood of the development of systems for neural control of selective attention.

Chapter Fifteen, co-authored with M. S. Gunther, examines the clinical application of the ideas presented in this monograph, but this time within the context of the neuro-psychiatric patient. Some clinical vignettes of persons with brain damage are presented and discussed, asking what a psychoanalyst can contribute as a member of a treatment team. *Psychoanalysis has much to offer patients with psychological and brain deficits; but they in turn have much to teach psychoanalysis about mind–brain relationships.* The stories of real patients, attended by real mental health professionals, illuminates the limitations and benefits of our current knowledge, and highlights the critical need for reaching across disciplinary boundaries to improve our success rate. *Interdisciplinary teams are simply more effective than going it alone in the sense of using the insights of just one discipline.*

Finally, the Overview Chapter summarizes specific principles underlying useful mind–brain correlations derived throughout this monograph. These principles are compared to those reported in *Mapping the Mind*, to better synthesize my research efforts over the past several decades, and also in my follow-up book, *Emotion and the Psychodynamics of the Cerebellum* (2009).

As you might expect from any collection of papers largely by a single author, there are inevitable gaps, errors, overlaps, idiosyncracies, and redundancies. The limits of my insight and those of mind–brain science generally cannot fail to stand out; yet one need not be embarrassed by such limitations. For as noted above, there are advantages in simply describing, as clearly as possible, what remains as yet unclear. I believe, in fact, it is principally our ability to describe sufficiently what we do *not* know well enough that determines how much more we can personally learn. For no one searches intensively for what they believe they already possess! And the same is true for entire fields of science. *Knowing that our psychoanalytic knowledge is incomplete is a significant part of what assures the future success of the field of psychoanalysis, for it keeps us searching for newer better answers to old questions.* But these answers do not need to come just from psychoanalysis proper.

Fred Levin

NOTES

1. Edelson (1988) believes—contrary to the assertions of Grünbaum (1984)—that in principle psychoanalytic hypotheses could be validated on clinical grounds alone. However, he agrees that such studies have never been performed. Consequently, for the moment, validation/refutation in psychoanalysis can only be determined in terms of the congruence of hypotheses with the known functioning of the central nervous system. As Levin (1991) was probably the first to point out, extraclinical validations may also take place through the resort to the findings of cognitive psychology and communications science. It should be noted, however, that these disciplines are also obliged continually to revise their theories in the light of advances in (developmental) neurophysiology.

2. The congruence of our views has led us to collaborate in a number of ways, including some input on my part as Levin was thinking through his chapters on consciousness in the present volume. Levin shares authorship in circumstances that many others would not even grace with a note of acknowledgment.

SECTION I
RETROSPECT

CHAPTER ONE

The philosophical background to Freud: thinking about thinking*

Fred Levin

et's begin with an exploration of some of the philosophical issues that are raised by contemporary psychoanalytic theory,[1] concentrating on a line of development of philosophy of mind in which the major nodal points are the contributions of Aristotle, Kant, and Freud. *Philosophy of mind has an impact on several aspects of psychoanalytic concern.*[2] *One such area is how our philosophical beliefs about such things as knowledge acquisition might influence psychoanalytic theorizing and the way we treat our patients.* A second area concerns creativity,[3] which I conceptualize as depending foremost upon one's ability to temporarily suspend personal belief systems in favor of alternative beliefs. In turn, I assume that the ability to suspend belief varies directly with the extent to which such belief systems function as dispensable parts of one's self.[4] I further assume that mental health is associated with a cohesiveness of the self, in the sense of personal belief systems that are relatively

* An early version of this paper was presented to the University of Illinois Medical School, Circle Campus, Department of Psychiatry, September 15, 1991, Chicago, Illinois, and published as Levin, 1995d.

independent of each other and not required for thinking generally (see Chapter Three), nor for our self-esteem.

Of course, the topic of knowledge acquisition has a rich history in our field and analytic scholars have written often and insightfully about such matters, such as Rapaport (1951b, especially pp. 721–723), Waelder (1962), Hartmann (1964), Holt (1967), Schlessinger et al. (1967), Klein (1968, 1976), Gill (1976), Basch (1976), Modell (1978, 1993), and Gedo (1986). There are also many excellent general works on the subject by non-analysts, for example, White's philosophical monograph (1982, especially chapters four and five), Kent's mathematical–neurophysiological treatise (1981), and Eickelman's learned discussion of the interface between knowledge and culture (1985).

This chapter is organized in the following manner. The discussion begins with a definition of epistemology and a sample of three variations of the central epistemological questions that are the subject of this chapter. There follows a review of the decisive contributions of Aristotle, Kant, and Freud, in particular, examining how their work forms a developmental sequence. *It is easier to comprehend the philosophical foundation of a psychoanalytic theory of learning, which this monograph aims for, when it is viewed in the larger context of a philosophy of mind.* Along the way, some case material is presented to illustrate the clinical relevance of some of the points discussed.

Epistemology: background and definition

According to the dictionary (Random House, 1988, s.v.) epistemology is "a branch of philosophy that investigates the origin, nature, methods and limits of human knowledge". One of the major epistemological questions can be expressed variously: "How do humans acquire knowledge from perception" (Aristotle; from the fourth century BCE)? Or, "How is it possible that reasoning arrives at conclusions which coincide with the outcome of processes occurring in reality?" (Rapaport's rephrasing of Leibniz's question, quoted in Gedo, 1986, p. 78; originating in the seventeenth century). Or, "How can the apparatus regulated by the pleasure principle (i.e., the drives) be also adapted to reality?" (Rapaport, 1951b, pp. 721–722, n. 6; from the mid twentieth century). *Clearly, the historical perspective demonstrates the question asked evolves over time, as the various sciences involved (including psychoanalysis in modern times) differentiate themselves from philosophy. And most importantly, there can be no doubt that the way the question about knowledge acquisition is posed necessarily influences whether and how it is answered.*

Knowledge can be operationally defined as that information which people can recall or demonstrate which is most valued by some subgroup within a given culture. Psychoanalysts do not usually think of themselves as being much concerned with knowledge in the abstract, but rather with the experience of an individual as he comes to know, believe, or feel something in particular to be true. In principle, however, analytic investigation sometimes is remarkably similar to the perspective of philosophers who ask general questions about the use of evidence. Moreover, there are times when analysts, like philosophers, collect evidence for the purpose of constructing generalized theories, especially of human motivation and/or personal experience.

Later, in Chapter Thirteen, I will present Rapaport's thinking about human development, showing how he integrates the views of Freud, Piaget, and Hartmann. Rapaport essentially describes the classical psychoanalytic concepts of introjection, identification, and a structuralization process in which aspects of the self's experience of another person who is loved and/or admired becomes enduring acquisitions in the form of mental functions. What is most interesting, however, is that we can deviate from the traditional analytical perspective yet describe exactly the same learning phenomena from the point of view of the progressive widening and deepening of databases of the mind–brain (see Chapter Four). Obviously, we are considering no less than two completely different yet complementary approaches to knowledge acquisition.

The change in orientation between Chapters Four and Thirteen, which will become obvious to the reader, represents my attempt to integrate the psychoanalytic with modern cognitive psychological and neuroscientific frameworks. It is my belief that *interdisciplinary viewpoints help our psychoanalytic theorizing, just as they were decisive for Rapaport's original creation of a psychoanalytic theory of learning* (about what he considered "structuralization"). Obviously, one reason why interdisciplinary efforts succeed more than some other approaches is that by their very nature as compromise formations they involve the temporary suspension of old belief systems that favor the ascendancy of new paradigms (see below).

An important step in this monograph, it turns out, is refining and extending Rapaport's psychoanalytic learning theory. This first occurs when Gedo and Goldberg create their hierarchical, developmental model (especially as modified most recently by Gedo, 1993a,b, 1997). This has the advantage of being consistent with data from child development, neuroscience, and psychoanalytic studies. That is, the Gedo model, like Rapaport's, is rooted in an interdisciplinary framework and has a very broad applicability. Of course, many details of such a modern learning theory need to be filled in, but now there can be little doubt that the outlines of such a general conception are gradually coming into focus.

But what are the implications for psychoanalysis of a general theory of learning (as is also considered in Chapter Thirteen), or an updated theory of transference, with its reference to memory priming and to judging similarity (as appears in Chapter Four)? Still more specifically, under the influence of what theory/theories of mind do we think and act with patients in the consulting room?

It would be possible, were one versed broadly in the philosophy of psychoanalysis or of mind, to write *in extensa* about the various philosophical nuances of such theorizing. Rapaport (1951b) in fact does so when he constructs his PhD thesis on the subject of philosophical contributions to the idea of mental association, matters that are part of his personal preparation for thinking about thinking psychoanalytically. However, because of the obvious inevitable limitations of time, space, and our personal knowledge of philosophy, the following discussions can do no more in each era than to consider various idiosyncratic outlines of the contributions of scholars such as Aristotle, Kant, and Freud to the present discussion. Interestingly enough, however, this does not prevent some useful creation of new theory, to fill in the gaps in our knowledge.

Aristotle: curiosity about psyche sets the stage for empiricism

Aristotle is important to our discussion about knowledge because he is arguably the first person we know of to employ an experimental/empirical approach to the study of novel human knowledge (Barnes, 1982). In fact Aristotle is the one who originates the idea of category without which we could not contemplate varieties of knowledge, and he also invents a vocabulary to describe logical thinking tersely. Perhaps even more important, however, is the fact that Aristotle further establishes the first general "rules of validity," thus making it possible for anyone after him to acquire scientific knowledge in the consensually validatable sense (Grene, 1979, p. 69).

Unfortunately, a portion of Aristotle's work seems to have been mistranslated from the original Greek into Latin by medieval religious scholars in a manner that has confused our appreciation of the man and his approach to novelty. Specifically, the word "psyche" is mistranslated as "soul" rather than in the way I believe Aristotle intends (Barnes, 1982, p. 65). Let me explain.

Judging from the twelve volumes of Aristotle's complete works (Ross, 1955–1962), *a better translation of "psyche" would appear to be "mind"* in the following sense: "that agency, that is, that interior, localizable part of the human body (and the bodies of animals), that is capable of learning (i.e., acquiring knowledge) from sense perception" (Aristotle in Ross, 1955–1962, *Analytica Posteriora*, 100b05). Aristotle is an enormously curious man. He thus believes that "psyche" (meaning "mind" in the above sense) is the proper study of science, not religion, and that through such techniques as comparative anatomy and physiology it ought to be possible to understand (mental) activities and the life process itself (Aristotle in Ross, 1955–1962, *De Partibus Animalium*, 641a25–30). Aristotle's novel idea of "psyche" thus helps free his mind to extend his scientific observations beyond his personal religious beliefs, that is, to keep the two domains separate.

The major reason Aristotle does not make clear that his primary interest is in mind–brain as we presently understand these terms is because during his Age no one understood the true role of the brain in mental activity. In fact, the brain in ancient Greece was believed to be merely an agent for cooling the blood, which was thought to be heated by the heart. The idea of the time was that mental activity suffers when the brain fails in its presumed cooling function, and this is how damage from blows to the head was explained in ancient times. However, even though Aristotle's anatomy and physiology are wrong regarding the brain, there seems to be no doubt that he is writing about the nature of mind (and what will eventually be localizable as brain) from an experimental, biological perspective. Moreover, his approach at times involves dissections carried out by Aristotle himself. The fact that his father was a physician no doubt played a decisive role in Aristotle's pragmatic approach to biology.

Early in the twentieth century, debates occur such as those between Russell and Poincaré, over whether knowledge is the product of logic or intuition. This debate, however, really begins 2,300 years ago when Aristotle introduces the concept of "category." For this purpose he borrows a Greek word that, in the legal parlance of his day, means "that of which a person is accused [that is, a *type* of crime]" and adapts this concrete reference word to designate abstract, logical *kinds* of "predication" (Ryle, 1971, p. 67). By predication, he means the predicate of various sentences such as "Socrates is a man" or "Socrates is mortal." Aristotle lists ten (sometimes fewer) general types (of predicate or "categories"): such things as "quality," "quantity," "relation," "substance," "state/condition," and so on (p. 67). It is hard to tell from Aristotle's work how universal or particular he believes such categories to be.

It is virtually impossible for us to imagine mental life without a concept of "category" in the Aristotelian sense, so we may easily underestimate the revolutionary advance he creates by coining the term. Aristotle's contributions to epistemology are thus multiple: (1) at the same time that he creates a terminology he also (2) gives us a systematic analytical method for abstract notation (i.e., a symbolic logic) in which letters stand for premises (for example, "If A, then B"), and (3) he then uses these conceptual tools extensively to analyze the thinking of his time (i.e., *Aristotle discovers "mind" as a subject of study in the scientific sense, and for him mind includes the study of biology*). Most crucial to our discussion (4) *he asks how perception leads to knowledge,* and (5) he establishes rules of validity to apply to our answers to questions generally. Each of these contributions is, of course, momentous; however, the fourth and fifth contributions seem decisive for epistemology, for *without a question about mechanism we would remain hopelessly mired in religious belief;* moreover, without rules of validity there could be no science as we know it, that is, in the sense of a discipline with empirical observations and reproducible results.

The clarification of the mistranslation of the word "psyche" as "soul," to which I refer above, is extremely important historically, because this is what makes it possible to appreciate Aristotle's distinctive achievements. What is crucial would appear to be the distinction between Platonic and Socratic idealism/vitalism on the one hand and Aristotelian empiricism/materialism on the other, that is, between a belief in ideal forms, conceived of as inseparable from religious experience, versus experimentally based categories, conceived of within a scientific matrix, wholly separable from religion.

In short, if one believes that Aristotle's scientific writings explore matters that pertain to the existence of a Supreme Being and an immortal soul, as some religious scholars do, then one necessarily sees Aristotle and his theories differently (and falsely, I believe), as a link in a chain of idealism/vitalism that extends from Socrates and Plato, through Aristotle, to the present time. On the other hand, if one sees Aristotle as publicly preoccupied in his scientific writings with science alone, but *willing to temporarily suspend his personal religious beliefs* (for example, while pondering the anatomical and physiological facts that bear on understanding the mechanisms by which sensory perceptions become organized as knowledge), then one will see Aristotle (truly) as the champion of a separate rationalist, scientific philosophy that flowers after another 2000 years (in the seventeenth and eighteenth centuries). In my opinion, the debate between idealism/vitalism versus empiricism/modern materialism invariably but inappropriately inserts itself into scientific debates whenever discoveries are experienced as threatening to one's belief system, whether religious or scientific. And this is not without clinical implications for psychoanalysis.

Immanuel Kant: the influence of mind on perception lays the foundation for neuropsychology

It is impossible to discuss philosophy of mind or theories of learning without reference to Immanuel Kant. To begin with, Kant alters Aristotle's meaning of category significantly.[5] Interestingly for this discussion, Kant's form of empiricism is uniquely complex, including as it does several incompatible yet important ideas (Collins,

1985), an idea I shall elaborate upon shortly and compare with Freud's epistemology. Most important, however, is Kant's recognition that there can be no empirical observations without the influence of mind; that is, that mind influences perception, which is no longer seen as a passive process. In fact, Kant postulates that external reality itself is nothing but a construct of mind, and essentially has no independent existence, a truly subjective empiricism (Collins, 1985).

The key to Kant's appreciation of the mind's influence on perception is his understanding that our very concepts themselves belong to the framework of knowledge; that is, they represent "ways in which the propositional structures extracted in logical theory function as the controlling principles of natural knowledge" (Ryle, 1971, p. 69). Thus, although our categories "provide an objective basis for knowing the world . . . there . . . [must be] times when mind is incapable of unfettered, intuitive insights" (Walsh, 1971, p. 220). Another way of saying the same thing is that in place of perception is apperception, a process that involves covert emotional influences of various kinds.

Consequently, Kant generally divides the world into two parts: the "noumenal", associated with what he designates as "practical reason, "final truths, and the "thing itself" ("Das Ding an Sich"), which he imagines to be fundamentally unknowable; and the "phenomenal," associated with lawfulness, causality, and determinism, and which is knowable on the basis of something he calls "pure reason" (Walsh, 1971, pp. 219–220). Put differently, these two domains relate, respectively, to either those things that are important to us because they have moral value and authority (but are not subjectable to proof), or those things that have truth value (and can or must be subjected to proof), such as scientific theorizing.

As an interesting aside, one can say that Kant resembles Freud in his willingness to live with the inconsistencies or complexities of his thoughts and not have to tidy them up with simplifying theories; hence, he develops a cumbersome philosophical system that is nonetheless reflective of some important internal reality of mind. Unlike Freud, however, Kant does not elaborate any theory to begin to account for the existence of simultaneous, conflicting ideas in the mind; in fact, he is not interested in doing so because his purpose is different.

Kant's aim seems to be primarily to clarify the importance and structure of scientific method while simultaneously establishing the necessity and value (in practical terms) of human morality. In other words, Kant's philosophic creativity is facilitated by his temporarily and selectively suspending his belief systems.

Kant is excited by the power of Isaac Newton's discoveries and he wishes to emulate Newton's scientific approach, yet without giving up his personal metaphysics, that is, his belief in God, free will, and an everlasting soul. (It is of course an interesting question, to what extent one ends up modifying one's personal philosophical, scientific, or religious beliefs in order to be able to be truly creative over extended periods of time.)

Philosophers of Kant's day offend Kant greatly by trying to prove their metaphysics (i.e., religious doctrine) rather than merely being content with belief. Kant's response is to debunk the details of their logic, arguing that "[while] there . . . must be answers to man's causal questions about empirically ascertainable events . . . there can be no answers to parallel questions about supposed states of affairs transcending human experiment and observations" (Kant in Ryle, 1971, p. 69). Here again, as in the foregoing discussion of Aristotle, we see a philosopher–scientist attempting a disciplined analysis of a subject matter in a manner that attempts to neutralize insofar as is practical the effects of his personal religious belief system, but which he also agrees beforehand is in principle impossible. *One can see in this self-conscious creativity of Kant a foreshadowing of Freud's discovery years later of the surprising existence of simultaneously incompatible ideas in the mind.*

But there is, thus, no doubt that by creatively introducing into philosophy the idea that the objectivity of (experimental) observations cannot be taken for granted Kant moves us imperceptibly closer to what will eventually crystallize as neuropsychology hundreds of years later. The key step in this later development will be the shift from Kant's idea of mental influence, to the modern idea of mind–brain's active role in seeking out perceptions that are needed, and therefore discovered in the real world. That is, our mind–brain tells our eyes what to look for, and "seeing" selectively fulfills this inner request (or need) for information. It is also apparent that without a Kantian notion of mental subjectivity, Freud could never have conceived such a concept as transference.

Yet at the same time as we are grateful to Kant for identifying the general influence of emotion in perception, we can wonder why he is not able or willing to further specify the role of religious and other emotions in his own thoughts. As Cavell (1988) puts it, Kant waffles on a number of questions about the nature of knowledge, leaving us with a notion that truth value depends merely upon "its consistency with a system of beliefs" (p. 864). But the answer can only be that *in creating the category of the "noumenal" Kant is preserving his own religious beliefs from scrutiny by placing them in the logical category of "Ding an Sich," which is by definition that which requires no further examination. Of course, he is also protecting himself from the scrutiny of others* because in Kant's day opposing or challenging religious teachings brought with it the danger of severe penalties from those authorities who also controlled the universities (and a large part of life itself). For example, in spite of Descartes's earlier efforts to stand up to Rome, the right to think freely was not yet conceded as an academic or basic human right even to geniuses like Kant.[6]

Freud: the unfettered investigation of mind

Of course, it is unfair for us to ask of Kant what we accomplish today only with the aid of psychoanalysis, and with the constitutional right to freedom of thought. For it was not until Freud that humankind began to examine mind systematically, that is, to turn the scientific perspective upon those aspects of mental life that Kant decides or needs to leave unexplored. Moreover, even modern scientists (or philosophers) may find it difficult at times to acknowledge the extent to which humankind's observations and innovations emanate from or are potentially in conflict with private aspects of our "psyche."

Psychoanalysis represents both a body of knowledge and a method of investigation; as such it contributes to the epistemological discussion with which I began this Chapter. Freud's major contribution to a philosophy of mind lies in three related ideas: (1) his introducing affects into the debate (in his theory of conflict and drive) (Modell, 1993); (2) his unique method of solving the problem of objectifying the subjective, which had become an intractable problem within philosophy before Freud (Modell, 1993), and which will be described presently; and (3) his postulation and examination of a Dynamic Unconscious (Holt, 1967). In Freud's (1915e) epistemology there can be no doubt of his utilization of Kant:

> In psychoanalysis there is no choice for us but to assert that mental processes are in themselves unconscious and to liken the perception of them by means of consciousness to the perception of the external world by means of the sense-organs . . . The psychoanalytic assumption of unconscious mental activity appears to us, on the one hand, as a further expansion of the primitive animism [narcissism?] which caused us to see copies of our conscious all around us, and, on the other hand, as an extension of the connections undertaken by Kant of our views on external perception. Just as Kant warned us not to overlook the fact that our perceptions are selectively conditioned and must not be regarded as identical with what is perceived though [the] unknowable [i.e. Das Ding an Sich], so psychoanalysis warns us not to equate perception by means of consciousness with the unconscious mental processes that are their object. Like the physical, the psychical is not necessarily in reality what it appears to us to be. We shall be glad to learn, however, that the correction of internal perception, will turn out not to offer such great difficulties as the correction of external perception, that internal objects are less unknowable than the external world. [p. 171]

Philosophy wrestled unsatisfactorily with mind until Freud. Thereafter, philosophers have benefited greatly from his creation of psychoanalysis and its novel insights into the nature of mind–brain, even although they may freely object to some of Freud's specific conclusions. In a series of discussions, Arnold Modell (1978, 1993) makes explicit how Freud's epistemology works toward a solution of the so-called philosophical paradox of objectifying the subjective.

Freud's primary philosophical method is to carefully sustain an ambiguity in his description of mind by alternating between statements that describe mental activities in scientific terminology (that is, from an external observer perspective) and statements that anthropomorphize mental agencies in a highly experimental language (Modell, 1993). In this way, he weaves together the Weltanschauungen of two major perspectives: the human, reflective sciences ("Geisteswissenschaft") and the impersonal, natural sciences ("Naturwissenschaft"), a distinction that goes back at least

to Vico in the eighteenth century (Modell, 1978, p. 648). This distinction will be considered further below under the rubric of varieties
of knowing.

The topic of Freud's epistemology is further covered by
Hartmann (1960), who summarizes the situation neatly in his
pioneering comments on psychoanalysis and moral values. As
Hartmann notes, although psychoanalysis has no Weltanschauung
itself, this

> does not, of course mean that the analyst will underrate or depre-
> ciate the . . . significance of "Weltanschauungen" in the individual
> or in society. [Moreover,] while the analyst learns to keep his
> personal values from intruding into the analytic situation, *this does
> not generally lead to the detachment of his interest from [such]* . . .
> concerns. Quite naturally, analysts and others acquainted with
> analysis will use its data and hypotheses also in their practical
> approach to questions of a moral, social, political, or artistic nature.
> What psychoanalysis can give them in this respect is increased
> psychological understanding . . . [p. 61, my emphasis]

According to Hartmann, "*a systematic psychology of 'moral behavior,' including the genetic [i.e. developmental] aspect, had hardly been in
existence before Freud*" (p. 24, my emphasis). Continuing, "in clearly
rejecting any and all religious creeds and systems, [Freud, as scien-
tist] did not reject the moral aspects of the Western tradition. He
wished, however, that one could establish these on nonreligious
grounds" (p. 18). As with Aristotle and Kant, Freud is a deeply
moral man; where he differs is in his curiosity and perseverance in
studying the personal origins of all things, morality, religion, and
science included.

In short, as analysts we are well aware of Freud's accomplishments in penetrating the privacy of mental life, to the point of
appreciating the origin of (individual) morality itself, something
which even Plato asserts cannot be understood properly without
our knowing the nature of man (Hartmann, 1960, p. 25). Thus we
have come full tilt from Aristotle's beginnings in creating a scientific orientation as something independent of religion (that is,
which allows the study of "mind" scientifically in relation to the
temporary suspension of various belief systems) to Kant's clarifications of observational bias in perception (with his willingness to go

quite far in suspending belief, although obviously on a selective basis), to Freud's exploration of unconscious mental life (based on his radical willingness to suspend belief seemingly without limit). Along the way we can more easily see how only gradually in human history is brain discovered, long after the discovery of mind; how long it takes humankind to be aware of the subjectivity of the mind's observations; and how resistant all humans are to facing their unconscious depths, whether they be scientists or philosophers. It has also taken a very long time for religion and science to coexist.

CHAPTER TWO

Psychoanalysis and the brain*

Introduction

H aving commented upon the philosophical basis of psychoanalysis, we are ready to begin our journey into understanding as much as possible of mind–brain. We are living
during a worldwide scientific revolution in which knowledge of the
brain and behavior is expanding dramatically, leading to a convergence of psychological and neuroscientific viewpoints. In
Edinburgh, Trevarthen (1989, 1995) has illuminated the micro-
orchestration of mother–infant communication, while in the United
States Demos (1985), D. Stern (1985), Basch (1975, 1976, 1983),
Lichtenberg (1983, 1989a,b), and others have clarified details of
infant development, which make it apparent that we begin our lives
with many surprising abilities that facilitate bonding. The newer
work on infant development can be seen as properly following
upon the pioneering child research of Anna Freud (1965), Melanie
Klein, Winnicott (1960, 1969), Spitz (1945, 1965), and many others.

---

* An earlier version was published as Levin, 1995e.

MacLean (1985) has created a triune brain theory from which Antrobus, Ehrlichman, Werner, and Wollman (1982), Baer (1989), Moore (1988), and others have derived many significant insights. In fact, it was MacLean who coined the term "limbic system" and, along with Papez, mapped out the anatomical details we now take for granted, as if its role in affect had always been understood. Today, MacLean continues his research in Washington on such subjects as the relationship between speech, language, bonding, and the programming of the thalamostriate division of the limbic system.

In Edmonton, Pierre Flor-Henry (1983a,b, 1985) has explored various correlations between psychopathological states and right-left hemisphere asymmetries, while Lassen (1987, 1994a; Lassen and Ingvar, 1961), in Copenhagen, Denmark, and Ingvar (1979), in Lund, Sweden have pioneered an extraordinary brain-scanning technology that allows visualization and quantification of regional differences in cerebral blood flow in "real time". These pioneers have provided some of the first maps of the brain in the psycho-physiological realm (in parallel with other special non-invasive techniques for brain mapping such as magnetic resonance imaging, CAT scanning, BEAM [functional MRI], and positron emission tomography). *The specific advantage of brain-mapping* (Roland, 1981; Roland & Friberg, 1985; Friberg & Roland, 1987; or virtually any of the works of Ingvar or Lassen), *is that it provides opportunities to test out hypotheses about mind–brain and behavior.* Drugs and their receptor sites can even be spatially localized by such means, and changes in neurochemical and physiological parameters can now be observed and compared before and after various treatments.

In England, Crow (1982, 1986a,b,c) and Reynolds (1987) have elucidated the pathophysiology of "positive" and "negative" symptoms in schizophrenia, especially the functions of the left temporal pole and frontal cortex. In the United States, Andreasen and colleagues (1994), using magnetic resonance imaging (MRI), have found abnormalities in the thalamus that theoretically could explain the symptoms in schizophreniform illness. In Norway, Retterstol (1983, 1985) has patiently conducted thirty(plus)-year follow-up studies on most of the paranoid schizophrenics in his country, while in Japan, Saitoh and colleagues (1984a,b) have extended Crow's work with detailed electrophysiological studies of variables of attention in conditions of severe ego disturbance, and Kim, Ugurbil, and Strick (1994) and Ito have greatly expanded our knowledge of the cerebellum's contribution to learning (paving the way, for example, for research on cerebellar problems in other conditions entailing a severe ego deficit, including infantile autism). Ito's (1981, 1982, 1984a,b, 1985a,b, 1986, 1988, 1993, 1998) work builds dramatically on his earlier studies with Sir John Eccles and Szentágothai (Eccles, Szentágothai, & Ito, 1967), the result being that neurotic and psychotic illnesses are now more clearly definable in terms of basic neural control mechanisms.

Neurologically informed psychoanalysts such as Reiser (1984, 1990) at Yale, Basch (1983) and Gedo (1978, 1981, 1984, 1988, 1991b,c, 1997) in Chicago, Schwartz (1987a,b) in Washington, DC, Sashin (1985; Sashin & Callahan, 1990) in Boston, Moore in Atlanta (1988), and Hadley (2000) in Lake Geneva, to name just a few, have sought to establish further clinical correlations between mind and brain, working toward a unified theory of mind–brain and behavior. Such a theory would be the psychological equivalent of what in theoretical physics is called by Hawking (1988), only half jokingly, the "Theory of Everything".

In addition, a large number of basic brain scientists, including Kandel (1976, 1998; Kandel & Spencer, 1968), Chugani and Phelps (1986), Geschwind and Galaburda (1985), Kent (1981), Kety (1982), Lashley (1950), MacLean (1985), Merzenich and colleagues (1984), Pribram (1962; Pribram and Gill, 1976), Sperry (1950, 1952, 1968, 1983; Sperry & Zaidel, 1977) have made invaluable contributions to our basic scientific understanding of such phenomena as learning, memory, and brain plasticity. In fact, it is virtually impossible briefly to summarize any area of interdisciplinary brain research without leaving out significant, or even critical, research. My list here is but a tiny sketch.

And for this reason, this monograph can provide only a highly selective sample of the rapidly expanding domain of mind–brain investigation, choosing necessarily from what lies close to my own interest and knowledge. It is my hope, however, that the examples presented here will not be too far removed from what is important and representative within the larger field.

Moreover, despite much progress, we should not congratulate ourselves on how much we know, since any monograph on mind–brain will necessarily leave many questions unanswered. *First there is the awesome complexity of the brain itself, the investigation of which is probably the most difficult task mankind has ever undertaken.* Real understanding of the brain will take our best efforts for generations to come.

A second reason relates to long-standing philosophical and religious debates that depreciate man's striving toward an integrated understanding (see Chapter One). Most notable has been the debate between dualism–vitalism (as represented by the line of thought extending from Plato through St Augustine, Descartes, Leibnitz, Spinoza, Eccles, and Popper) and modern materialism (as represented by Hippocrates, Galen, Aristotle, Democritus, Pelagius, Hobbes, Kant, Armstrong, and Freud). This debate hinges upon whether all aspects of mental life are capable of being understood in terms of fundamental brain mechanisms. Although this seems to me to be a correct assertion, the position I hold is the more pragmatic one that at least some aspects of mind and some findings in brain (chemistry, anatomy, and physiology) may now be successfully related to each other.

A third reason for the difficulty in performing interdisciplinary studies of mind–brain is the fact that our medical education system tends to produce two somewhat exclusive categories of specialists: neuroscientists relatively uninterested in mind and psychiatrists/ analysts relatively uninterested in brain. Those who retain a keen interest in both have risked rejection by both groups.

Yet psychiatry and psychoanalysis have benefited greatly from research on mind–brain correlations, so it would seem vital that these continue. The ideas of Gedo, Lichtenberg, and Sameroff, who have incorporated updated, neuroscientific knowledge (in the form of multiple, complex "functional–motivational systems") into their revised, psychoanalytic models, demonstrate the awesome utility of interdisciplinary research. In my earlier monograph, *Mapping the Mind* (1991), I delineate in great detail the rapidly evolving field of mind–brain studies. In a brief chapter such as this, I have far fewer options: I can concentrate on an overview, or I can pay attention to small areas of the larger field that feel critical. I have decided on the latter.

During the past few decades we have witnessed an explosion of knowledge in the area of neurotransmitters and research on neurons and neuroglia.[7] We have progressed far from Schildkraut and Kety's (1967) original catecholamine hypothesis to much more complex theories describing the expanding number and spatial distribution of the large number of psychoactive substances produced in the body (not merely in the brain). Several examples stand out as exemplifying the enormous complexity of this one branch of research: there is recent work on the broad distribution of nitric oxide, and the localization of a multiplicity of brain peptides (for example, those in the hypothalamus reported by Makara, Palkovits, and Szentágothai (1980)), and the similar diversity of neurotransmitters in the basal ganglia, especially the striatum (Graybiel, 1984; Iverson, 1984). These latter two structures of the brain constitute critical control structures or systems with an inner organization that boggles the mind, in some cases seeming to reduplicate much of the complexity of the entire rest of the brain in microcosm.

As Yamawaki and colleagues (1994) have summarized, current work on depression no longer focuses simply upon monoamines, but on serotonin (5-HT) and 5-HT2 receptors and on dopamine, which has proved decisive in the area of psychosis research. Depression, ego disturbances, and disorders of movement represent related phenomena often encountered in clinical psychiatric and psychoanalytic practice.

Other psychopathologies have become the study of intensive biological studies with psychological implications. Flor-Henry (1985), as noted above, has creatively described the relationship between some exhibitionistic psychopathology and disturbances of hemispheric asymmetry (observable by EEG), attempting to elucidate the basic pathophysiology involved. In a similar vein, Harrow (1994) has created a model of schizophrenia that integrates the biological and the psychological, noting an imbalance between frontal and limbic areas of the brain that he believes relates to problems with synaptic density. In a nutshell, Harrow assumes that high stress causes heightened cognitive arousal during the acute phase of schizophrenia. The result is an intermingling of personal concerns and wishes into conscious thinking and a selective disorder in monitoring one's own ideas. The monitoring difficulty is probably secondary to an impairment in the effective use of long-term stored memory regarding what is socially and contextually essential and/or appropriate.

Complementing Harrow's work, Crow (1982, 1986a,b,c) has provided evidence that in all likelihood schizophrenia represents several different illnesses, at least one of which (in right-handers) is probably a retroviral disease contracted *in utero* as a result of the mother's having influenza during the second trimester of gestation.[8]

Molecular biologists have even begun to locate and reproduce the genes that lead to various mental disorders. Genes causing a significant number of illnesses have now been located, including several genes that might be causative of manic–depressive illness (MDI). We have clearly come very far since the days of Abraham's and Freud's original biological and psychodynamic speculations about MDI (then known as circular insanity) and schizophrenia (once called dementia praecox).

Infantile autism, obsessive–compulsive disorder, and panic disorder, to mention additional clinical examples, represent further areas in which considerable interdisciplinary research has occurred in the past decade. When I entered medical school, these topics barely seemed on the agenda; at the present time, specific medications (e.g., selective serotonin reuptake inhibitors, or SSRIs)[9] have been introduced in the United States which help the latter two conditions, and several drugs have been tested for the first condition in Japan. In addition, the attention drawn to such brain structures as the cerebellum (by many workers in the psychiatric field, especially including Ito) has resulted in more careful investigation of the role of cerebellar pathology in areas such as learning disabilities, and in infantile autism.[10] This does not negate the pioneering insights of psychoanalytic observers such as Bettelheim, Winnicott, Bowlby, Spitz, Provence (Provence & Lipton, 1962), Modell, Kohut, and others regarding the importance for recovery of a loving, nurturing, human environment, but it certainly allows for a fuller consideration of how environmental and experiential factors might interact with genetic loading, and it supports the utilization of combined treatment approaches.[11]

Another prominent area of research concerns anxiety syndromes, including post traumatic stress disorder (PTSD) and panic attack syndrome (PAS). Following Freud's work on war neuroses during the First World War and Grinker and Spiegel's work in the Second World War, a younger generation has expanded knowledge of these disorders from the Vietnam War experience as well as from man's increasingly traumatic civilian life-style. For example, research on PAS includes studies (at Washington University Medical School in St. Louis) that show abnormal metabolic activity in the right parahippocampal gyrus, reduced by the tranquilizing drugs (e.g., alprazolam) useful in treating this condition.

A second example of modern research on a variety of what Freud called the "traumatic neuroses" (as opposed to the so-called narcissistic neuroses) concerns obsessive–compulsive illness (OCD). Baxter (1990) has suggested the possibility that this illness may relate to alterations within the striatum that prevent the normal (caudate-based) inhibition of motor, affective, or cognitive patterns, which then become repetitive, that is, "obsessive" or "compulsive," depending upon which area of the caudate or lenticular nucleus is affected. Clearly, there is substantial interest in the basal ganglia (cf. Graybiel, 1984), and there is much to learn and appreciate about those brain areas that eliminate irrelevant information, inhibit repetitive cycles, or gate the flow of sensory input. In this regard, we can expect a concentration on prefrontal, cerebellar, anterior cingulate, and basal ganglia mechanisms in the future, since these areas appear critical for neural control.[12] They are also increasingly visualizable by the latest non-invasive scanning technology.

Neuropsychoimmunology is still another novel area that barely existed a few decades ago but that now makes its own unique contribution to mind–brain integration. We have long appreciated that feelings influence the course of physical illness. Long ago, Cannon (1942) described "voodoo death," and we have the example of couples who have lived together for years not infrequently dying within a short interval of each other (and the same is known to occur with animals living together in zoos). Now, thanks to experts who combine knowledge of immunology and neuroscience, we are in a better position to appreciate more exactly how the brain affects the course of many physical illnesses, such as altering vulnerabilities to infectious disease, cancers, and toxic or viral exposure. We can also better appreciate how the immune system feeds information into the brain itself, functioning as a kind of "radar" regarding bodily events outside the central nervous system.

Cells of the immune system are capable of producing neurotransmitters, which are released into the peripheral blood. In this research domain, Biziere (1994) has written eloquently as follows: *"We are more aware of research on how the CNS affects the immune system (IS), but significant research is currently afoot to study . . . neuropsychiatric disorders which may result from normal or abnormal immune responses . . .* leading to excessive concentrations of certain cytokines within the CNS" (p. 21, my emphasis). Cytokines are produced by, and released from, immune cells but pass through the blood–brain barrier. Clearly, this discussion could be extended considerably; however, at this point, I prefer to focus instead upon details of particular areas of major psychoanalytic interest. Those curious about details should consult Reiser (1984); Schwartz (1987a,b), and Flor-Henry (1983a,b, 1985).

Freud's "Project for a Scientific Psychology"

Although Freud never published his "Project" (1895), there can be little doubt that his "psychology for neurologists" represents a Rosetta stone for understanding Freud's theoretical writings, particularly, for example, chapter seven of *The Interpretation of Dreams* (1900a). As Strachey (1950) describes, Freud was not afraid of brain:

> Freud's attempted approach seventy years ago to a description of mental phenomena in physiological terms might well seem to bear a resemblance to certain modern approaches to the same problem. It has been suggested . . . that the human nervous system may be regarded in its workings as similar to or even identical with an electronic computer – both of them machines for the reception, storage, processing and output of information. It has been plausibly pointed out that in the complexities of the "neuronal" events described here by Freud, and the principles governing them, we may see more than a hint or two at the hypotheses of information theory and cybernetics in their application to the nervous system. To take a few instances of this similarity of approach, we may note first Freud's insistence on the prime necessity for providing the machine with a "memory"; again, there is his system of "contact-barriers" [a description of the neuron hypothesis, which Freud anticipated before other neurologists gained fame through its discovery and description], which enables the machine to make a suitable "choice", based on the memory of previous events, between alternative lines of response to an external stimulus; and, once more, there is, in

Freud's account of the mechanism of perception, the introduction of the fundamental notion of feed-back as a means of correcting errors in the machine's own dealings with the environment. [pp. 292–293]

Strachey refers to Pribram's (1962) detailed elaboration of Freud's "Project," and reference should also be made to Pribram and Gill's book on the same subject (1976).

By all accounts, Freud invented an early version of the idea of a cybernetic or information-processing system, much as he discovered the "neurone hypothesis" in this early manuscript (Basch, 1975). We may consider some of the reasons why Freud failed to understand defense against perceptions. Freud began with the belief that "in order to prevent the generation of excessive anxiety one must be able to defend oneself not only against unmanageable aspects of instinctual stimulation, but also against re-experiencing or recalling potentially traumatic perceptions from the external world" (Basch, 1983, p. 125). *Freud understood that repression could protect against instinctual derivatives (endogenous stimuli) but felt that perceptual activity and consciousness constituted a single system which did not allow the possibility of defending against external perceptions, with their strong or significant sensory quality. This was Freud's error* both in the "Project" and in his letter no. 39 to Wilhelm Fliess.

But in 1911, as Basch notes (*ibid.*), Freud temporarily recognized the gap in his previous understanding when he stated (correctly), "a system living according to the pleasure principle must have devices to enable it to withdraw from the stimuli of reality" (1911b, p. 220). Basch traces Freud's movement toward solving this problem to his paper "The loss of reality in neurosis and psychosis" (1924a), in which Freud speculates that whatever the mechanism is that protects us from reality perception, it functions like repression and must involve "a withdrawal of the cathexis sent out by the ego". Freud again correctly concludes that in neurosis "a piece of reality is avoided by a sort of flight, whereas in psychosis it is remodeled" (1924e, p. 185). The problem was Freud had difficulty holding on to his insight.

Basch (1983) makes the same point:

It has been established in the field of perceptual psychology that contrary to Freud's [erroneous] hypothesis [that] Pcpt=Cs,

perception and consciousness are neither identical nor simultaneous. *Perception precedes consciousness by a measurable amount of time,*
and given the complexity of the neuronal network [of the brain],
there is ample opportunity to evaluate the significance of that
percept and judge its suitability for consciousness. [p. 149, my
emphasis]

Basch underscores this point when he notes that

the data-processing capacity of the brain has now been established
to be in the neighborhood of ten trillion bits or decisions per second
[and therefore most brain activity is part of the dynamic uncon-
scious], while approximately only ten bits of information per
second can be admitted to conscious awareness. [*ibid.*].

To put this differently, *the answer long sought by Freud as to how
we defend against perceptions is as follows: we retain in memory perceptions per se, but defend against these by lending them various levels of
personal significance ranging from "highly significant" to "essentially
inconsequential." Such a disavowal of meaning is an extremely important
psychological defense mechanism,* originally described by Freud (but
nearly lost in translation). The rediscovery and clarification of this
defense we owe to Franz Michael Basch (1983).

Psychoanalysis and the two cerebral hemispheres

A most critical contribution to clinical psychoanalysis is Basch's rediscovery of the psychological defense of disavowal and its distinction from
denial. Disavowal is the downplaying of the personal meaning of a
recognized, accurately perceived event, accessible to conscious and
preconscious memory; in contrast, in denial a piece of reality is
completely non-existent to the ego, substantially perceptually
distorted and/or not accessible to memory at all.[13] In addition,
work on this distinction contributed to the search for connections
between such phenomena as psychological "defenses" on the one
hand and neurophysiological mechanisms on the other (Levin and
Vuckovich, 1983). One way to further explore such terrain has been
to start with what is known about the differing roles of the two
cerebral hemispheres.[14]

The two hemispheres essentially constitute two brains and are obviously capable of sharing or sequestering their internally or externally generated experiences. Sperry (1968) has pointed out, however, that they share one "consciousness". Cortical morphological differences between the hemispheres have been observed before birth. Handedness is essentially a reflection of "brainedness" (Annett, 1985), and the archeological record suggests that it goes back millions of years. According to Levy (1974), approximately 89% of the human population is genotypically right-handed, and most (99.67%) of this group is left-hemispheric-dominant for language. Of the 16% of phenotypic sinistrals, 56% have left-language dominance and 44% right-language dominance. Females show less cerebral dominance than males; that is, their brains are more symmetrical regarding the parsing of various functions. These asymmetries have profound implications for the nature of human experience, as well as for the responsiveness and recovery rates to brain injuries. For example, aphasia, which was studied by Freud (1953 [1891], 1891) extensively, hits males more devastatingly than females, and the male degree and rate of recovery from aphasia are much lower than for females. Clearly, there are critical differences between the brains of men and women, a point rarely entertained in developing a psychology that would apply to both.

It will help to further review some of the differences between the hemispheres. The following comments apply to a right-handed individual (i.e., someone who is left-brain-dominant for language). The right hemisphere is a leading part of the brain's systems concerned with intuition and the formation of gestalts, the processing of tactile input, visuomotor and spatial skills, facial expression, the prosody (metrical composition) of language, time synthesis, and tonal reproduction and recognition, exclusive of musical scores. The musical quality of speech is extremely important, since without this we find it extremely difficult to encode or decode speech's emotional meaning(s).

Thus, although the left brain is usually described as dominant with regard to language, this so-called "dominance" is really a gross oversimplification. For example, the right brain also makes a major contribution to language, especially as regards word fluency, prosody (the musical quality of speech), and verbal memory (Tucker, Watson, & Heilman, 1977). Moreover, although the left hemisphere contains Broca's and Wernicke's areas, which control systems for the transformation of thoughts into motor speech (Broca's), as well as the encoding and decoding of abstract ideas into language (Wernicke's), the right hemisphere contains areas that are the counterparts to these two left-sided language areas (Kandel, 1976, 1998). These right-sided areas (located in analogous positions to Broca's and Wernicke's area on the left) are what we use to create the affective components of language which complement our language's formal syntactical and phonological structures.

The left hemisphere is primarily associated with serial experience, with logic and reasoning, and with most of the learning that we associate with school. Such information has been called "explicit" or "declarative" knowledge by research psychologists, indicating that it is retrievable by direct, language-based questioning. This is in contrast to "implicit" or "procedural" knowledge, which is characteristic of some of the brain's other memory systems—for example, the vestibulocerebellar system. In this system, information is stored as a motor memory and is most easily retrieved through "priming"—that is, by action modes or sensory stimulation. It may help to note here that when we identify enactments in a psychoanalysis, we are able to see that they provide the necessary "priming" for the recovery of some of the early (preverbal) events in the patient's life, though they are not exclusively limited to that period.

Thus, it follows that *some significant, and probably early experience is captured in a form that will not be tapped by our analysands unless the proper sensory stimulus is provided within the analysis. From this perspective, one could make an argument that the analyst who is more willing to talk (say at those times when the analysand is trying to recall something that is just out of reach and becomes silent for some extended period of time because his recall efforts are failing, and he needs help) will stimulate components of the analysand's missing memory* through spontaneous comments, by means of the evocative effect of the tone of the analyst's voice, visual imagery, and so forth (see Levin, 1991, for a detailed discussion of the complicated aspects of such interventions; see also Gedo, 1978, for further examples and theoretical commentary on this point).

When Freud (1953 [1811]) wrote extensively on aphasia as a cerebral disconnection syndrome, he was in effect not only advancing a novel refutation of the narrow, anatomical localization models of cerebral function of his day but establishing a perspective that could serve multiple purposes. Freud's approach would now be called a general systems perspective, in which "a mental phenomenon corresponds to each part of the chain [of events], or to several parts. *The psychic is, therefore, a process parallel to the physiological, a 'dependent concomitant'*" (1953 [1891], p. 55, my emphasis).

In other words, mind derives from neural activity. Freud was to apply this same perspective repeatedly, elaborating upon what he felt to be the elements of a system subserving multiple mental faculties. Thus, he attempted to describe their system relationships. Employing Freud's systems perspective, *one might consider a somewhat novel definition of "conflict" as that state in which the system relationship of the two hemispheres becomes disturbed.*[15] This includes most importantly the possibility of functional interhemispheric blocks between the hemispheres. That is, if the hemispheres are capable of sharing information with each other or with other areas (such as the prefrontal cortex), then they are also capable of blocking out such connectedness.[16] A brief description of the possible manifestations of interhemispheric blocking follows, along with a discussion of its mechanisms (Levin & Vuckovich, 1983; see also Levin, 1991). Basically, the position generally taken is that the "willful" control of the flow of information within the mind–brain occurs by some unknown process akin to the manner in which regional cerebral blood flow increases in association with spontaneous thinking (Roland & Friberg, 1985).

If one imagines an isolated left hemisphere then one's whole brain is then operating with only the cognitive perceptions of the experience in memory, but without much if any emotional coloring, which is usually right hemispheric. (Here, I intend "isolated" in the sense of being without input from the right hemisphere—that is, without emotionally weighted information clarifying the degree and quality of the personal meaning[s] of an event). It is easier to see how this isolation of emotions makes it harder, or even impossible, to understand the personal significance of the disavowed event, just as it is difficult to establish the meaning of a message when it is communicated in the emotionless computer voice used by the telephone company. Such "black and white" pictures, or words without emotional coloring, illustrate the internal state corresponding to the psychological defense of "disavowal" that I am trying to delineate.

In contrast to the case of disavowal, one can imagine a system *without left hemisphere input. One would then have the presence of some significant quantum of affect; but the whole brain would be without the specific memories of an "event" to go along with the (right hemispheric) affect, hence the affective state itself might well be unintelligible.* This would coincide with what is usually termed "repression." It was thinking along such lines that originally gave rise to the idea that interhemispheric communication blocks might provide a fundamental explanation for certain psychological defenses (Levin & Vuckovich, 1983, pp. 179–186; Levin, 1991; Galin, 1974) such as disavowal and repression.

Some may believe that this hypothesis regarding a possible correspondence, or even an isomorphism, between repression/disavowal and left/right or right/left interhemispheric blocks is either wrong or of little clinical relevance to psychoanalysis; however, the following considerations and examples may help persuade the reader not to discard the hypothesis immediately, especially since it also has the advantage of being testable experimentally.

If the two cerebral hemispheres are functionally differentiated as described above (with the right brain particularly orientated toward affect, prosody, and facial expression, the left toward formal logic, rules, and syntactical language) then there is the possibility that during psychoanalytic work *what the analyst facilitates is basically a bridging between the analysand's hemispheres* by being sensitive to the "language" of each hemispheric input simultaneously (see Levin, 1980). This increases the information available to the whole brain.

For example, the analyst might help with the visualization of emotional intensity by overcoming disavowed affect, and potentially help as well with the retrieval of forgotten (repressed) perceptual details, to which specific affect attaches. In this manner, *isolated information in part of the nervous system would become inputs for the rest of the brain, and the overall information system would become functionally enlarged.* From this perspective, one aspect of the integrative function that we know to be an attribute of analytic process would become understandable in terms of integrative brain functions and known psychological variables (such as disavowed feeling states and repressed perceptual details). Some clinical case material may help explain further the relevance of such research to psycho-analysis.

The first comes from Galin (1974), who reports on the following case from Sperry's split-brain research. The experimental subject described here had her corpus callosum severed for the experimental treatment of epilepsy:

One film segment [of Sperry's research] shows a female patient being tested with a tachistoscope. . . . In the series of neutral geometrical figures being presented at random to the right and left [visual] fields, a nude pinup was included, and flashed to the right (nonverbal) hemisphere. The girl blushes and giggles. [The experimenter] asks 'What did you see?' She answers 'nothing, just a flash of light', and giggles again, covering her mouth with her hand. 'Why are you laughing again [asks the experimenter]', and again she says 'Oh doctor Sperry, you have some machine'. [p. 573]

As Galin points out, if you did not know that this patient had a commisurotomy of her corpus callosum, you might interpret her behavior as demonstrating a number of perceptual defenses in order to avoid what appear to be embarrassing sexual feelings. You would be wrong. *Actually, her right hemisphere is reacting to something her left hemisphere has no knowledge of because of an anatomical disconnection from the right brain.*

Another example (without anatomical complications) will help clarify the phenomena under discussion even better and make still more credible the physiological and psychological correlations being asserted here. This second example is taken from the analysis of a psychoanalytic patient who began to talk in a detached, disavowed manner.

[While she talked] her analyst's attention wandered to the patient's left hand, which was shifting periodically into a "gun" gesture [completely] out of her awareness. When this gesture was called to the patient's attention, she responded by remembering that she had read in graduate school about right–left brain studies, including Ferenczi's observation that the left side of the body (the right hemisphere) appears more in touch with the unconscious. (The patient did not [at this] point know of the analyst's interest in the subject of right–left brain studies.) She simultaneously became aware of and experienced significant anger toward the analyst, which during the session she gradually was able to relate with increasing certainty to the analyst's upcoming vacation. Finally, at the end of the hour, she began to recall some specific memories of being taken advantage of sexually by certain parental substitutes in childhood [i.e., during the absence of her parents]. The patient was not immediately comfortable getting angry with her analyst for going on an upcomming vacation, which made her once again feel vulnerable. [Levin & Vuckovich, 1983, p. 185]

It is apparent that this second example is not unusual in psychoanalysis; in fact, the reader may wonder why such a mundane example is presented here. The answer is that *the only way to fully appreciate what the gun interpretation accomplished is to consider our unique perspective on interhemispheric communication blocks.* By interfering with her disavowal (that is, by pointing out to the patient the gun gesture, which she was unaware of), the analyst created a sequence of developments in which repression was unmasked or undone as well. Only then did the whole brain have all the information it needed to analyze the situation properly, and appreciate her anger about being abandoned.

Experience suggests that these two defenses (disavowal and repression) go together more often than can be by chance. If this is correct, then the mechanism of action of psychoanalytic intervention is being addressed by our attention to the details of the second case. First, the analyst becomes aware of the patient's disavowed state by finding his own interest drifting; but, unlike the patient, he does not dismiss her hand gesture as meaningless. Next, the analyst points out what the patient's left hand is portraying gesturally (viz., a gun). Then the patient becomes aware of her own disavowed affect of anger or rage. Finally, this affect leads her to memories of some personally significant but apparently disavowed "events" (in "episodic" memory) and associated repressed details (in "semantic" memory [see Basch, 1983]), which together allow for the integration of affect and cognition around the traumatic, developmental experience with parental substitutes (including the analyst). From the patient's perspective, this is like finding a hidden "gravestone" (that is, something "disavowed"), which now points to something deeply "buried" there (specifically, her "repressed" memories of being sexually abused by a caretaker).

As a sidelight, it is probably of no small significance that the two hemispheres come together (in terms of the first major wave of myelinization of the corpus callosum) during the oedipal period (around three and a half). This suggests that *one reason for the importance of oedipal-level anxiety, in addition to the well-known psychoanalytic reasons, is that during this period the child is experiencing a critical developmental shift in psychological defensive strategy*: he or she is passing from a time when "events" and wishes are non-traumatic, by virtue of the fact that the hemispheres are functionally isolated anatomically, to a period when such a functional separation can occur only as a result of some internal decision making within the brain to defend itself from feelings.

Put somewhat differently, one of the tasks of the oedipal child is to deal with the affects generated by the observations and correlations that he or she is increasingly capable of making. Before this age, it seems likely that the child is relatively protected by the anatomical separation of the hemispheres as well as by hemispheric immaturity itself. Afterward, defensive needs may require a reinstitution of the state of interhemispheric disconnection. This would have to be initiated by some internal decision-making process of the brain and have a physiological basis, resulting in a regressive isolation of the hemispheres; it would mark the beginning of the psychological phenomena we call repression and disavowal, and infantile amnesia would also be one of its manifestations.

It should be obvious that such defensive disconnection need not be total, since a quantitative threshold might make a significant qualitative difference, starting around the age of three and a half, when the two hemispheres become able to share information with each other, with the prefrontal cortex, and with other areas. Clearly, my explanation of disavowal and repression is not intended to be an all-encompassing explanation of all defensive phenomena; undoubtedly other defenses involve different neurophysiological mechanisms.

Two further notes. First, *the analyst seems to be in a favored position to recognize when the analysand is unaware of either a critical affect (right hemisphere input), a critical memory (left hemisphere input), or a correlation between the two*. Second, it is possible that what is described clinically as functioning in primarily a "hysterical" mode (favoring repression) or an "obsessive" mode (favoring disavowal) could possibly reflect a fundamental tendency to isolate the hemispheres on a physiological basis for the purpose of psychological defense or adaptation (Levin & Vuckovich, 1983; Levin, 1991).

Plasticity, learning, and psychoanalysis

I will now review aspects of the brain's plasticity, or capacity to adaptively alter its way of functioning. It is by means of integration of all of the different subsystems of the brain at various levels of organization that learning and "therapeutic" process occur. In other words, if one assumes that emotional growth involves learning, then our wish to expand our understanding of how psychoanalysis works (that is, to facilitate learning in the psychoanalytic setting) depends upon our understanding the basis of learning. (For details, see Albus, 1971, 1981; Alkon, 1985; Levin, 1991; Levin & Vuckovich, 1987; Lynch, McGough, & Weinberger, 1984; Rosenzweig & Bennett, 1976; Thompson, 1986, 1987; Young, 1978). In what follows, I review some of what is known about brain plasticity and its relevance to psychoanalysis.

Four adult mechanisms for learning are known: development of new neuronal branches and synapses, use of reverberating circuits, use-dependent modification of existing circuits, and the alteration of pre- and post-synaptic processes (Alkon, 1985, p. 1037). *All organizational levels within the nervous system are capable of change in response to experience and thus contribute to the learning process.* At the beginning of life, "the embryonic and newborn brain extends many more neural processes than will ultimately be employed by the adult organism. Subsequently, inappropriate neural connections will be pruned away by the death of nerve cells" (Snyder, 1984, p. 1255). This constitutes one major means of early brain synaptic organization and reorganization.

Of course, *optimal experience with caretakers is a critical factor in establishing optimal synaptic organization.* Experiments have suggested that in all likelihood no new neurons generally appear during our lifetime (Rakik, 1985), although new evidence suggests that the hippocampus[17] may lay down some new cells after maturity (Kempermann & Gage, 1998; Kempermann, Brandan, & Gage, 1998).[18] At present, however, no one knows how significant these new cells are for functioning or repair. The situation in humans may also be different in some respects than in avian brains, (Nottebohm, 1985), where new cells *do* appear during maturity which clearly expand functioning. The new hippocampal research, however, opens the intriguing possibility that in the future man may learn how to unlock the human potential for neurogenesis.

A distinction can be made between plastic change and learning. In a sense, any change in the tendency to respond can be seen as a simple form of learning; however, in lower animals this is usually referred to as "sensitization" rather than "discriminative [that is, specific] learning" (see Young, 1978, p. 83). Thus, although all patterned change in behavior represents learning, all learning does not involve complex, discriminative ability.

Psychoanalysts were sufficiently interested in the neurophysiological basis of memory[19] to invite the neuroscientist Kandel (1976, 1998), who won the Albert Lasker Award for Medical Research in 1983, and the Nobel Prize in 2000, to report on his findings at a plenary session of the American Psychoanalytic Association. He noted that at the microbiological level, short-term memory (much better understood than long-term) can be correlated with a neurochemical cascade involving known neuroactive substances. For example, in serotonergic neurons there is a sequential transformation of intraneuronal adenosine triphosphate (ATP) into pyrophosphate and $3'5'$-AMP (the so-called second messenger, or cyclic-AMP). These products cause the activation of ionic channels for calcium at the synaptic membrane level, and an alteration of the operator gene ensues that causes previously "unexpressed" genetic material in the nucleus of the nerve cell to express itself. In this manner, the neuron may respond to environmental factors by switching neurotransmitters, and thus participate in different chemical pathways.

Equally exciting, at the level of the somatomotor strip (the so-called cortical homunculus or map) Merzenich and colleagues (1984) have correlated learning with significant cortical cellular changes. They have shown, for example, that with the increased use of a finger (in monkeys and presumably also in man) the cortical homunculus changes, with the area (representing the involved finger) growing in size. Also, in amputation experiments, when a finger is removed, the cortical cells learn of the loss, and the cortical map changes so that the area of cortex previously representing the amputated finger now represents the fingers on either side of the lost digit. There can be no question but that learning is associated with changes at the cortical level and relates to the plastic manner in which cortical cells represent a given motor (or sensory) field.

From the standpoint of learning theory, *human development represents the acquisition of skills* (autonomous ego functions) *based upon (1) the release of various inborn biological potentials (deriving from the genetic blueprint) and (2) experience with other humans who encourage stimulus input, and are thus required for optimal development.*[20]

Most interestingly, the genetic blueprint is decisive not only for its specification of *what* is to be learned but also for *how* this learning is to be accomplished (M. Stern, 1988). For example, psychoanalytic work with individuals who suffer from learning disabilities has made it clear that we are not all born with the same internal programs for learning. In fact, some people appear to be substantially unprepared for learning within various realms without timely assistance.

In our examination of the subject of cerebral asymmetry, we discovered that some internal decision making is required in order to coordinate the hemispheres during the performance of any particular task. Specifically, it is helpful to match a given problem with the learning subsystem of the brain most adapted to this kind of problem. In a paper on brain plasticity, Vuckovich and I (1987) explored how such internal automatic decision making might occur. In particular, we make the case that the cerebellum, through the cortico-vestibulocerebellar subsystem, would seem to be a major candidate for coordinating such pattern matching within the brain.[21] In a nutshell, we are asserting that *the cerebellum handles thoughts the same way it handles movement.* Ito, whose work was cited at the beginning of this chapter, provides extensive details as to how this might be accomplished, and the interested reader will appreciate Chapters Nine and Ten of this monograph for Ito's latest ideas. Lest anyone doubt the significance of the cerebellum to ego development (Frick, 1982) and learning (Ito, 1984a, 1986), it has been established that infantile autism is likely a consequence of cerebellar malfunction (Hadley, 1989).

Brain scientists (see especially Galaburda, LeMay, Kemper, & Geschwind, 1978; Geschwind & Galaburda, 1985), social workers

(Palombo, 1985, 1987), psychologists, and educators have long been interested in the important subject of learning disability (LD). It becomes increasingly important that psychoanalysts also be aware and knowledgeable in this area, especially because without the proper understanding they may end up making such errors as misidentifying learning disability phenomena as "sadomasochistic" and creating psychodynamics that do not exist. The point is that *all hurtful, self-damaging, self-defeating behavior is not intended to be so at an unconscious level. Some individuals fail painfully because they simply do not know how to do something.* The school-age group with significant learning disability probably makes up close to 10% of the child population, and this may not be different at the university level. In my opinion, a similar percentage of adult psychiatric patients are also learning-disabled, and most of this group suffers as well from not ever having had testing, a proper diagnosis, or remediation. Many patients with LD eventually seek out psychoanalytic help, so analysts cannot avoid the need to become knowledgable in this important area.

One additional problem deserves a brief comment. Since LD is defined operationally as the inability to achieve satisfactorily in spite of normal intelligence, *the diagnosis of learning disability itself depends upon the precise assessment of intelligence.* But if the tester is not that familiar with LD testing, then it is easy to underestimate a person's intelligence (since the tester will not conduct the test in ways that allow for the patient's intelligence to be expressed) and thus miss the diagnosis of LD entirely.

Space does not permit an in-depth discussion of psychoanalysis and LD, but it is my opinion that special *care is required so as not to fall into the trap of misdiagnosing problems, misinterpreting motives, or improperly estimating a patient's abilities.* Palombo (1985, 1987) and Orenstein (1999) should be consulted for their thoughtful discussion of the clinical issues involved in psycho-dynamic work with individuals with LD.

At this point, a final comment upon the vestibulocerebellar system seems in order. This system has been described in detail (Levin & Vuckovich, 1987), especially with regard to its role in learning. Also considered under the rubric of brain plasticity is the capacity to acquire sensorimotor schema, and although those interested in learning have not always taken much notice of this phase of learning (with the prominent exception of Piaget, who starts from this perspective), it seems that over recent decades the role of motor learning has become an important topic within the psychology of learning in general.

Learning about oneself, others, and the (inanimate) world occurs first on the basis of vestibular and proprioceptive input, recorded by the vestibulocerebellar system (Chugani & Phelps, 1986). This fact is important for psychoanalysis because it means that our core sense of self is a reflection of a known system of the brain. Consequently, our ability to modify this core will hinge upon our developing a refined knowledge about this system (Levin, 1988b; also see Chapters Nine and ten of this monograph).

Some final comments on the evolution of psychoanalytic theory

Successful neuropsychoanalytic bridging should assist the search for better psychoanalytic models, just as psychoanalytic perspectives have intelligently guided neuroscientific research from the beginning. One such interdisciplinary model is the Gedo and Goldberg (1973) hierarchical, developmental model, as modified most recently by Gedo (1989a, 1993a; see also Levin, 1989; Lichtenberg, 1989a,b). This model is unique in a number of respects that are germane to the present discussion. First, it takes into account the prime data of clinical psychoanalysis upon which all other major, psychoanalytic models are based; thus, it is overarching. Second, it makes the time or developmental dimension explicit and is thus easier to apply clinically to both the shifting motivational–structural axis of a life course (see below) and the regressive and progressive moves within a treatment. Third, it is consistent with the intense work in the field of infant observation studies, as summarized by Lichtenberg (1983, 1989a,b), D. Stern (1985), Demos (1985), and others. Fourth, it is internally consistent.

Gedo's model is closely related to the ideas of Lichtenberg, who stated recently that "psychoanalytic theory is not at its core so much a theory of structure as it is a theory of structural motivation" 1989b, p. 57). After the fashion of Levey (1984–1985), Gedo (1989a), and Sameroff (1983), Lichtenberg describes how *the meaning of psychic structure changes throughout development,* identifying the following "functional–motivational systems" or goals which can serve sequentially as axes around which structural developments can be organized: "(1) the need to fulfill physiological needs; (2) the need for attachment and affiliation; (3) the need for assertion and exploration; (4) the need to react aversively through antagonism and/or withdrawal; and (5) the need for sensual and sexual pleasure" (1989b, p. 60). By acknowledging such multiple motivational goals that extend far beyond dual instinct theory and ego psychology, these psychoanalytic innovations are changing psychoanalytic theory in a most useful way.

To elaborate, the formal linkage of Gedo and Goldberg's (1973) model to Freud's reflex arc, structural, and topographic models is dispensed with in Gedo's current hierarchical model because of the incompatible assumptions among the traditional models. What Gedo retains is the developmental sequence that takes into account the multiple motivations described by Lichtenberg (Wilson & Gedo, 1993a,b). These specific motivations correspond roughly to Gedo's stages of self-definition, self-organization, and self-regulation. Moreover, Gedo (Lichtenberg, and others as well) retains the current psychoanalytic tripartite oedipal phase model of Freud, which appears in the hierarchical model as the stage involving the renunciation of incompatible wishes that threaten adaptive equilibrium.

What is interesting here is the general agreement that the meaning of "structure" changes throughout development (Sameroff, 1983; Levey, 1984–1985; Lichtenberg, 1989b; Gedo, 1989a). In other words, during each stage (mode) of development, the central organizing principle is seen to change: from *regulating stimulus input,* which is crucial at the beginning of life, to organizing around real objects with the goal of *forming a nuclear self,* to a stage wherein the functions provided by self-objects facilitate the further crystallization of a *cohesive personhood* (self), to a phase *governed by ego, super-ego, and id regulation,* and finally to a *conflict-free sphere* in which a hierarchy of goals and values is further arranged, appropriate to the subject's needs at a given time.

But what determines this changing fulcrum of development?

This question, a pivotal one for psychoanalysis, is answered by Gedo and Levin as follows: *the genetic blueprint itself determines the timetable* for changing motivational structure. Consider, for example, what is known about the genetic control system for biological development. Our DNA contains a small number of closely associated *master genes* (the homeobox) which have been conserved over a large number of species, the purpose of which is to control development—that is, the order in which the rest of the genes will be activated in the developmental sequence and presumably during the lifetime of an individual (Levin, 1989). What changes between species is not the overall sequence (for example, making a body axis, then adding limbs to it, and so on) but the details regarding what body plans or parts are to be used (e.g., which limb types added, and so forth). In the case of insects, wings are included in the step of forming limb buds upon an already established anteriorposterior body axis. In our own instance, the addition of human limbs occurs as the corresponding step. It follows that, for human psychological development as well, the sequence of appearance of motivational–functional systems conforms to a fixed, species-specific plan. What psychoanalysis is urgently in need of is a map of the neurological, developmental sequence and its rules of operation.

Some may argue that by including such factors as genetics and biological motivations Gedo, Lichtenberg, Sameroff, Levin, and others are generating models that are not truly psychoanalytic. But this would apply to Freud himself, since he too was struggling with the problem posed by the complexity of motivational systems. For example, in his "On narcissism" (1914c) Freud postulated narcissistic motives, which challenged the then psychoanalytic establishment with developmental ideas that were inconsistent with his own libido theory. He did the same thing again in *Totem and Taboo* (1912–1913) when he considered the role of magical thinking in narcissistic development, and, within the Vienna Psychoanalytic Society, when he observed that a case of Federn's did not represent a neurotic fixation (that is, something to be seen within the extent model of drives and defenses) but rather represented "infantile" arrest in development (Nunberg & Federn, 1975, pp. 145–146). Clearly, at this time in his theoretical thinking, Freud was aware of multiple, "functional-motivational systems." If he did not fully integrate his new insights into his theory of the time, we can sympathize, since he was then experiencing the need to defend psychoanalysis (in the form of libido theory) from attacks by Adler, Jung, and others.

Furthermore, theory innovators such as Gedo, Sameroff, and Lichtenberg are also following the lead of Anna Freud, Hartmann, and Rapaport. Anna Freud's concept of multiple lines of development is itself a precursor to a general systems theory perspective; it remains a very short step to the idea of multiple motivational goals at different phases of the life cycle (see Gedo, 1989a; Levin, 1989). Moreover, Hartmann's view of the evolution of the self involved an adaptive process of "autonomous ego development," by which he meant that the multiple motivational systems of brain biology needed to be integrated into our field. And Gedo quotes Rapaport as himself following a Piagetian schema in which, epistemologically, "the possibility of knowing is rooted in the organic adaptation from this basic root, a hierarchical series of thought-organizations [which] arises, in the course of maturation and development, culminating in reality-adequate thinking" (Gedo, 1986, p. 65). It is my belief that such "thought-organizations" are economically expressed by the theoretical revisions of Gedo, Sameroff, and Lichtenberg. Such revisions follow the best psychoanalytic traditions in attempting to develop models that encompass our ever expanding knowledge of mind–brain.[22]

Summary and conclusions

Psychoanalysis is changing so as to take into account the explosion of knowledge within neuroscience. The increasing knowledge of mind–brain is leading to a convergence of all the fields that study human behavior and experience, and some overarching, general theories that begin to approximate a general psychology are emerging. I have discussed the importance of this revolution for psychoanalysis in particular.

I have especially highlighted the work of Basch on the important subject of psychological defenses, as a point of departure for a more detailed examination of some basic brain mechanisms that may underlie defense. In the process, I have stressed the importance of distinguishing between such overlapping defenses as disavowal, repression, and isolation of affect. I have also considered the important role of interhemispheric information transfer in psychoanalytic interpretations and the possible role of brain asymmetry and information sequestration in the specific psychological defenses mentioned. Finally, I commented on the importance of brain plasticity and the possible regulating, integrating role of the cerebellum, cortico-vestibulocerebellar, and other systems in bridging the hemispheres. All these subject areas have a relationship to the phenomenon of learning, a central issue in all brain-related sciences and a subject of seminal importance to psychoanalysis.

Examples were given to suggest the utility and aptness of these interdisciplinary perspectives, particularly the phenomenon of priming of so-called procedural memories. Such priming may be initiated in analysis by enactments and reliving, thereby aiding the rediscovery of early memories. The special case of learning disabilities was also presented as a reminder of the complications that accrue when we fail to recognize that our diagnostic knowledge is sometimes seriously limited. Our patients rely upon us to be exquisitely careful about how we understand and interpret the maturation of their behavior.[23]

Finally, the discussion has touched upon some of the theoretical revision within psychoanalysis which is itself based upon the convergence of a variety of psychoanalytic and neuroscientific discoveries. My hope is that the kind of neuroscientific knowledge presented in this chapter will continue to be integrated with the best psychoanalytic research, so that psychoanalysis may remain a major contributor to the brain-related sciences, and vice versa.

SECTION II
PSYCHOANALYSIS AND GNOSIS

CHAPTER THREE

Learning, transference, and the need to suspend belief

Fred Levin

We are now ready to return more particularly to the questions raised at the outset regarding the search for a psychoanalytic theory of learning, and also a theory of transference. We could start with the second of the two theories (relating to transference) but cannot fail to rapidly advance to the first theory relating to learning, since transference is at least partially reducible to the mind–brain's system for acquiring refined, affectively meaningful information about the self and object world (i.e., expanding episodic memory). In what follows I will attempt to settle some issues that help us proceed with the deeper investigation of transference and learning of Chapters Four and Five.

Transference from its inception has been a complex idea. Freud's major depiction of transference rests on an image of the mind as a form of map, with known territory (the conscious and preconscious) and terra incognita (the unconscious). This powerful topographic metaphor of knowledge distribution within an imaginary space illustrates Freud's capacity to excite our imagination while simultaneously arousing our scientific curiosity. Most critical, however, is Freud's conveyed sense that the fabric of mental life is deeply conflicted as a universal condition, and that only when the mental "pieces" are properly recombined (through analysis) does the entire "puzzle" become intelligible (the so-called dynamic point of view).

Although Freud does not state his model of mind in explicit epistemological terms, clearly he believes that the confusion in understanding mind–brain is more apparent than real (as when he states (as cited in Chapter One) that the psychical is less unknowable than external reality, or asserts that, fundamentally, mental development is guided by discoverable variables, such as "sexuality" and emotional attachment, whose influence begins in infancy. Primary and secondary process transference (of reaction patterns, including affects) across a repression barrier, and combinations of condensation, displacement, symbolization, and other mental mechanisms are seen by Freud as component "threads" in a complex, mental "fabric" that expresses how man's sexuality plays out in its various aims, objects, and particularities.

I describe above how Freud approaches the intractable philosophical problem of objectifying the subjective by combining humanistic and scientific perspectives in a systematically consistent ambiguity. It seems also true, however, that some significant confusion for psychoanalytic theory necessarily results from this very same strategy. For example, the sequential theoretical modifications of psychoanalytic models evolved by Freud can cloud the picture and confuse our focus. Thus, after his momentous papers "On narcissism" (1914c) and on "The unconscious" (1915e), in which he explores respectively the narcissistic components of libidinal ties and the dynamic and systematic unconscious, Freud then constructs his so-called tripartite model in *The Ego and the Id* (1923b). The new model, however, can already be seen as a movement away from affects (such as sexual desire, murderous rage, incest taboos, castration, and humiliation) toward an impersonal theory of information processing. Of course, the matter of clarity is not helped by the mistranslation of Freud by Strachey, which is generally acknowledged to obscure the richness of Freud's emotional meanings in the cloak of a dry English scientificism (Modell, 1993).

In other words, the topographic model comes closest to Freud's tendency to creatively capture novel truths in the skillful interplay of ordinary terms; as such it is powerfully evocative and experience-near. In contrast, the later tripartite model seems dull, technical, and experience-distant by comparison. It is unfortunate that the gain of precision in the later creative clarifications of theory occurs at the apparent cost of colorfulness and aliveness of metaphor. In addition, the need to alternate subjective and objective perspectives in order to solve a philosophical dilemma not of psychoanalysis's making runs a further risk of adding a potential "rift zone" between our psychoanalytic models and our awareness of the feelings these same models are supposed to explain.

Such dilemmas remain a considerable challenge for us in the discharge of our duty to update and understand the scientific basis for what we observe in any psychoanalytic setting. Try as we may to be attentive to new observations in our field, or new observations in our clinical work with particular patients, it is easy to lose touch temporarily with either our humanity or our objectivity. In the face of such difficulty it would seem natural for the psychoanalyst to fall back upon rigid theoretical positions that essentially serve a defensive function. An important question is whether and how this can be avoided.

Before approaching this question directly, it may help us to briefly return to Rapaport's (and Gedo's) theory of learning (the details of which we cover in Chapter Four). The core of these theories is the Freudian idea that first and foremost in learning is the subject's powerful emotional attachment to the object of desire. Everything hinges on this fact; that is, on the love, or respect, or intensity of the tie to the object, who is at some point no longer available to the subject in reality, but remains potentially available in working memory. In other words, the subject must be able to appreciate at some level the importance of his feelings about his relationship with the object before he can acquire aspects of the relationship in the form of enduring mental functions. In Freud's words, object loss leads to mental structure.

In Chicago's Psychoanalytic Institute, in particular, the theorizing of Heinz Kohut and his collaborators, has further refined our understanding of many subtle aspects of object ties and their relationship to the establishment of such things as enduring values, nuclear ambitions, the unfolding of inborn talents, and even to the so-called "cohesiveness" of the very self at the core of our being. It should be obvious from this work about self psychology that what Hartmann discusses under the rubric of morals, Rapaport under the heading of mental functions, and modern theoreticians such as Modell (1993) under the heading of "private self" are in essence all discussing the same thing: the flowering of the basic or core personality pattern of the individual, or how an individual comes into being with certain fixed features that identify that person as unique over time. Obviously, all such theories attempt to take into account the interaction of biological givens and environmental inputs, to account for such elements as each individual's core knowledge and methods of acquiring and modifying it over time.

But the insights psychoanalysis has gained over its years of closely observing humans tells us unequivocally that *learning is not any single thing*: sometimes it will be seen as a specific content of the mind, equivalent to adding quantifiable bytes of information to a computer. At other times, however, what is learned becomes a core part of one's self, intrinsic to our personhood (that is, necessary for our very functioning). With this perspective in mind, it should be easier to understand why it is that some knowledge acquisition will also be dispensable, or at least, function in a manner such that its influence *can* at times be usefully minimized willfully by the individual, whereas other knowledge will play a continuous role in mental activity, involving as it does desires at our very core. *In other words, some beliefs can never be dispensed with, even temporarily, because they constitute core psychic structure without which thinking itself cannot occur in decisive areas.* Let me elaborate upon this idea.

I believe I am asserting that *our belief systems will only be dispensable or suspendable if they are not part of the core of who we are and if we are not dependent upon them for thinking itself.* For if our scientific, religious, or other belief systems are so central to our makeup that they can never be even temporarily suspended, then this fact of dependency can or will impact on our scientific and therapeutic work whenever our work requires the suspension of belief for us to see something novel that we have not seen and/or appreciated before. As Modell has noted, this may reach a peak where such beliefs relate to one's hidden grandiosity; but it appears likely that *any belief system may prevent the acquisition of any new belief if it can never be held in abeyance.*

Religion and science are sometimes antithetical, at other times coincident and/or mutually supportive. Humankind does not really have the freedom to get along without either. For this reason

I personally doubt Hartmann's assertion that Freud actually completely eliminates the religious factor from his life. Rather, it seems more likely, as I suggested in Chapter One, that Freud's (and by extension, our own) ability to concentrate during prolonged periods of analytic activity stems primarily from his ability to *temporarily* suspend his beliefs and see where things go. Since such belief systems are inevitably part of most of us, however, we should have no expectation that we can easily think entirely independently of our private "theories" without the assistance of psychoanalytic freedom.

Put differently, perhaps the only kind of truth we can know is a retrospective truth, one that is understood deeply only after considerable investment in time and patience. This is certainly the case of those personal truths discovered in psychoanalysis. I believe the study of the works and the lives of Aristotle, Kant, and Freud (Chapter One) suggest this would also be the case for significant learning within any setting, and not just within psychoanalysis.

At this point it seems appropriate to present some clinical case material to illustrate some of the ideas noted above.

Clinical cases

Case 1

A middle-aged deaf man presented for psychiatric care after he became afraid that his hearing son would soon leave home. His anxiety about loss was massive, but what was most difficult was that during the first interview with me he signed too quickly for me to understand him and he insulted me for my stupidity in not understanding his signing. However, he *did* sign very clearly and slowly that he hated Jews, men, and doctors! I answered that for this reason it would be better for him to be interviewed first with another person, a woman, someone much more fluent in sign language than I was at the time. But I made it clear that afterward I would return, and that I hoped we could work together.

When I returned, to my surprise and dismay this patient was willing to meet with me for therapy, and we made arrangements. All of the beginning sessions involved his asking me to help him in one way or another, most of which I attempted to accomplish. Sometimes I had to help him make urgent telephone calls (at the time portable TTY machines did not exist, nor did the telephone company relay service by which the deaf can get free translation assistance in receiving and sending messages). At other times I felt placed in impossible quandaries involving making arrangements for him, where he would change his schedule and expect me to accommodate him by changing my own right away. Usually, after some discussion, we found a compromise time, but often not until tempers had been tested severely.

Most troubling, however, was his intense rage. Later, when the treatment came to a highly successful planned termination after about three years of collaboration, I asked him why he had been so angry when we started out. He laughed and signed: "I felt then that life as a deaf person was so hard for me, why should I make things easy for you!" By this time I had developed considerable affection for him. But along the way he pushed my capacity for empathy as hard or harder than anyone I have ever worked with.

Why did this treatment work? My expectations at the beginning were of disaster. Once, for example, he threatened to kill someone with whom he was angry. It was all I could do to help him calm down and convince him that such action would be wrong. Finally, I threatened to call the police if necessary. I said I would call the intended victim if I did not get credible reassurances that my patient would drop any plans for attacking this person. It was quite frightening. But the fascinating thing is that somehow, in spite of everything, we were gradually learning to trust each other. Yet this was in contrast to how we felt when we started out on our journey. Then we decided to go against our initial impressions that the situation was totally hopeless. He really began with the thought that I was the worst therapist he could possibly have been given. I felt the same: I could not imagine a worse patient.

Later we discovered, however, that *when we suspended our beliefs about each other, things began to happen that facilitated closer collaboration.* Ultimately, we turned out to be very precisely well matched to work together. I loved his cranky intensity, especially his ability to express his thoughts clearly, even though they were very often insulting. His intelligence was quite impressive. He in turn greatly appreciated my ability to concentrate on entering his world, the world of the deaf, with him as my guide. And I believe in this I was a bright student of his.

Without a doubt his world felt terrifying to us both, that is, the hearing world in which deaf people can be essentially *persona non grata*. I learned from him about hearing people who could be cruel to the deaf for no other reason than that the deaf were different. He told me how someone had attacked him viciously in an elevator, nearly injuring him seriously, when the person asked him to step aside so they could get out, and (of course) my patient had done nothing (since he had not heard that person speak). Life was full of hearing people not taking into account his deafness.

I made so many mistakes in treating this patient that it was amazing to me that he continued with me at all. Often I did not understand his signs (I was learning sign language at the time), so he not only had to explain his difficulties, but teach me his language simultaneously. He had to laboriously finger-spell the meaning of his signs whenever I forgot them, which was often!

Yet in spite of everything, there was progress in both of us. Especially poignant was a joint session with his son. The son was hearing and had been the patient's ears from childhood. Now seventeen, he was hoping to head off to college; but how could he abandon his father? By the end of the session we were all crying. Part of what made things progress, I believe, was our ability to assume that we each were working as best we could, and that we did not mean to hurt each other by what we were doing or not doing. The son did not want to hurt his father by his leave taking; he only wanted a chance to grow up on his own, without the burdens of parenting his father. And the father was not trying to hurt his son by hoping he would not leave; he really loved his son and did not know how he could manage without him. Yet he felt if he could get along with such a stupid therapist as I was, he could possibly get along satisfactorily without his son as translator.

If we had been "reasonable" at the beginning of treatment we would never have worked together. Luckily, we suspended belief and acted on the assumption that we might be wrong and, in fact, we both were, and often! I will always remember this wonderful, brave patient and at times I wonder how he is doing. This case as much as any other reminds me of how often we can be mistaken in judging people by surface features, and how crucial it is to suspend belief until we have facts to fill in accurately the gaps in our knowledge.

Case 2

An exorcism assists psychodynamic insights. A middle-aged African American woman presented with free-floating anxiety in relation to being placed under a curse by someone who belonged to the same Cajun culture. Listening to the patient and her history, it was obvious that one could understand her plight from several different perspectives: either from the viewpoint of an ongoing psychotic process (in a schizophrenic or possibly borderline person) in which persecutory delusions were dominating her thinking, or, from the perspective of her cultural belief that, having been cursed, she required exorcism. Questions to her about her culture, and the evidence she used for judging whether she had been cursed or not, proved inconclusive. A complete mental status examination was not formally conducted, but close listening and observing convinced me finally that there was no obvious thought disorder. After working with this patient for months, however, it became increasingly obvious that if she was psychotic in a paranoid sense, this seemed localized to the experience of her believing herself cursed, and to nothing else in her life.

One day she asked me how I felt about her having an exorcism! I responded, somewhat surprisingly even to myself, that I could well understand this wish, given her upbringing and experience, and if she felt this would help, then why not go ahead with it. After all, she clearly knew much more about such things than I did. I also added, however, that I hoped that whatever she decided to do we would continue to talk about her experience and understand it.

Within a week she had arranged for an exorcism, which proved highly effective, after which we were able to continue analyzing what appeared to be the residual of a deleterious relationship with what sounded like a deeply disturbed mother. At the end of her treatment she thanked me sincerely, especially for my being understanding about her culture. *I had respected her beliefs, and this had been decisive.* Her recovery has lasted all these years, so far as I know. By termination she was anxiety free, and had some significant insight into her problems, in particular, the role of her mother in repeatedly humiliating or not accepting her. In the process of exploring her childhood memories she also discovered that much of her source of pride and strength emanated from her Cajun culture, which now appeared less fearful when experienced as separate from her experience of her mother. Diagnostically, I was unable to rule out a psychotic process. It was unclear, however, if she herself was psychotic, or if we had witnessed the memory of a psychosis that belonged to her mother and which the patient experienced in her early childhood (and re-experienced in her treatment).

Although my patient experienced me as accepting, actually I was somewhat defensive about listening to someone tell me about such things as spells and exorcism. This became obvious to me when I realized that I first considered this belief system to be something that separated my patient and myself from each other. That is, until I remembered enjoying *Fiddler on the Roof*, which is, of course, saturated with similar Jewish superstitious beliefs that undoubtedly influence me as her beliefs influence her.

Fortunately for our collaboration, I also felt willing to suspend any defensive use of my scientific belief systems, so with my patient's permission I had entered her world, temporarily, with her as my guide. In a similar way, undoubtedly, she suspended her skepticism about working with a Jewish doctor, whatever this meant to her. *Because we were each able to suspend belief and judgment about the other we were able to temporarily share experiential space in which collaboration and mutual trust held sway.* Our differing backgrounds became incidental to the meeting of our minds, our joint concern for sharing feelings and ideas about what might explain her fears, and finding approaches to their resolution that did not violate her precious values and beliefs.

Such examples could be multiplied from everyone's practice. I believe enough has been presented, however, in the two cases above to clarify at least my concrete meaning of the pressure the analyst is under to temporarily suspend beliefs for the purpose of allowing a sufficient level of neutrality and openness to new ideas. This, of course, serves as a model for the patient's own temporary suspension of belief, which allows for creative solutions to old problems. It is our job as analysts to do everything we can to support such constructive temporary suspensions of belief. And, of course, in doing so we are following in the footsteps of Aristotle, Kant, and Freud.

Summary and conclusions

This essay follows from our study of the epistemology of Freud's work as mapped out in Chapter One, wherein Freud is part of a developmental line that starts with Aristotle's experimentalism and builds upon the empiricism of Kant. Freudian *psychoanalytic theory, especially the postulation of a dynamic unconscious, represents a decisive turning point in the philosophy of mind* (and the history of science), which can be seen as having stagnated in this respect before the invention by Freud of psychoanalysis.

A major conclusion from the review of the history of philosophy of mind is that *creative thinking requires the ability to temporarily suspend one's systems of belief,* although it is recognized that this may be problematic depending upon how intrinsic one's belief systems may be for the functioning of the self. *The temporary suspension of belief is what allows us to go beyond our current beliefs,* in effect, to think the unthinkable. Aristotle did so when he allowed himself to ponder scientific questions apart from the religious beliefs of his time. Kant made a further inroad into such suspension of belief when he thought deeply about proofs about the existence of God, a soul, and free will, concluding that these beliefs cannot be proven in the same way one can prove scientific facts. He made still more progress (and set the stage for neuropsychology) when he observed that there can be no observations that are free of theory, that perception is really apperception. And Freud revolutionized science and contributed to philosophy by temporarily suspending his personal religiosity or spirituality in order to plumb the depths of the human psyche and discovered the Unconscious Mind.

Through very clever strategies Freud was able to begin to solve the philosophical paradox of being objective about subjectivity (or one might say, subjective about objectivity). But the danger today is that we may use such strategies as his to avoid being open to further change. The challenge is how to hold on to the insights of the past while continuing to discover and create new observations. In the present chapter I try to bring together some of the philosophical issues raised in Chapter One (and as prelude to Chapters Four and Five). In my opinion, the key to further advances in finding workable theories of learning and of transference lies in two directions: the first is the building and testing of our theorizing through interdisciplinary perspectives, something this entire monograph aims at; the second is to use our psychoanalytic methodology in the service of improving our ability to temporarily suspend our various belief systems as a means of opening up ourselves and our patients to newer and better theories. Our scientific creativity requires that our beliefs remain dispensable. And our patients cannot learn without a similar openness.

CHAPTER FOUR

The special relationship between psychoanalytic transference, similarity judgment, and the priming of memory*

Fred Levin and Ernest W. Kent

H umans create databases from experience that they deepen and enlarge over time. It is the product of this deepening and enlarging process that we call knowledge. Knowledge keeps us safe from danger and enhances our chances of reaching wished-for goals. Of course, some knowledge is wrong in that it leads to faulty conclusions or unsuccessful adaptation. For example, how much of the content of this essay is correct may be difficult to say at this time. This last observation points out the importance of continually testing and therefore updating our knowledge bases.

Within the psychoanalytic situation, the analyst and patient engage the patient's complexity, experiencing together crucial countertransference and transference states that become a major object of their study. Over the years, psychoanalysts have learned how to tap this vital, conscious and unconscious dialectical stream of information about feeling states, behavior, and cognitive

---

* Earlier versions of this paper were presented May 19, 1994, to the American Psychoanalytic Association in Philadelphia, PA, and on October 7, 1994, to Psyche '94, The International Symposium on Mind–Body Problems, Osaka University Medical School, Osaka, Japan. It was published as Levin, 1995f.

patterning. The resulting self-knowledge and working through of feelings greatly facilitate the mastery of conflict and emotional growth by means of updating and improving the key knowledge bases upon which our adaptive skills depend.

This chapter attempts to explore more deeply the mystery of transference. It suggests that *what analysts call transference involves the transfer of knowledge and the creation of expert systems.* In a nutshell, the understanding of one's personal knowledge alters its organization, making it both more accurate and useful (i.e., more like an expert system). Clearly, psychoanalysis looks to psychology to help understand how knowledge is transferred between content domains (that is, to identify the governing principles involved). Similarly, psychoanalysis depends upon neuroscience to understand better the basic machinery and mechanisms by which knowledge bases are created, modified, and tapped within our brains.

Yet psychology and neuroscience must depend upon psychoanalysis to better appreciate the significance of such a covert human phenomenon as transference, into which our affects are organized and which so significantly influences human knowledge organization and decision making. This is because psychology and neuroscience do not routinely include information about the highest level of man's psychological and affective organization, as is manifest through transference. Cognitive psychology in particular has also had great difficulty integrating affect into its models.

The core of *this chapter centers upon what appears to the authors to be a special relationship between psychoanalytic transference, the judgment of similarity, and the priming of memory. Our idea, briefly, is that these three processes use closely related machinery of mind and brain.* Addressing the relationship between these three processes, therefore, should help us bridge psychoanalysis, cognitive psychology, and neuroscience, bringing us a step closer to a basic scientific understanding of how mind and brain work.

Definitions and clarifications

Some definitions and clarifications seem in order. To begin, the central concept of *transference* traditionally refers to a tendency toward "displacement of patterns of feeling and behavior, originally expressed with significant figures of one's childhood, [onto] individuals in one's current relationship," including of course one's analyst (Moore & Fine, 1968, p. 92). A number of qualifications are important: (1) transference always involves affects, and any affective gestalt or ego state can become a transference; (2) transference invariably arises in attunement or reaction to persons (in one's environment or in one's memory); (3) some psychoanalytic scholars no longer consider transference to be disintegration products of the drives, but rather modes of cognition (Gedo, personal communication, 1994; Modell, 1993); and (4) given the above descriptions of transference there can be no question that *transference always involves judgment of similarity comparing past and present figures (or, put differently, that various real-life situations prime affects, which in turn lead to transference).*

Turning now to psychology, *judging similarity* (and difference) can be based on superficial or deep structural correspondence (Gentner & Ratterman, 1991a,b) and has been considered "one of the most central theoretical constructs in psychology," pervading virtually all theories of cognition (Medin, Goldstone, & Gentner, 1993, p. 254). Later in this chapter we shall introduce a model of mind that updates one introduced by one of us (Kent, 1981). *In our new model of mind–brain we shall attempt to show how priming and similarity can be defined in terms of coactivation of elements in the model that relate to attentional and motivational states.* However, for practical purposes at this point in our discussion, the reader should merely consider that "transfer of learning is said to hinge crucially on the similarity of the transfer situation to the original training context. An important gestalt principle of perceptual organization is that similar things will tend to be grouped together" (Medin, Goldstone, & Gentner, 1993, p. 254).

Most important for this chapter is what seems to make experts better than novices, namely, their familiarity with certain paradigms and their consequent advantage in judging similarity and transferring relevant knowledge between content domains. (By the way, we apologize for using similar sounding terminology to mean different things here: transferring knowledge means what it seems, transferring information from one content domain to another; and this is different from transference, by which we always mean "psychoanalytic transference").

Finally, regarding neuroscience, the *priming of memory* generally refers to the effect of perception on recall within specific brain memory systems. Some memories are declarative (some say representational or explicit), whereas others are procedural (or implicit), and a characteristic of the latter is that "a substantial part of the information may be stored at a few discrete loci, e.g. synapses in the [neural] network. *What is stored is the altered probability for a stimulus-evoked response, and retrieval is actually the readout of the information in the reflex*" (Dudai, 1987, p. 403, my emphasis; also see Levin, 1991).

In other words, *some past events captured in the mind–brain are principally retrieved only when part of the original experience creating them recurs. The evocation of such retrieval is called priming.* Perhaps some examples will help. If I sing the beginning of a song, you may be able to remember the rest of it, even though it is long forgotten, because of the stimulating effect of your perceptual experience. Similarly, if as the result of brain injury you lose your ability to walk (having "forgotten" the engrams), should I place you in water you may, by virtue of re-experiencing the movement of your legs, begin a swimming movement and subsequently recover the ability to walk (Sacks, 1984). In fact, this is how Oliver Sacks recovered his ability to walk after a serious fall.

Declarative and procedural memories appear to involve different brain circuitry. Specifically, declarative knowledge ". . . is affected by lesions of the limbic system, especially the hippocampus, amygdala, and mammillary bodies. In contrast, the . . . [procedural system] probably requires the participation of the basal ganglia and cerebellum" (Dudai, 1987, p. 404). Because transference probably involves both declarative (explicit) and procedural (implicit) memory, it seems likely that the corticolimbic, corticostriatal, and corticovestibulocerebellar circuits would each be involved in its case. Detailed attempts to further buttress these claims have been made elsewhere (Levin, 1991).

In what follows, we shall compare and relate the three processes that are the principal subject of this essay from a number of perspectives. We shall also diagram, describe, and compare dynamic models of mind–brain in which these processes can be seen as parts. The reader may then judge for himself if we have established a sufficient basis for further study of *the interlocking nature of priming, transference, and judging similarity.* Table 1 summarizes the points already made.

Table 1. Subprocesses and their properties.

Subprocess at issue	Transference	Judging similarity	Priming memory
Investigating discipline	Psychoanalysis	Cognitive psychology & neurophysiology	
Defining characteristic	Displacement of feelings from old to new figures	Comparing structural similarities	The part reads out the whole
Memory type	Declarative, procedural	Declarative, procedural	Procedural
Relevant brain structure	Limbic (hippocampus, amygdala, mamlary bodies)	Limbic	Basal ganglia (striatum), cingulate cortex cerebellum, limbic thalamus

Models of mind and brain

The reader will wonder how the three processes under examination might fit into current models of mind–brain. Of course, such efforts to systematically relate functions across disciplines are extremely rare (Chapter Two; also see Levin, 1991, and Reiser, 1990, for a review of such efforts). We shall present and illustrate our ideas about how such a synthesis might begin.

Figure 1 (see p. 62) depicts an updated version of the model of mind–brain organization presented earlier by one of the authors (Kent, 1981). First, some general remarks about the model. The model is simultaneously parallel and hierarchical, with four major divisions noted: an input (sensory/perceptual) system, and output (motor) system, a goal selection system, and a "world model." In addition, where in the system interaction occurs with the external world is made explicit. Proceeding upward, one goes from large numbers of synthesizers to small numbers of integrators, from concrete to abstract, and from spinal cord toward cortex. The arrows in Figure 1 show schematically the general direction of information flow or activity (which can be described as roughly clockwise).

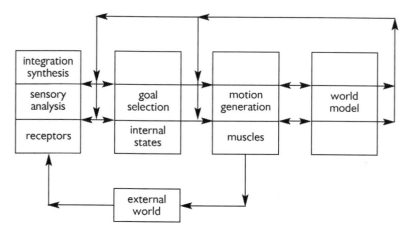

Figure 1. A conceptual representation of the basic organization of the brain's architecture. The organization is both parallel and hierarchical. The four major functional systems (input, goal direction, world model, and output) are shown. Each of the major systems is assumed to connect with each other at high, low, and intermediate levels of processing and interconnections with other systems at each level. Many data paths may exist in the system. Square areas indicate databases in which massive amounts of information are processed simultaneously, in parallel. Arrows indicate sites of major interactions between systems.

Because of the importance of this model it will be useful to describe its workings. The central goal-selection portion becomes an input to a "world-model" that represents the system's internal construction of hypotheses, models, beliefs, and so on, about the nature of the external world. At each level there are linkages as follows: a feedback loop would be established between the world-model and the sensory processing system in which input from the sensory processing system would be evaluated and used to update the world-model. Input from the world-model would also be used to present hypotheses about expected sensory input (based on world-model contents and current actions). On the other side (of the diagram), input to the world-model from the action-generating system would provide the modeling system with information concerning current actions which would allow it to predict states of upcoming sensory input. In turn, the world-model would return to the action-generating system hypothesized results to be worked on the world as the result of planned actions. In particular, it would use the input from the goal-selecting system to identify goal-relevant stimuli (by modeling anticipated sensory input) and generate appropriate attention directives to the sensory processing system, thus providing the action-generating system with the information on predicted consequences of planned actions with respect to goal-relevant stimuli.

The question that seems important to us at this juncture is where would one place priming, similarity judgment, and transference within the updated model of Kent? An approximate answer appears in Figure 2(b) (a blow-up of the goal selection system). Within Figure 2(b), priming is depicted at the lower end of the model because of its known relationship to the perception of motor output activity. In contrast, transference and similarity judgment are diagrammed as running the entire length of the goal selection system because they are known to involve multiple levels of abstraction depending upon whether based upon superficial or deep comparisons.

A more complex answer to the question of localization within the model of Figure 2(a) will be attempted in the next section (see also

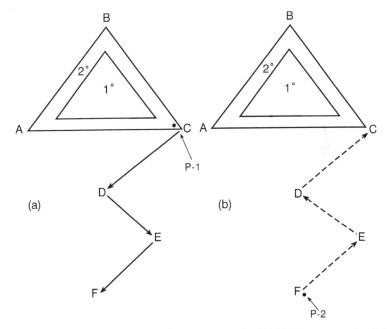

Figure 2. In the left triangle case the "association" of C–D–F starts at point P-1 which is an intrinsic pointer to an important connection of points D, E, F to what the triangle "represents". The dotted lines in the right triangle's connection indicates that this connection of the triangle with D, E, F is false, since it starts from point P-2, which is *not* related to the triangle. Sometimes "associations" have only superficial similarity.

pp. 94–95, Chapter Five, for further discussion of Figure 2(a) and (b)). At this point, however, we shall move on to the work of Hadley and Gabriel, which we believe to be highly complementary to Kent's model. We shall then use these three models to further illuminate something that might be called motivation, discrimination, or simply thinking with the goal of solving problems.

We shall begin with Hadley's perspective on the limbic system. The circuit (Figure 3) that is judged to be crucial motivational machinery for mind–brain involves a cortico–hippocampal–amygdala–striatal–hypothalamic–cortical loop (Hadley, 1989; also see Cloninger, 1991). According to Hadley two basic organizing principles are involved in any such motivation or goal selection: (1) "the maintenance of familiarity of neural firing patterns" based especially on limbic (notably hippocampal) comparator mechanisms, and (2) the use of pleasure-unpleasure affect signals for steering behavioral choices through a matching/mismatching process" (p. 337). The motivational system depicted schematically in Figure 3 shows the basic flow of information within the limbic circuit (p. 339). Hadley's description of comparator mechanisms and matching–mismatching processes clearly highlights the important role of comparing gestalts and judging similarity.

We now move on to the research of Gabriel of the Beckman Institute, University of Illinois. Gabriel (1991) has been investigating the brain's patterns of excitation in association with discriminative learning in rabbits. The changing patterns of firing of individual brain cells and clusters of brain cells demonstrate the performance of two fundamental neural computations: (1) "motor priming (centered in the striatal motor areas)" and (2) "event-processing (centered in the cingulate cortex and limbic thalamus)" (p. 11). The former system primes motor patterns but cannot encode, recall, or interpret information. The latter system encodes, recalls, and interprets events but has no effect on motor priming. We will first describe Gabriel's experimental paradigm in our own terms, then in Gabriel's terms. In general, the rabbits must make choices in matching to sample, for which they can receive rewards (or avoid punishments) if they are successful. The key point to note is that, remarkably, *Gabriel has been able to place the electrodes in the rabbits' brains so that the oscillographic patterns associated with learning can be identified and followed, from region to region.* As Gabriel states:

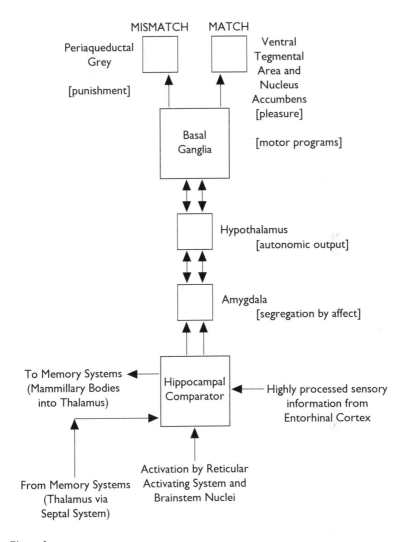

Figure 3.

The predictive cue presented to a trained rabbit [first] elicits the established topographic retrieval pattern in the limbic thalamus [meaning, a pattern already identified as the oscillographic signature of a particular learned relationship between a perceptual event and a behavioral response]. The pattern is [next] projected to the posterior cingulate cortex, where it is compared to the "historical" mnemonic template [which is the pattern associated with past success]. [On the one hand] if the [current] pattern matches the [historical] template, [then] cells in the cingulate cortex send a command volley to the motor system. [On the other hand] if a match does not occur, the learned [motor] response is suppressed and [something called] the anterior cingulate cortical recency system is activated [the purpose of which is] to encode novel mismatch-generating events. [p. 11]

By the way, so far as we understand it, Gabriel's reference to *historical mnemonic template* is a neural firing pattern which he actually identifies experimentally, and not something that he merely hypothesizes.

Figure 3 also illustrates how *all levels of processing within the limbic circuit involve comparisons between goal states and intermediate states*. In a manner similar to Hadley and Gabriel, Kent describes what he calls "the basic equipment of the brain for rational thought [meaning problem-solving, goal-directing thought processes]" (Kent, 1981, p. 203). For Kent, this involves the following: *selective attention* to goal-relevant features of both input and internal states; *suppression of output* to goal-relevant features of both input and internal states; *suppression of output* temporarily pending evaluation of the projected outcomes of possible actions; *defining intermediate goal states* on the basis of similarity to the desired goal states; and finally, *targeting temporary goals* on the basis of current and past associations with goal relevant stimuli.

Now our conclusion: We perceive a close relationship between Hadley's, Gabriel's, and Kent's ideas. Kent's are the oldest, yet they neatly describe in operational terms the steps involved in discriminative (i.e., rational) thought and their temporal relationship. Hadley's and Gabriel's viewpoints cover much the same ground but take into account some of the latest neurophysiological research on goal selection, and also describe some of the functional anatomy involved. By combining the viewpoints of these three scholars *we can begin to appreciate how complexity gets built into the variety of cognition which we are calling judgments of similarity*. Because input relative to needed judgments about similarity is likely to occur at multiple levels within the "information bus" of the limbic circuit (forgive the computer term "bus" for the information highway within a computer program linking the various data flow paths), therefore similarity judgments will differ substantially, because some will be based on superficial characteristics, while others will be based on deep, structural similarity. In other words, *we are hypothesizing that the differences in kinds of similarity judgment themselves result from the amount of information that gets included in the comparison;* that is, quantitative differences create qualitative differences when critical thresholds are reached (compare with Galatzer-Levy, 1978).

How similarity judgment and priming might be conceptualized in the revised model of Kent

Kent's revision of his earlier model provides a more sophisticated, plausible, and detailed depiction of mind–brain operation, and one that better lends itself to the task at hand of appreciating the relationship between a number of complex variables. Priming in such a scheme could be understood simply as a coactivation of certain elements in the model as follows: (1) by similarity to elements in the model with current sensory input and (2) in relation to input from motivational systems. Another way of stating this with precision mathematically is that within Kent's mind–brain model the recursive (i.e., reiterated) estimation evaluation in the sensory-input/world-model module provides a feedback loop onto similar stimuli, the result being that the model will have a tendency to accept the input as relevant to the model of the target of the motivational state. In essence, we are attempting to describe how *relevance* appears in the model, and how priming and similarity judgment neatly dovetail in the model's operation. The beauty of such a model, of course, is that it also corresponds with known patterns of functioning of mind–brain.

We apologize for the mathematical language employed in this section, but we wish to describe accurately something that will allow a better appreciation of certain relationships, so we ask the reader to bear with us temporarily, and will try to make things clearer before long. In particular, what we are interested in here is a new way of understanding similarity judgment and priming in the revised model (of Kent) we are putting forward. We would suggest that the brain system we are describing might be modeled mathematically (conceptualized) as a system input space[24] spanned by various primary sensory attributes (e.g., luminosity, color, retinal location, time of occurrence, etc.). Technically, this would include values for each point location within the so-called input space together with all their partial derivatives to about fourth order. Such a space (termed technically a "jet bundle") provides essentially a model of the local sensory input to fourth order (that is, to great detail), for each point in the theoretical input space. To this one can add a scale dimension so that the local neighborhood (or collection of input space points) is represented at various sizes but with decreasing resolution. In such a space, any stimulus will have some vector distance from any other. *One could take this vector distance as a measure of similarity* (and thus concretize the concept of similarity). If, then, we let the attention function provided by the world-model project the vectors representing any two stimuli onto some relevant subspace of interest, this may well decrease the vector distance (in other words, increase the similarity) between any two stimuli relative to others, *so the perception of similarity becomes a function not only of the stimuli themselves, but of the attention function, which in turn may be influenced by motivational states or planned actions.* If our logic eludes some readers, we beg to suggest that what we have just stated is merely an attempt to describe how Kent's revised model can itself be used, with mathematical strategies, to emulate mind and brain activity (as on a computer) as well as to operationally define *attention* and *motivation*. In fact, it is the very ease of performing such an emulation that lends plausibility to the model itself.

The criticality of similarity categorization for organizing databases of mind–brain

Gentner's work on similarity posits a central importance for similarity judgment as a process at the core of human cognition. Yet similarity from her perspective actually seems to her decomposable into a number of kinds of similarity judgment, and these probably fall as well into a rough developmental sequence (Gentner & Ratterman, 1991a,b; Medin, Goldstone, & Gentner, 1993). *It thus becomes possible for us to compare Gentner's view on the judging of similarity with our psychoanalytic conception of the transference phenomenon.* First, like similarity judgments, transference hypothetically expresses a variety of components. Second, the components in the case of both similarity judgment and transference probably reflect as well a developmental sequence or process. (We cannot prove this assertion, but it would seem plausible given the evolving nature of transference over the life-span.) Third, both transference and similarity judgment can be seen as serving the larger function of organizing and expanding the knowledge bases of mind–brain. For the purpose of this essay, it thus becomes important to carry our comparison of transference and similarity judgment as far as possible to better understand how these processes might further connect. Let us explain.

Transference to others in our growing-up years, or to other adults, including our analyst, involves bringing into alignment at least two sets of characteristics, namely, those associated with interpersonal experience from different eras. Based upon Gentner's research, including her own attempts to emulate similarity judgments on computers, similarity judgment seems to proceed most easily by a two-step process. The first step seems likely to be a match according to superficial or surface features, which assumes that surface similarity is often correlated with deep or structural similarity. Gentner notes that such a method will inevitably result in errors, but it is computationally "cheap" (Gentner & Ratterman, 1991b, p. 41; also compare with Newell & Simon, 1985). The more costly similarity mapping computations are then only performed on the "winners" of the first, approximate matching process. Obviously, as experience gradually occurs in any particular content domain, a natural tendency to eliminate errors will appear based on the creation of "expert systems."

Reasoning by analogy, *one reasonable inference is that the psychoanalytic transference represents a critical early stage or "probe" in the initial surface-matching process*, which might or might not be borne out by further, costly similarity-mapping computations. *Thus transference allows us gradually to bring into focus deep structural similarities and thus gain in our understanding and appreciation of past and present experience by comparing them.* In other words, *transference is a step in the creation and deepening of the details of expert systems.* Levin makes a similar point when he speculates about the possible evolutionary value of the transference phenomenon itself (Levin, 1991, chapter 8, especially pp. 169–171; see also Chapter Five of this monograph).

The exact details of the similarity-judging system, however, are not crucial to the argument introduced at the outset of this essay that similarity judgments are likely a core part of the goal selection system of mind–brain, and the major element from which psychoanalytic transference emerges on the basis of contextual clues and the priming of memory.

Conclusions

Specifically we have noted that *at the core of the transference are two general processes that would seem to characterize all goal-directed thinking, namely, the judging of similarity (and difference) and the priming of memory*. In previous publications Levin (1991, especially chapter 1) has discussed the importance of allowing priming to generously invade the psychoanalytic situation. In this essay we are more specifically suggesting that *priming in the form of transference facilitates not only the retrieval of information, but the deepening of our internal knowledge bases as well, so as to form expert systems*. This would seem to be the consequence of repetitive cycles of priming our memory for old solutions that are usable for new problems, and the judging of similarity sufficiently to apply solutions only to appropriate cases (i.e., the refining of such judgments).

The core of the entire cognitive system of the brain would thus appear to be a system for making various kinds of refined judgments of similarity and difference. Psychology is learning about similarity just as neuroscience is learning about priming. But the key to our understanding human behavior more comprehensively would seem to be appreciating the relationship between priming, similarity judgment, and our emotionally meaningful psychoanalytic transferences. This is because *it is only our transferences that code for the highest level of meaning within the human system of goal selection;* moreover, only transference accounts for affects that undoubtedly organize memory along lines of similarity of feeling.

Some will object to the juxtaposition of judging similarity, priming memory, and the psychoanalytic transference, believing that this contributes little or nothing to the difficult task of understanding any of these phenomena. However, along with Ricoeur (1981) we hold that "all new rapprochement runs against a previous categorization" (p. 234) which disturbs us significantly and requires the suspension of belief, at least temporarily (see Chapter Three). Based upon the evidence and reasoning presented, *we would argue that these three phenomena are closely enough related that they likely employ sufficiently similar mind–brain machinery to make studying them in tandem advantageous.*

To add to the plausibility of our speculations we have also taken the time to elaborate on earlier models of mind–brain, generate a new model, and describe how it can be used technically to emulate the kinds of similarity and priming activities that we believe are key parts of the mechanisms of such models. The result is that *transference becomes less mysterious when it is broken down into subprocesses that can be studied and related to each other, such as we attempt to do in this essay.*

We have thus come full circle, to appreciate how *transference functions as a critical means of keeping our knowledge updated, so it can function better as an expert system.* We have also seen how this proceeds by means of steps that involve comparing past and present affective (emotionally meaningful) experiences, and transferring such knowledge from one domain to another. Finally, we have presented a detailed model, capable of emulation by computer, of how mind and brain work with regard to the variables under discussion: judging similarity, priming memory, and our psychoanalytic transferences. In our opinion this model is both sophisticated and supported by many facts about mind–brain operation culled from cognitive psychology, neuroscience, and psychoanalysis. Of course, this does not prove the model, but it does make it compelling.

CHAPTER FIVE

Integrating some mind and brain views of transference: the phenomena*

Fred Levin

Introduction

This chapter[25] builds on the insights of Chapters 1–4 and further examines novel interdisciplinary perspectives on transferential learning phenomena. Extra-analytic information about the more general set of phenomena that constitutes transference enhances both clinical work and psychoanalytic theory construction. As we have seen, making correlations with ideas from cognate fields accelerates the contribution of psychoanalysis to more general scientific theories (Waelder, 1962). At the level of clinical theory, Merton Gill saw interdisciplinary analyses as highly relevant attempts to understand psychoanalytic phenomena from the broadest perspective possible.

Some notable interdisciplinary efforts have appeared on the subject of transference: for example, Fried, Crits-Christoph, and Luborsky (1992) have documented the existence of transference phenomena outside the clinical context of psychoanalysis, thus confirming what psychoanalysts and cognitive psychologists have long inferred, that the transference concept has utility in explaining behavior generally and is not restricted solely to the clinical setting.

Also, Forrest (1991a,b) has discussed transference as a brain phenomenon susceptible to derangement in conditions such as the misidentification syndrome. Forrest (1994b, 1997) further warns us against splitting our thinking and clinical approaches to patients into partial domains where biological and psychological approaches are conceptualized as unrelated entities.

Priel and Schreiber (1994) have approached transference from the perspective of chaos theory (an approach pursued in detail in Chapters Eleven and Twelve). Chaos theory is a branch of nonlinear dynamics that identifies hidden order in data that otherwise appear random. Whether we are observing the rate of a faucet's dripping, the beating of a heart, or the electrical activity of the brain, it is now possible to find orderliness in nature in an unprecedented way that allows for predictions and, at times, effective interventions that reorder systems.

Priel and Schreiber's work shows that during analysis psychologically significant developmental points appear to cluster in temporal patterns that can be technically characterized in terms of mathematical objects known as "strange attractors" (Levin, 1996b). Strange attractors are indicators of chaos, a state of rapid doubling that occurs at a rate related to the Feigenbaum constant, a number in nature much like the number we call *pi*. "The term 'attractor' derives from the observation that if a system in phase space [defined below] is near an attractor, it tends to evolve towards the state represented by the attractor" (Çambel, 1993, p. 59). For example, from the perspective of attractor theory, the complex movement of a decelerating pendulum toward a fixed point is seen as conforming to an attractor rather than being controlled by gravity. The term *phase space* denotes the theoretical space in which a point moves according to a set of equations that cover its position, velocity, and acceleration (*ibid.*, p. 44).

Priel and Schreiber's nonlinear dynamical study of transference opens the door to analyzing the associative structure of transference and related memory phenomena in standard terms that cross disciplinary boundaries. Such results make psychoanalysis more interesting and accessible to scientists of other backgrounds (Levin, 1995a) and show that the insights of psychoanalysis can sometimes advance knowledge in other disciplines.

I aim at two specific goals: (1) to reconcile what is understood about transference from within the field of psychoanalysis proper with what is known about transference from extrapsychoanalytic perspectives; and (2) to describe explicitly, using a combination of traditional and nontraditional perspectives, a number of specific circumstances and neurocognitive mechanisms through which transferences result in learning.

The psychoanalytic and extrapsychoanalytic perspectives on transference presented below include some of our latest ideas about transferential learning mechanisms, along with neural net theory (Forrest, 1995), work on the relationship between transference and the zone of proximal development, or ZPD (Wilson, 1995; Wilson & Weinstein, 1996), and research on schema theory (Lichtenberg, 1989a; Slap & Slap-Shelton, 1991; D. Stern, 1985). The extrapsychoanalytic perspective on such psychoanalytic process also dovetails nicely with psychoanalytic inquiries aimed at formulating better answers to such questions as what actually motivates transference. (By *motivates*, I mean *what moves transferences* in the sense that some complex inner mechanisms create the transference clinically, transferring our feelings onto individuals other than those for whom the transferences were first created.)

Transferences offer unique opportunities for expanding the meaning and depth of experience.[26] This follows from their tendency to sometimes lead us into mistaken judgments of similarity which then become potentially analyzable clinically under specifiable circumstances, as Freud discovered long ago (Levin, 1980, 1988b, 1991; Levin & Kent, 1995). *Specific supporting details and correlations presented here from the perspectives of psychoanalysis, cognitive psychology, and neurophysiology should create an indelible picture of transference phenomena as something of great power and undeniable interest to both clinicians and theoreticians.*

Yet bringing together in one place interdisciplinary work on what is relevant to a basic science understanding of transference inevitably also highlights how much remains to be explored. If transference were considered analogous to a spiderweb into which insects sometimes fly, then our current level of understanding of transference (as a psychobiological phenomenon) would be equivalent to the simple assertion that insects fly into webs. It is as if nothing more were required of us to account for the behavior of these hapless insects than to simplistically describe it. However, since insects clearly *may not* invariably benefit from their "mistakes," any more than transference patients automatically benefit from their transferences, so we need to search for a deeper explanation for such unusual behavior.

However, in the case of insects and spiderwebs, actually a few years ago an article in *Science* explained in a surprising fashion exactly why insects fly into webs. We begin with the fact that spiders fabricate their webs out of two distinctly different silky materials woven together, each with its own refractive index. The resulting web, when seen from the experiential perspective of the insect's visual system, looks roughly like three intersecting lines (i.e., something like the letter Y). To the same insect's visual system, flowers also look like Ys. As a result flies are more often ensnared in webs than would occur by chance alone, because webs and flowers happen to look alike to the flies' visual system.

What I am asserting by analogy with the spiderweb is that *transference is a very complex set of phenomena that deserves at least as much interdisciplinary attention as science accords the behavior of insects.* For example, sometimes transferences function primarily as resistance, with little that is obviously useful or insightful growing out of them at all.[27] In terms of our above spiderweb analogy, this would be equivalent to the insect dying in the web. At other times, however, transferences are exploited by analyst and analysand for therapeutic ends, and insight accrues from psychoanalytic exploration. This is analogous to an insect approaching and, upon closer scrutiny, avoiding a web (which is very tempting) by learning to distinguish between various kinds of web-related percepts. But, most important for our discussion, there are special times when knowledgeable individuals will recognize transferences even extraanalytically: they can then make use of this information to facilitate further learning. This would be analogous to our hypothetical insects learning permanently to avoid webs. We wish to understand specifically what determines such different outcomes, especially periods of unusual transferential learning.

To exploit our understanding of the potential consequences of transference clinically *we need to expand our knowledge of transference as a psychobiological phenomenon.* Like anything in nature that has evolved and survived in a particular species, transference phenomena must have an identifiable set of functions. What are the likely functions of transference? Under what circumstances are these functions potentially adaptive, that is, when might they promote human learning and survival, individually or collectively? Another way of putting the question would be to ask, What precisely motivates transferences? *Attempting to answer questions such as these can only enhance our ability to exploit the transference clinically.*

Freud's definitions of transference: resistance and adaptation

Freud first used the word *transference* in *Studies on Hysteria* (Breuer & Freud, 1895d) to describe "transferring on to the figure of the physician the distressing ideas . . . from the content of the analysis" (p. 302). The transference phenomenon was seen essentially as a "false connection" (pp. 302–303; see also Stone, 1995, p. 111). In Chapter Seven of *The Interpretation of Dreams* (1900a) we find Freud's most generalized definition: The transfer of the intensity of an unconscious idea to a preconscious content (pp. 562–563).

In the famous Dora case, Freud (1905e) asks "What are transferences?" and answers as follows:

> They are new editions or facsimiles of the impulses and phantasies which are aroused and made conscious during the progress of the analysis; but they have this peculiarity, which is characteristic for their species, that they replace some earlier person by the person of the physician [i.e. the patient's psychoanalyst]. [p. 116]

In other words, transference involves the attempt to relive past wishes or actual experience with people who were once important to them.

Freud elaborates these ideas in five major papers spanning the decade from 1910 to 1920. In the last of his five lectures on infantile sexuality and neurosis, Freud (1910a) notes the tendency of every neurotic in psychoanalytic treatment to develop affectionate feelings toward the analyst, thereby reviving old, unconscious fantasies, wishful and mostly sexual. These wishes, previously bound via compromise formations into neurotic symptoms, are in essence set free by the psychoanalytic situation.

The conscious derivatives of these unconscious sexual wishes set free in treatment—as transferences—may undergo various fates:

as Freud recognized, they can be ignored by the patient through various mental activities; they may be re-repressed, disavowed, or denied; they may spur the patient to seek gratification, or they may lead to psychological growth and insight. Most advantageously, the patient may consciously evaluate the transference and perceive its harmful outcomes. In theory, transference wishes may then be renounced (in response to the "voice of reason"), leading to the resumption of developmental trends that had long before been interrupted but which are now free to evolve safely and as a source of insight rather than a rationale for action or acting out.

After mentioning that transference first becomes the strongest weapon of the resistance, Freud (1912b, 1914g, 1920g) notes how in transference love the patient is in essence repeating rather than remembering, thereby avoiding the painful affect that would be associated with reexperiencing repressed memories that might provide an entrée to insight. Freud's remedy (1915a, 1916–1917) for the resistance of insisting on the analyst's help in the satisfaction of erotic wishes is as follows: the analyst needs to call attention to and analyze the meanings of the patient's transference wishes while simultaneously avoiding "acting in" with the patient.

In summary, Freud's emphasis is on the motivation of transference as resistance and on its relation to what has become known as the repetition compulsion, but also on the opportunity transference offers for insight based on the application of the proper psychoanalytic technique for dealing with it. To this extent, Freud attempts to explain the conundrum of the repetition compulsion. However, nowhere, except in Freud's generally rejected work on the death instinct, are explanations given for the psychological origin of repetition itself.

The question thus remains: How can we begin to place these precious Freudian perspectives within a larger conceptualization of transference as a ubiquitous learning phenomenon not limited to the psychoanalytic situation (Fried, Crits-Christoph, & Luborsky, 1992)? And how can we understand transference repetition and explain transference as both resistance and road to cure?

In a cogent discussion, Stone argues (1995, p. 114) that quantitative factors determine whether transferences lead to healthy or neurotic solutions. In his experience, transferences frequently "become an enduring and formidable component of resistance structure, always subject to 'renewal' through well-worn channels" (pp. 114–115). Stone's observation would appear to raise an important objection to my thesis, for if transference is a dramatic expression of resistance, how then can one assert that there is any adaptive aspect to transference? The brief answer is as follows: *the therapeutic use of the transference phenomenon clinically renders it adaptive.* Wilson and Weinstein (1996) explain some of the cognitive details (to be discussed later), which dovetail neatly with the neurocognitive descriptions I will offer regarding the specific circumstances and mechanisms that empower transferential learning.

No one doubts the awesome power of transferences in human behavior. Nonetheless, Pfeffer (1961, 1963) and Schlessinger and Robbins (1983) demonstrate clearly that during psychoanalysis, despite the resilience of transferential patterns, their recurrence in fact does change. Hence, within the mind of successfully analyzed subjects the mechanism of transference persists, but cycles of recurring conflict and its resolution take place within greatly abbreviated time spans as the analysis progresses, so that *the influence of transference on overall behavior gradually becomes significantly limited.* In terms of our earlier analogy, unlike the "mistakes" of insects flying into potentially lethal spiderwebs, these cases of transference behavior in humans in analysis often result in new learning and an enhanced ability to distinguish behavior in similar and dissimilar situations.

To summarize, the word *transference* has at least two possible meanings. One, more narrow, relates to the purely clinical situation and to questions of how analysts might best respond to the patient's transference at any given time. But the second meaning—the subject of this chapter—involves how we understand the set of transference phenomena more generally.

Reconciling the adaptive and the resistance perspectives on transference requires several additional lines of argument. The first asserts that *what is resistance from the perspective of the analyst is at the same time adaptive from the perspective of the patient.* Patients immersed in a transference are essentially operating in a primitive mode of cognition. As Freud discovered, what appears and acts in treatment as a transference resistance is also the most significant instance of reexperiencing decisive early childhood events in transaction with the analyst within the treatment context. *When properly appreciated and analyzed, transference repetition leads to resolution of conflicts.* In a nutshell, Freud taught us how to capitalize upon the transference, bringing conviction along with insight about hitherto unfathomable psychic dispositions.

A second integrative approach to the differing nuances of Freud's transference definitions would be as follows. If we assume that transference resistance represents perseveration in a mismatch (between the potentialities of past and present objects), the function of analytic intervention would be to show that there is an alternative preferable to the patient's transference perspective. Thus, transference repetition could be viewed as a miscarriage of the adaptive advantage of repeating. *In patients with an adequate defensive repertory, however, it seems that it is only through such things as dreams and transference repetitions that unconscious thoughts become knowable.* Seen from this perspective, transference repetition is crucial for adaptation. *It functions as one of a number of mechanisms humans have evolved for reprocessing the unconscious (primary process) language of the brain into symbolic terms we can comprehend and evaluate* (see Frank, 1969).

Transference resistances (as distinct from transference repetitions) also have utility for the patient. By means of what we label resistances, patients defend themselves against more novelty than they can process at a given time (Moraitis, 1988, 1991; Wilson & Weinstein, 1996). Viewed in this light, *transference resistance is a purely unconscious process that protects against overload.* Freud has shown us that the analysis of unconscious resistance (in the form of transference) is fruitful precisely because *it permits putting into consensual language what in the absence of transference would remain unspeakable and thus unrememberable.*[28]

It should be stressed, however, that in arguing that transference can be adaptive I am not asserting that transferences invariably result in learning or positive behavioral change; obviously, transferences often become formidable obstacles to adaptation and to treatment. I am suggesting rather that transference enactments, in and out of psychoanalytic treatment, are instances of repetition that contain within them the potential for change, depending on what happens next.

In the psychoanalytic situation, the analyst attempts to assure that what happens next will generally involve interpretive insight regarding the transference, rather than infantile gratification or further defensive complications. (Sometimes, however, we analysts are simply too obtuse to meet the challenge of helping the patient clinically.) Outside psychoanalysis, chance factors will obviously play a greater role in deciding whether transference repetitions result in learning, that is, whether a self-analytic process will obtain.

This discussion of the possible adaptive significance of transference in creating profound learning opportunities gives rise to an additional crucial question: In those instances where proper management of the transference could eventuate in learning, *how might we further our detailed understanding of the subprocesses involved so that we might optimally exploit for the patient's benefit the learning opportunities presented by the transference?* This is the subject of the remainder of this chapter. The question is important clinically, because if we do not understand how transference works we may lose opportunities to facilitate transferential learning in our patients and to allow them thereby to achieve the maximum benefit from psychoanalytic treatment.

Transference data, brain scans, and critical learning thresholds

This section describes (1) the thought processes that give rise to transference and (2) the neural substrates and mechanisms that support these processes. We will learn how the patient's active interest and attention coincides neurophysiologically with the establishment of simultaneous activation patterns in parts of the brain that lend themselves to recollection and synthesis in the form of "aha" reactions. *The topic of metaphorical transference interpretation (MTI) is introduced as one provocative agent for exceeding a critical learning threshold.* In this manner, the topics of similarity judgment and the priming of memory are introduced and then connected with working memory activation. Eventually, they become the subjects of more detailed focus in later sections of this paper.

Luborsky, Bachrach, Graff, Pulver, and Christoph (1979) have shown through the study of transcripts of psychoanalysis that examination of the three-minute period preceding particular "events" can result in significant insights into causal connections. In another study (Levin, 1980) I examined all the "aha" reactions in a five-year analysis and learned that this interval often begins with the use of a metaphor on the part of the analyst, one that attempts to characterize the transference in a novel way (see also Levin, 1991, chapter one). These metaphorical transference interpretations (MTIs) seem to enhance or prime the various kinds of "aha" experiences (i.e., to facilitate integration and/or insight).

Comparing these findings about "aha" reactions with certain findings of Lassen, Ingvar, and Skinhøj (1978), whose research pioneered brain scanning with radioactive xenon 133, I observed (Levin, 1980) two significant basic patterns in their scanning data. First, when people are significantly interested in what they are attending to, they appear to activate *simultaneously* their primary cortical association areas for touch, hearing, and vision; when people are engaged only half-heartedly, however, these same brain areas activate *serially*. What is the significance of these differing patterns of activation?

In MTI, the simultaneous activation pattern predominates. That is, when patients attend to a fascinating metaphor, they also experience complex intersensory bridging activity that accesses memory and inspires insight. But how does this occur? First, the bridging appears to draw together, into a neural net, brain areas concerned specifically with intersensory integration. Second, the transference metaphors (in the MTI) stimulate insights by the following means: (1) metaphor invokes crucial covert connections between experience in more than one sensory modality; (2) metaphorical interpretations invite the mind to connect with several levels of experience simultaneously; (3) the connections formed also depend on judgments of similarity and difference (Levin, 1991, pp. 145–164); and (4) the complexity of the bridging initiated by MTI bears a relationship to brain plasticity, interhemispheric mechanisms of defense and control, and to self-regulation within the vestibulocerebellar system (Levin & Vuckovich, 1983, 1987). Unfortunately, these last domains of inquiry are clearly beyond the scope of the present chapter.

What should be appreciated here, however, is that *transference influences critical learning thresholds within mind–brain*. The analyst's and the patient's entrée to such learning potential is through their joint and individual awareness and interpretation of transferences as they occur. In the sections to follow, we will come to better understand how transferential learning depends on the activation of working memory. In our attempts to understand the neurophysiological and neuropsychological basis for transferential learning, it may also help us to keep in mind the following: when cognitive tasks become difficult, areas of neural control such as the cerebellum and basal ganglia become active in recruiting "more neural tissue into each area of the [neural] network" (Just, Carpenter, Keller, Eddy, & Thulborn, 1996, p. 116), which increases the probability of effective problem solving. Thus, it seems likely that these centers for neural control and the subsystems they represent are caught up in transferences in significant ways.

A *thought experiment*

To better conceptualize "microscopically" what happens both clinically and experientially during the psychoanalytic transference, I ask the reader to join me in the following thought experiment (Levin, 1991, pp. 9–10 and chapter 8; 1994). Imagine you are falling through an imaginary landscape, namely, the virtual space (of personal transference categories) of your own mind (see Figure 4, p. 84). During this free fall imagine, as in a dream, that you land at various levels within this concretized mental hierarchy (represented in the figure by overlapping triangles). If you join me in this imagery, we may use it to appreciate some theoretical possibilities for understanding component subprocesses of the transference phenomenon that relate to transferential learning.

The image of mentation depicted in Figure 4 illustrates at least three different dynamic aspects of transference. First, *transference involves a regressive shift* (indicated by the free fall).[29] *A second aspect concerns the locus of the movement which is through the hierarchical levels of mind*, as represented by the same overlapping triangles. A conceptualization of the regressive and progressive swings through such a mental hierarchy has been presented by Gedo in his hierarchical-developmental model (Wilson & Gedo, 1993b). *A third aspect of transference concerns judgments of similarity*, which might be what connects specific points in the various triangles with one another (see, e.g., Levin, 1991, chapters 1–2). In other words, when we develop a current transference, we are connecting some experience of the present person with a similar experience of someone from our past.[30]

Figure 4.

Returning to the visual image in Figure 2 (see p. 63), let us apply two contemporary interdisciplinary perspectives to the subject of transferential learning mechanisms. The first is Vygotsky's "zone of proximal development," or ZPD (Wilson, 1995; Wilson & Weinstein, 1996; see also Kohut & Seitz, 1963, especially as regards a close cousin of ZPD, namely, the zone of progressive neutralization). The second is M. Stern's (1988) teleonomic (i.e., adaptive) viewpoint.

Wilson and Weinstein explain how "the ZPD works in tandem with the transference, . . . allowing for the possibility of internalization" (p. 167).[31] What is important about the ZPD viewpoint is (1) that it reinforces the value of thinking of transferential learning as *something occurring within the context of a teaching–learning dyad*, and (2) that "proximal" development clearly implies *temporal proximity in a sequence of information processing*. It will help to explore the ZPD concept further.

Let's start with Wilson and Weinstein's view of the relationship of the ZPD to the transference phenomenon. They begin with a question that appears deceptively simple: "What furnishes transferences with their motivational impetus?" (p. 196). They answer as follows:

The ZPD provides [a] context . . . The transference is not a tool for change without the ZPD. Unless the internalizing function of the ZPD is harnessed, the transference will endlessly repeat what will continue to be unresolvable conflict. Brenner (1982) declared that the transference is ubiquitous, and the primary distinguishing factor of the clinical situation is that the transference is gathered rather than dispersed. Yes, of course, this is so, but something additional must now be appended: gathering [the transference] is not enough without its conjunction with the ZPD. The ZPD precedes and undergirds the transference and provides the transference with its mutative potential. The interactive context brings to life the latent potential of the intrapsychic. [p. 196]

Wilson and Weinstein's comments about the relationship between ZPD and transference move us closer to understanding some fundamental aspects of transference motivation—namely, that *within transference relationships the cognitive goal is mastery in learning and that the method involves avoiding overstimulation.* But the reader will appreciate that the ZPD concept, in its current form of elaboration, is in itself insufficient to provide a comprehensive explanation for how transferential learning flows *from operating inside the ZPD but outside the transference.* However, Wilson and Weinstein seem correct in assuming that a variety of technical factors are involved in the facilitation of transferential learning, but we are left wondering exactly what these factors might be.

In their focus on the relation of ZPD to transference, Wilson and Weinstein seem clearly to be elaborating Gedo's sense that much of our clinical work with transference involves therapeutic methods "beyond interpretation"—that is, that [the use of psychological defenses] such as pacification, unification, and optimal disillusionment play a role in optimizing learning within a given transference (Gedo, 1979).

The second interdisciplinary perspective on transference motivation flows from the research of M. Stern (1988) on night terrors. Here, Stern points out how people awakening with night terrors seek out a soothing other, to whom they almost invariably describe the content of their fears; in other words, they are guided by strong interpersonal needs. Stern believes such communicative acts have both transferential and evolutionary (i.e., adaptive) consequences.

According to Stern, sharing fears under the circumstances of night terrors tends to enhance internalization.[32] In essence, Stern is describing how individuals with structural deficits (and thus a tendency toward night terrors) are motivated to seek help from others at times of difficulty. Like Freud and recent proponents of the ZPD concept, M. Stern concludes that *certain unstructured personalities are motivated toward regressive transferences because such states invite caretaking, are psychologically adaptive, and thus carry the potential for structuralization.*

Briefly, the perspectives on transference discussed in relation to Figure 4 appear to share certain underlying assumptions, namely: that transferential learning (1) involves some dynamic flux between hierarchically organized levels of mind and brain; (2) bears a direct relationship to the degree to which patients consciously compare similarities between the various contents of the differing hierarchical levels of their mind and brain; and (3) inevitably involves a supportive dyadic experience. The second point seems quite important and is the subject of the next section. The third point, dealing with transference as a two-party system requires elaboration.

In the process of transference reenactments between people, at least two major possibilities arise. On the one hand, the enactor may fulfill his transference expectations by an appropriate choice of object; on the other hand, even if the enactor fails to find a willing partner for a transaction based on a transference, he may nonetheless benefit from observing and experiencing his frustrated expectation in an interpersonal context. Developmentally, all of us potentially benefit from learning the characteristics of those people who might actually meet our transference wishes, and to distinguish these characteristics from the qualities of those who can be expected to frustrate them. Obviously, we also need to recognize the optimal (i.e., not overwhelming) circumstances in which transferences become usable sources of insight. This, in fact, is part of *learning how to make use of human relationships.* Such knowledge can be acquired through repeated transferential experiences that are potentially understandable psychoanalytically.

Let us now take stock. No one has yet provided anything comparable to a complete set of answers to the original question: In those instances where transference appears to lend itself to learning, how might we understand the detailed processes involved? In addition, we do not completely understand everything that motivates transference. But we are beginning to possess a number of ideas that suggest that *transferential learning works in conjunction with a number of factors that appear to relate to working memory activation and the crossing of certain affective thresholds for recollection and insight.* Similarity judgments and the priming of memory also seem involved in the sense that knowledge about our affective life is organized within memory and might well restructure itself in a useful way under the right circumstances.

How, then, should we proceed? I suggest we consider in more detail the specific roles of similarity judgment, and memory priming, as they effect the psychoanalytic transference. It turns out that this orientation can help explain more about what is meant by finding computationally "cheap" ways to discern deep similarity, and thus ways to transfer knowledge between content domains (Levin & Kent, 1994, 1995). We will, of course, reiterate some of what we learned in Chapter Four.

Second, under the rubric of transference motivation, I will go into more detail about the relation of my perspective on the computational efficiency of transference to the other viewpoints mentioned above: the ZPD, neural net theory, and the work of D. Stern, Lichtenberg, Slap, and others on schemas, scripts, and prototypes. These viewpoints provide further support for our position regarding computational efficiency as a key part of the mechanism of transferential learning and will perhaps further clarify aspects of the debate over what generally motivates transferences. These perspectives on computational efficiency will also be compared with those of Forrest (1994a,b, 1995, 1996a,b, 1997), who shows that arguments about what is computationally "cheap" are not as circular or teleological as they may appear, but derive from an attempt to appreciate transference as a crucial step in a cognitive/affective sequencing of information processing that builds and exploits emotional databases of mind and brain. Finally, I will conclude this paper by delineating the role played in transferential learning by spontaneity and free association, decisive factors in learning facilitation sometimes overlooked by previous investigators.

Computationally "cheap" ways to discover deep similarity

Those familiar with the arguments of Chapter Four should merely proceed to the following section. The psychoanalytic topic of transference significantly overlaps the topics of similarity judgment and memory priming in the domains of cognitive psychology and neurophysiology (Levin & Kent, 1994, 1995). These overlapping domains of knowledge thus reflect how different specialties have tackled what appears to be one phenomenon, however complex and variegated it may be.[33]

To clarify, consider that *clinical transference in psychoanalysis is clearly based on some perceived structural similarity* between past and present situations, or between patterns of behavior with the analyst or with some other person. *The priming of memory in neuropsychology refers to a similar process whereby experiencing part of any previous perceptual pattern leads to the recollection of the rest of the pattern.* Clearly, priming memory and judging similarity can be related to transference states when we react with a transference to persons in the here and now, since something in our experience of them serves as an important clue to similar past experiences recorded in memory. In slightly different words, the present partial transference experience could be seen as priming the recollection of a larger generalization regarding past experience. These points, summarized in Table 1, also are strongly supported by the psychological explorations of Gentner and Ratterman (1991a,b), the neurological research of Gabriel and colleagues (1991), the conceptual work of Hadley (1989), and the neurocomputational work of Forrest (1996a).

But how does this interdisciplinary synthesis further our understanding of the mechanisms of transference as an adaptive phenomenon possessing learning potential? Gentner and Ratterman (1991a,b) have shown that similarity judgments seem to be preferentially performed in ways that are computationally cheap for memory. This means that *transference is essentially the mind–brain's way to find and exploit deep structural similarities the recognition of which is of adaptive advantage to the individual and the species; that is, transference allows this to be accomplished in a manner that is computationally cheap.* The expression "computationally cheap" here means requiring less time and less allocation of working memory.

Finding deep similarities is important because this is what allows us to compare past and present situations properly and *to transfer solutions from old to current problems* with a reasonable expectation they will apply. According to Gentner and Ratterman (1991a,b), when people judge things to be similar, they usually assume that the similar surface features they have identified in making the match in fact overlie a deeper structural similarity.

What is particularly interesting is that superficial and deep similarity do often run together (but, of course, not always). That is, there is a decided adaptive advantage of similarity judgments, in the sense that the mind–brain has learned to perform a more detailed analysis (to see if indeed there is a deep structural similarity) only upon those matched items that have already met the test criteria for a superficial judgment of similarity. In the case of transference, the way this works is that we test further for someone's potential for enacting with us deep aspects of our transference experience only if that person's appearance or behavior bears a superficial resemblance to past objects. In this way, an economical search is entertained for deep structural similarities that can enhance the odds that transference needs will ultimately be met (Levin, 1995a,b; Levin & Kent, 1995); on a statistical basis, we waste little time and save considerably on working memory.[34]

It will help to indicate why I am repeating that a saving of time and working memory is important. The quality and quantity of any person's life depends on the number and quality of adaptive (successful) decisions they make per unit time. Since decision making depends principally upon working memory, any saving of working memory or the time it is used guarantees that the individual will improve his or her overall decision making.

One final note before leaving the notion that there is psychological advantage in what is computationally cheap. Although this is not obvious, both direct and indirect benefits accrue from the introduction of mechanisms that simplify cognition. On the direct side is *the acceleration of learning secondary to the reduction in computational demand*, as noted above. But perhaps even more important is the advantage, on the indirect side, that *the increment in learning activity itself interferes with the uncontrolled repetition of behavior*. That is, *the reason behavior becomes repetitive in the first place is because the rate of learning has stopped or at least slowed down considerably; what psychoanalysis often accomplishes is the restitution of efficient learning within an individual. Once we are learning again, our behavior may very well demonstrate an enhanced capacity to search for novelty and experimentation, leading to new structure rather than old tendencies toward repetition, automaticity, and defensiveness* (Levin, 1991).

What motivates (moves) the transference?

To analyze what motivates transferential learning, it will help to summarize our conclusions to this point and compare the viewpoints presented with those of the following researchers: Wilson and Weinstein (on ZPD); D. Stern, Lichtenberg, Slap and Slap-Shelton, Luborsky, and Horowitz (on prototypes/schemas); Forrest (on neural networks); and Gedo and Wilson (on hierarchies of goals and values).

As noted, the debate within psychoanalysis over what motivates transference begins with Freud: drive defense theory (transferences represent archaic unconscious wishes transferred to current objects and can serve as powerful resistances to insight or as vehicles of change); remembering versus action theory (transferences represent reenactments that are substitutes for remembering, but repeating does not necessarily mean working through); and Freud's discarded theory of a death instinct (transferences reflect Thanatos in conflict with Eros, that is, either a deeply ingrained repetition compulsion to restore a prior state or a tendency moving the organism toward increasing entropy).

The debate over the motivation of transference has been reconceptualized by the contributions of D. Stern (1985), Lichtenberg (1983, 1989a,b), Slap (Slap & Saykin, 1983; Slap & Slap-Shelton, 1991) and others as representing schemas, prototypes, or scripts. Slap and Slap-Shelton (1991) have delineated a perspective on schemas in the greatest psychoanalytic detail. Building on the Piagetian view of adaptation, they identify two components: assimilation, "the modification of perceptual data to fit preexisting internal structures or schemas," and accommodation, "the modification of internal representations or schemas to fit reality" (p. 50). Citing Bartlett (1932) as the first to describe schemas, they quote his definition of the schema as "an active organization of past reactions or of past experiences" p. 48). Horowitz (1988), they note, uses schemas "as a way of understanding various mental states and transference experiences of the patient" (p. 43).

From this it should be clear that schemas, though smaller units than transferences, can be used to explicate them. Schemas of various kinds divide the inner world into enduring organizations of self and objects, goals and values, personality patterns, types of relationships, and mental states (Slap & Slap-Shelton, 1991, p. 43). The key to schema theory is that adaptation requires both assimilation and accommodation; however, when *emotional disruptions occur in accommodation*, the child "seeks out the experience or stimulus that has created the disequilibrium in order to accommodate to it" (p. 50). Only then can the child learn and develop optimally. In other words, *the child creates and attempts to exploit a transference in order to master what it has experienced as traumatic.*

Freud's concepts of transference and of repetition compulsion enter into the equation because

> once a repression of an instinctual wish or impulse has occurred, any new experience that stimulates a similar impulse, even if the experience is not in itself threatening, will lead to further repression. . . . [Thus] certain categories of experience remain sheltered from the processes of the ego [that is, they are repressed]. [p. 51]

Repressed schemas cannot be modified so as to take into account new information.

In other words, as applied to learning and transference, these schemas or prototypes are based on memories of *affectively loaded, traumatic interpersonal experience* that *can fuel transference reenactments*, based as they are on repressed schemas that are otherwise unavailable for learning. Such schemas abstract out of experience some general expectations and are presumably elicited (primed) by anything that resembles the original experience. Luborsky's work on the core conflictual relationship theme, my own work on MTI, Horowitz's concept of the role relationship model, and D. Stern's "representation of an interaction generalized" (RIG) are examples of the schema approach to studying transference (Gillett, 1996).

The schema approach to transference, like the theorizing of Wilson and Weinstein, Gedo, and myself, unites affective, psychodynamic, and cognitive psychological perspectives on the transference phenomenon. Although, models of schemas are also clever integrations of Freudian and Piagetian psychology, the schema approach may not ultimately lend itself to determining what motivates the transference microscopically; instead the approach may merely delineate how the patterning of transference demonstrates that transference is in essence its own motivation.[35]

For example, Lichtenberg's study of schemas and prototypes suggests to him that motivation best parses into a handful of motivational systems, but even his sophisticated attempt to integrate infant observation studies into psychoanalysis using schema theory requires that the self system be understood to be "the primary integrator of all motivation" (Wilson & Gedo, 1993b, p. 320). Yet this would appear to relegate an unclear function (motivation) to a still more ambiguous system element (self); lacking further specification, Lichtenberg's conception of self regulation and motivation seems circular.

Posner and DiGirolamo (1996) lend further support to theorizing (such as Gedo's) that emphasizes the decisive role of values and goals. Their research on visual attention, based in part of the work of Carbonnell (1981), leads them to conclude that "an important aspect of [any] coherent [theory of] behavior is to have a set of goals . . . that can control current behavior" (Posner & DiGirolamo, 1996, p. 23). From this perspective, what motivates transference is its ability to move the individual toward actually achieving goals and values, particularly those that already have an inner relationship to currently or previously desired states.

Where Gedo, Wilson, and I differ among ourselves is over which factors contribute most decisively to transferential learning. Gedo and I believe that the analysis of resistance (in the form of transference) is most fruitful because it permits putting into consensual language what without transference would remain unspeakable and unrememberable. Gedo and I focus predominantly on the affective and cognitive components of transference repetitions, what earlier I called "mechanisms . . . for reprocessing the unconscious (or primary process) language of the brain into symbolic terms." Wilson and I are most focused on determining the precise agency for transferential learning, whereas Gedo differs from us in his focus on integrating such cognitive/affective details into a refined, overarching psychoanalytic theory.

Most specifically, I have introduced the issues of similarity judgment and knowledge transfer into the debate over what motivates transference. Since these topics have been extensively explored within cognitive psychology, they offer psychoanalysis a crucial database for comparison. Wilson and Weinstein's theorizing supports my view of transference, even if in citing the ZPD they have created a special category the examination of which largely remains ahead of us. More specifically, their ZPD approach is very much in keeping with the work of Wilson and Gedo (1993a) and of Levin (1991), which attempts to round out a psychoanalytic theory of learning.

A further cognitive aspect of transference concerns the perspective of neurocomputing (also called connectionism or artificial intelligence theory), the mathematical simulation of thinking and behavior (Levin 1995b; Levin & Kent 1995). This subject has been recently reviewed from the psychoanalytic vantage point (Forrest, 1995; Olds, 1994; Palombo, 1992). For example, regarding mathematical physics and attractor models (see Section IV of this monograph), Forrest points out that Freud (1900a), in his description of the dream processes of condensation and overdetermination in the election of the elements of dreams by *scrutin de liste* (p. 284), "based his theoretical structures at first on a neural model, just as neural net modelers do" (Forrest, 1995, p. 60; see also Palombo, 1992). Forrest believes that "the new logic and practice of neurocomputing . . . resembles not merely cognitive but also psychodynamic human mental operations, and simulates a broad range of learning, pattern recognizing and problem solving" (p. 68). Neurocomputing thus justifies the return to quantitative and economic perspectives in psychoanalysis, including attempts such as mine to identify computational costs in relation to transferential learning (Forrest, personal communication).

Continuing Forrest's line of reasoning, Olds (1994) points out that *neural networks are capable of brainlike behavior and learning* in a mode of classical conditioning (p. 586). As such "they provide models which psychoanalysts might use as metaphors for psychic function" (p. 589). Still more specifically, Olds notes the close correspondence between the analyst as recognizer of important regularities in the analysand's associations, and the neural network as a pattern recognition mechanism par excellence (pp. 599–600). Olds, citing Slap's work on schema theory, presents a view of transference as based on perceptual errors. Olds further connects schema theory with the recent paradigm shift within psychoanalysis from thinking in terms of "inborn tendencies and . . . the enactment of early-instilled conflicts [or programs]" to emphasizing empathy, transference distortion, and "expressive interaction" (pp. 602–603).

I have suggested that transference seems to employ an efficient strategy for judging similarity, one that involves *priming and the subsequent transfer of knowledge* between content domains—for example, from past solutions to present problems. As noted above, *this emotional learning perspective on transference eliminates the need for postulating a repetition compulsion.* If one considers mental illness from the viewpoint of interrupted or blocked learning, then *it simply makes sense that behavior should become repetitive—since when learning stops behavior automatically repeats.*

Spontaneity and free association

To understand the extra assist transference provides learning, we should next consider how *free association, through activating working memory, creates learning "windows."* Freud's systematic application of free association in psychoanalytic exploration was a brilliant procedural discovery in light of later neuroscientific evidence that learning is easier when the learner is freely associating rather than merely reacting to outside influences (Levin, 1994, 1995b). This is also the conclusion on learning localization by Posner (Posner, 1988; Posner & Raichle, 1994; Posner & Rothbart, 1994a,b, 1995) in this country and of Lassen (1994a,b) in Scandinavia. During spontaneously initiated activity, primary sensory association cortical areas are activated for the sensory experience involved, but "without the input or output machinery" (as Lassen puts it in a personal communication).[36] In short, *during free association and free recall experiments, modality-specific aspects of working memory appear to be significantly activated.*

To clarify, let us depict learning in Figure 2 (see p. 63) (Levin, 1994; Levin & Kent, 1994). A, B, and C represent three functional areas of the brain united in a neural network to accomplish a specific task. For example, let triangle ABC be an element in the visual system, where A, B, and C are specialized modules for capturing motion, form, and color analysis in a unified, dynamic visual image. If we assume that triangle ABC also represents a specific body of visual knowledge (within its boundaries), then we might diagram an expansion of visual knowledge by connecting triangle ABC to points D, E, and F.

The expansion of knowledge in Figure 2 (see p. 63), however, can be accomplished by at least two possible routes. In the first (a), connected with *free association*, one would start from position P-1 and build from C toward D, E, and F. In the second method (b), connected with *being overly led by another person* in our learning, one starts from position P-2 and builds from F to E to D, and then finally to the triangle ABC.

If one compares these routes, learning proceeds faster and more easily when the learning starts from P-1 rather than from P-2. That is, learning is better in the case of free association, namely in case (a), rather than in case (b). This is because P-1 lies continuously within the area of activated working memory. In other words, within the boundary of triangle ABC working memory is active, and the location of P-1 within this area is precisely what makes enhanced learning possible. P-2, however, is outside of activated working memory, and thus starting from P-2 guarantees that the appropriate working memory will not be activated and that the necessary extension of knowledge will not occur as easily.[37]

Patients who are freely associating are not only remembering and rethinking specific subjects; they are simultaneously activating their working memory for the same subject domains they are remembering. Working memory is what is required for learning to occur through the manipulation of particular kinds of data from memory (or the formation of facilitating connections within the mind–brain). Recall that it is working memory that allows for intentional change in ongoing computations (and thus in databases of mind and brain).[38]

In summary, it appears likely that *transferences, precisely because they are spontaneously initiated by patients, share with free association the activation of working memory for the kind of affective experience coded into the specific transferences involved.* This means that learning itself will be enhanced by the activating effect of emotion-laden transference on working memory.[39] *In other words, subjects engaged in periodic transference behavior, by dint of their free associating and generally high level of self-initiated activity and memory priming, greatly facilitate their own learning (see Levin 1991, Chapters 11–12). Without transference, therefore, the learning of our species would be lessened, because working memory would be less fully activated at the time of the experiences that we need to internalize.* In terms of the preceding discussion of transference motivation, transferences create learning opportunities to the extent that they enable the modification of sequestered (repressed) schemas or prototypes, a process that optimally involves the activation of working memory.

Concluding remarks

In discovering transference, encouraging spontaneity, and devising the technique of free association, Freud not only uncovered phenomena that are enormously important in the clinical practice of psychoanalysis (and psychotherapy); he also drew our attention to processes that may be exploited for learning and thus for survival. Learning to change behavior, however, is never easy, and learning from the transference requires substantial efforts from patient and analyst. Nonetheless, *psychoanalysis (and only psychoanalysis) systematically teaches individuals how to capitalize on transferential learning.* The analysand learns from the example of the analyst, who points out transferences and their possible significance (see Gardner, 1989); analyst and analysand also discover and respond to many nonverbal communications beyond interpretation (Gedo, 1979) that facilitate transferential learning.

This chapter illuminates a number of unique perspectives on how transference involves complex forms of bridging within the mind–brain. It synthesizes what is known from the study of transference at the clinical level (regarding emotional enactments) with what is understood about transference from basic science (interdisciplinary) perspectives. Various "microscopic" viewpoints on transferential mechanisms and circumstances have been presented to detail the relationship between transference and learning.

The psychoanalytic/transferential facilitation of learning in humans can be seen as an evolutionary movement from fairly fixed reptilian (brainstem) control mechanisms, to somewhat more flexible, early mammalian (limbic) control mechanisms, to highly flexible, advanced mammalian (corticocerebellar and brainstem basal ganglia related) mechanisms of neural control and adaptive learning (Levin, 1991). The last level clearly hinges on control via a hierarchy of goals and values. Moreover, *by learning how to exploit the transference for its optimal learning potential,* we convert a potentially dangerous perceptual "mistake" based on a mismatch into an opportunity to reprocess the unconscious imagery (primary process language) of the brain into symbolic, speakable, rememberable, and useful terms.

SECTION III
CONSCIOUS AND UNCONSCIOUS SYSTEMS

CHAPTER SIX

Some additional thoughts on attention*

Fred Levin

Introduction

A young driver suddenly comes to a screeching halt as he realizes that his car has entered an intersection against a red light and is perilously close to pedestrians. The surprise on his face makes him look as if he just awoke from a bad dream.

A self employed business man fires his secretary and then gradually discovers that he is unable to stay organized and properly attend to many accounting details which begin to seriously overwhelm him.

A grammar school student with an otherwise nice disposition becomes surly with her parents after realizing that once again she has forgotten to turn in a homework assignment, and will not get academic credit for her efforts.

An analyst listens to a patient freely associate and is surprised to find herself thinking of the very last time she spoke with a dying friend. Returning from this reverie, however, she recalls that at

---

* An earlier version of this paper appeared as Levin, 1997g.

the beginning of this same session the patient had innocently mentioned in passing the name of a particular friend he might visit on an upcoming trip. The analyst knows that this close friend of the patient is suffering from cancer. The analyst comments on her own associations, and with this the patient gets more in touch with his current fears about losing his friend to cancer. He had been aware of these thoughts earlier in the session, but was defending against them.

Each of the above situations concerns selective attention, a variable that quietly functions behind the scenes of most lives so long as it does so successfully. When this function fails, however, the seamless experience of life itself can begin to unravel, sometimes disastrously. It behooves us to examine carefully what exactly attention is and what factors may influence the shape of its deployment. After examining this subject I shall return to the specific examples given to make some further comments about each case.

Psychoanalysts, of course, have their ideal of so-called "evenly hovering attention"; however, although there is well documented evidence that both the patient and the analyst can learn to pay attention to the fluctuation of their thoughts, it certainly does not appear that the result is ever "even" or "regular". In this sense, the ideal would appear to be a theoretical fiction, although a useful metaphor nevertheless. Maybe the best one can hope for regarding attention is that during each analysis the participants (that is, both analyst and analysand) will feel free enough to comfortably experience their own and each other's attentional shifts while simultaneously observing and remaining curious about when and how these shifts occur. In addition, of course, both parties need to appreciate the significance of these "resonances" for such things as their ongoing transference relationship.

Attention also bears important relationships to learning, the facilitation of which is perhaps the central subject of this monograph. For example, what I will later describe as the anterior attentional system relates directly to what has been called explicit learning (and memory) and is blocked by distraction; while what I shall call the posterior attentional system relates to implicit learning and memory (which is learning without the conscious recollection of the experience that one is learning) and this is not blocked by distraction (Posner & Rothbart, 1994a).

These brief introductory remarks should highlight the importance of attention to life and to analysis. The remainder of this discussion delineates *attention* from an interdisciplinary perspective. This Chapter also builds on two previous papers bridging psychoanalysis and cognitive neuroscience (Levin, 1995b, Levin & Gunther, 1996). It does not, however, attempt to elaborate on the relationship between psychoanalytic learning and attention *per se*. Those interested in this subject should consult Levin (1995b, 1997d).

Some definitions may help at the outset. *Attention* refers to our conscious awareness of what is happening in the here and now. *Selective attention* refers to the fact that whenever we choose to focus on some things we leave others out, depending, presumably, upon what is of interest to us at the time (that is, depending upon our motivations). Put differently, signals compete for our attention. *Motivation* refers to the idea that perception, action, and thinking tend to follow deeper level priorities which are set according to some inner hierarchy of values and goals. Thus, if our brain decides that the time to eat is approaching, instructions are relayed to our various sense organs to begin to investigate the availability of food.

Consciousness obviously plays some role in the ensemble of activities which I am attempting to describe; somewhat surprisingly, however, *understanding the role of consciousness in brain design is much more complex than it appears*. For this reason, Section III of this book is entirely devoted to the subject (see also Levin, 1997a). The reader will further appreciate how, in our effort to understand consciousness, we shall make use of many of the insights of Sections I and II.

Motivation is still another complex topic; it was touched upon in Chapter Five, and will be examined in more detail in Sections IV and V (see also Lichtenberg, 1989a,b). Fortunately, deferring some of these topics relating to attention will not detract too much from our present discussion, since our focus at the moment concerns shifts in attention, their role in information processing, and their meaning for clinical psychoanalysis.

Perception is the process of taking in experience by means of particular sensory modalities. Of help is the Freudian notion of perceptual defense, that is, the idea that humans in general are not ready to fully accept what they see, hear, touch, etc. unless it fits with their current inner needs. Put differently, reality, like memory, is a highly filtered construct. Each experience recreates reality or the memory of it. Thus, the so-called defenses of denial, disavowal, projection, etc. allow us to adjust the current register or perception of reality according to our momentary psychological needs. It should be clear from this description of mental processing, however, that *in our effort to wrestle with what generally underlies shifts in attention, we are engaging a new subject, namely, the need to create and preserve a privately useful reality, or a "private self"* (Modell, 1993).

So let us update our thinking about how unconscious cognitive mechanisms provide selectivity and privacy of attention, and how this manifests itself in our patients. For this purpose it will help to review some recent work in the area of the so-called executive control network (ECN), a terminology that denotes the highest level system of the brain which enables us to establish and maintain control over our mental processing in an efficient manner. Some detour into neuroanatomy and physiology is inevitable, but I hope this will help some readers better appreciate how things are accomplished in the mind–brain, that is, how brain makes mind, rather than adding a level of complexity to an already difficult subject.

The core executive control network

Posner and Raichle (1994) describe an experiment in which subjects must attend to a particular location on a TV monitor and press a key when a specified target appears. We will call this the primary task. So-called secondary tasks are then added to the primary task. These tasks involve such things as counting backward from a fixed digit or monitoring a series of spoken words for the appearance of a target word. To help differentiate primary from the secondary tasks using scanning, only the primary task requires a movement as a response. Posner and Raichle learned that the secondary tasks essentially delay the time required for the primary task. They interpret this as indicating that *"visual orienting requires access to [an] . . . executive [control] network [ECN]"* (p. 177), *that is, to an overarching specialized system that pays attention generally and not just visually. As we shall see, the anterior cingulate gyrus and basal ganglia play a crucial role in providing exactly these functions.*

There is a second important variation of their original experiment. When they use as subjects patients with damaged parietal lobes on the primary task alone, as expected, delays in the primary task occurred, especially when the target to be tracked appeared in the visual field opposite to their lesion and at a location other than where the subjects were attending (that is, in a part of the visual field controlled by the parietal cortex). This is because *parietal lobe damage is known to interfere with the ability to detach from objects that have captured our interest.* What was unexpected, however, was that when these same parietal damaged patients were engaged in the combined (primary and secondary task) experiment, their reaction times were slowed only very slightly and they were not slowed at all when images appeared on the side controlled by their lesion.

From this second experiment and its unexpected results Posner and Raichle concluded that "not only does visual orienting require access to the executive network . . . but *operations performed by the executive network are quite different from those performed by the visual orienting network*" (p. 177). *In other words, a more general system for executive control seems involved and it is obviously capable under certain circumstances of taking over for the visual system.*

One final comment about this experimental paradigm: these researchers also discovered ". . . [that] if a target is detected in [one] stream of information, the chance of detecting a simultaneous target in another stream is greatly reduced" (p. 178). It appeared to them that what they were studying in these various experiments was what is usually meant by fluctuations in consciousness, "at least in the form of focal awareness" (p. 178).

Posner and Raichle divide the ECN into anterior and posterior components. *The anterior involves the anterior cingulate gyrus and basal ganglia, and is responsible for selecting objects of interest, zooming in on these, and for overall attentional control. The posterior system is made up of the superior parietal cortex, pulvinar, and superior colliculus. This system enables subjects to detach from what is of interest and move on to new interests.* Detailed descriptions of the subfunctions these researchers have called "next", "scan", "name", "zoom", etc. are covered in Posner and Raichle's book, and elaborated upon in the numerous bibliographic references they cite therein.

Important for our discussion, Posner and Raichle cite evidence that supports their conclusion that consciousness as focal attention requires the activity of the anterior cingulate. First, in a semantic monitoring task the anterior cingulate shows stronger activation as the number of targets increases, without corresponding increase in task difficulty. Second, the anterior cingulate activates when subjects are asked to evaluate multiple target attributes, such as form, color, and motion. Third, feelings of effort in visual target detection coincide with those times when the anterior cingulate is activated, whereas clearing one's thoughts is associated with deactivation of the anterior cingulate.

Extensions of the ECN

Having described the basic components of the ECN, I wish to add some complicating facts. In addition to the anatomical structures noted in the basic network, it is important to describe other structures that contribute decisively to the ECN. You may think of these components as an extended system that is available to the anterior and posterior parts of the executive control network; in essence, they are extensions of the basic system without which the basic system could not accomplish much that is interesting or important.

It will help to name these structures and say a word about each of them. They include the following: the cerebellum, corpus callosum, amygdalar and hippocampal systems (on both sides), the basal ganglia, the orbital frontal cortex, the left posterior parietal cortex near the angular gyrus, the reticular activating system, and the left frontal cortex near Broca's area. (The amygdalar and hippocampal systems will be reviewed in Chapter Eight and will not be elaborated upon further here.)

Working memory, according to Posner (personal communication, 1997) involves two major components. There is a content specific component and an executive control. Posner believes that the content specific information is present in the left lateral frontal and left posterior parietal cortical areas, perhaps separate for different domains. For example, he believes verbal material requires the left frontal area near Broca's area as well as the left posterior parietal area near the angular gyrus. But as noted above, Posner feels that *overall control of working memory is not domain specific* and this involves the medial frontal cortical system, namely, the anterior cingulate gyrus. The reader may be confused by the current literature on working memory that varies significantly from author to author. However, *most researchers appear to agree with Posner that the anterior cingulate and (orbital) frontal cortical areas are both decisive.*

The basal ganglia are well known to provide control over movements and ideas, for recognizing the appearance of redundancies (meaning recurrent thoughts and actions), and for setting limits when necessary in their cycling within mind–brain. I am referring particularly to the research on obsessive compulsive disorder (OCD) (Baxter, 1994; Schwartz, Stoessl, Baxter, Martin, & Phelps, 1996), and also to recent research on childhood Group A beta hemolytic streptococcal infections where injury to the caudate may contribute to OCD clinically as an "interval clock" mechanism of the brain gone awry (Baker, 1996; Morell, 1996). Perhaps we sometimes need to repeat activities or thoughts when we cannot compute time duration.

Importantly, *the corpus callosum is not just the band of neurons connecting the hemispheres but is true associative cortex.* Sperry, Trevarthen, Levy and others have demonstrated that it plays a role in matching hemispheric systems (some lateralized, some not) with the task at hand, through what they call *metacontrol.* It also brings together nonverbal and verbal intelligence with affect and knowledge systems (Levin & Vuckovich, 1983; Levin, 1991).

The cerebellum in particular, does much more than regulate movement; one of its prime functions ". . . is to learn to predict and prepare for imminent information acquisition, analysis, or action" (Allen, Buxton, Wong, & Courchesne (1997). This research confirms pioneering studies in the late 1970s and early 1980s by Heath and others on patients with cerebellar damage, by Ito on the vestibulocerebellar reflex, and by Frick and myself on the cerebellum and neural control in relationship to learning and psychological development.

The reticular activating system has long been known to play a role in general arousal. This contributes to the precise control executed by the anterior cingulate in forming systems tuned for specific cognitive tasks. In essence, the cingulate's job involves recruiting an ECN which is matched to the task at hand, including the necessary databases of mind–brain bearing on this task. Along the way the ECN creates the felt experience of self awareness (consciousness), cohesiveness, intentionality, and autonomy (see also Levin, 1997e).

Some clinical applications:
the executive control network at work

At the outset I introduced vignettes relating to selective attention. I will now make brief comments on these cases, and attempt to describe how I believe problems with the ECN may demonstrate themselves in the clinical situation (i.e., analysis or psychotherapy). The first vignette was of a young man whose car screeched to a halt, narrowly missing some pedestrians. As psychoanalysts we naturally would think of a mix of conscious and unconscious impulses that could generate such behavior. What needs to be added, however, is that it is possible for an individual's attentive behavior to fail because of physiological disturbances in the ECN. Only examining the detailed history, including the physical and mental status of a person will tell us the extent to which specific behavior is determined by conflict or by other factors. As we considered in Chapter Two, a significant number of learning-disabled children grow into learning-disabled adults. Some of these individuals also suffer from attention deficit disturbance with or without hyperactivity (ADD or ADHD). This population may show clear-cut evidence of brain damage on neurological examination; it most certainly shows problems with such variables as short term memory and selective attention on neuropsychological testing.

The self-employed businessman with difficulty tracking customer accounts was seen in treatment and tested by an expert in LD (i.e., learning disabilities). The diagnostic impression of his analyst, confirmed by psychological testing, was that he definitely suffered from an attention deficit disorder (ADD) without hyperactivity. The history also confirmed his symptoms started during his childhood, and all *DSM-IV* criteria for the diagnosis of ADD were met. Treatment with stimulants resulted in immediate significant gains in his ability to concentrate. In addition, he selected to continue his psychotherapy in order to sort out the significance of this new diagnosis for his sense of self.

The grammar school student who got into trouble with homework, a common enough problem, is being observed by her parents and not in treatment. Her psychological testing is currently inconclusive. The probability remains that there is some developmental delay that is showing itself as at least a transient dysfunction of the

ECN. Unless she would be worked up medically, and / or in psycho-therapy or analysis, it would be difficult to make any further characterization.

The example of the analyst whose attention drifted to a reverie of being with a dying friend was presented to remind us that our analytic listening involves fluctuating attention as a normal event from which we learn. Such ego capacities are sometimes surprising in their depth and range. Most importantly, they can be improved if we become aware of and practice them, and if we discuss with each other the data of our scientific observations and the ways in which we use analytic data to make various inferences. In fact, the very scientific status of psychoanalysis depends, to a significant extent, on such matters as how we collect, utilize, and test our evidence.

Now some further suggestions as to how disturbances in aware-ness / attention might present themselves in treatment. The first example (covered in detail in Chapter Eight) concerns patients with disturbances of consciousness. *Gedo (1996a,b), reviewing a lifetime of psychoanalytic work, describes patients who demonstrate disturbances of consciousness during their analysis, something that was actually quite rare in his experience (three out of seventy patients). But importantly, each such patient had experienced disturbing trauma during their first year of life that continued for significant periods thereafter. Howard Shevrin (1992, 1997a) has indicated that one mechanism that may play a role in such cases is that proper perceptual tags are not attached to such traumatic experience, so that memory becomes unreliable.*

That is, some traumatized patients become unable to differenti-ate properly between what is a memory of a thought or wish vs. a real event; and they also have problems recalling the circumstances associated with their trauma. For Shevrin, such categorization of experience is *the* principal function of consciousness (attention) and is required for the proper organization of memory and a number of self-related functions.

A second example would be an analytic patient with a non-optimally functioning parietal lobe. Such posterior attentional pathology would require special care in helping the patient to prop-erly detach his interest from subjects or objects of interest. This kind of difficulty would need to be distinguished from ADHD / ADD or from obsessive compulsive behavior. Put differently, such symptoms as difficulty distracting oneself from compelling subjects may result from a variety of pathological mechanisms, including our focus here, a malfunction of the parietal system, which ordinarily allows detachment and thus smooth transitions from one object of interest to the next. The analyst of such a patient with parietal lobe pathology would therefore probably wish to make use of the fact of observing himself subtly but repeatedly assisting the patient in making critical transitions in thinking, and properly categorizing them.

A third example might be classified as a disturbance in metacontrol, following Trevarthen and Levy's terminology. This kind of patient will be relatively unable to match a particular task at hand with the optimal mind–brain machinery suited for such problem solving. This kind of decision making requires an intact corpus callosum, under the guidance of the anterior cingulate gyrus. Here, the analyst's attention will be drawn inexorably toward questioning the nature of the patient's approach to particular problem solving.

Of course, as someone's psychoanalyst, we need to be careful not to overdiagnose executive control problems. For example, we might start to quickly dismiss as inappropriate a patient's surprising thoughts or approaches as if these are pathological *per se* just because they are unexpected. On the one hand, some patients will just be unusually creative. On the other hand, analysts cannot help but observe that some patients are likely to have problems with analyzing because they consistently approach certain problem domains from an idiosyncratic perspective. Gedo refers to such patients as apraxic; it should be noted that this does not imply that learning cannot occur and have profound effects, when ways are found within the patient's analysis to facilitate insight. Obviously, the diagnosis and facilitation of learning difficulties can be a very challenging but rewarding part of the work of psychoanalysts.

One final example. Consider a patient who consistently attempts to accomplish too much at once, but not because they are driven by a pathological need to achieve, a narcissistic sense of omnipotence, or some deep-seated masochistic impulse. In this case, the problem may stem from an executive malfunction in integrating the various components of the ECN, say a disturbance in the cerebellar module itself, which ordinarily improves the handling of thoughts with the same agility that it orchestrates movements. In this instance, the analyst's interventions (interpretations) may have the function of *simplifying the overall cognitive task by such measures as reducing the patient's memory load*, thus freeing the patient to concentrate more effectively on how to best arrange the elements in mind into coherent patterns. This may be accomplished, for example, by reminding the patient in timely and gentle ways of important related material from preceding sessions.

Please note, I am merely suggesting a few out of a very large number of possible interventions, but I think this last example (and the others above) should give some idea of what I mean when I suggest that the ECN deserves the attention of psychoanalysis. In fact, it seems probable that analysts are already thus addressing both neurophysiological and conflict-related difficulties through the tactful subtlety of their interventions. After all, the mind–brain does not change just because we shift our orientation at times between psychoanalysis and neuroscience.

CHAPTER SEVEN

Why consciousness?*

Fred Levin

Introduction

T he problem regarding consciousness, simply stated, is that no one has satisfactorily explained why consciousness is necessary (Shallice, 1988, p. 381). Solms (1997) bravely raises a number of questions about consciousness. After commenting on his work, I will survey some interdisciplinary perspectives and then attempt to describe what it is that consciousness might be doing.

For Solms, and for most psychoanalysts, processes within mind which are usually labeled subjective experience are no less real than so-called objective observations of the external world. Solms further argues, and I agree, that all perception involves conjecture about events, localizable either in the universe outside or in the one inside our self (Lassen, 1994a,b; Levin, 1991; Posner & Raichle, 1994).

The consciousness debate is muddied, however, when Solms introduces the philosopher Searle (1995a,b), who asserts, among other things, that consciousness is a mystery and that there could

---

* An earlier version of this paper appeared as Levin, 1997a.

be no such thing as an unconscious.[39] These untenable assertions of Searle are best answered by the research of psychoanalysis, including especially the research of Shevrin, Bond, Brakel, Hertel, and Williams (1996), which meticulously demonstrates unconscious phenomenology as well as the neurophysiological signature of unconscious process (as distinguished from conscious processing).

However, it would be wrong to dismiss Solms or Searle completely. Consider, for example, Searle's so-called Chinese room argument (Crane, 1995, p. 132; Searle, 1995a,b), which actually supports the application of psychoanalytic frameworks to questions about the nature of conscious processing (see below).

The Chinese room argument states that a man who exists inside a room, who uses various algorithms to translate English messages passed to him in Chinese and who is to pass these back, is not undergoing the same mental states as someone who actually understands the Chinese language, no matter how good the translation (Crane, 1995, p. 132). Searle uses this argument against those who argue what he calls the strong case for artificial intelligence (AI), namely, that computers (like the man who possesses mere translating algorithms) can indeed usefully model mind and brain. But for Searle, the strong case for AI is wrong because it asserts that the differences between human brains and computers can be ignored without consequences. Here I entirely agree with Searle. In fact, if the brain–computer distinction were trivial there would be no concern about consciousness, for both the human brain and current artificial brains (computers) would share exactly the same range of "states," which they do not. Yet the weak argument for AI, that we can learn much from attempts to imitate/simulate brain and mind on computers, seems more correct.

Combining some psychoanalytic and neuropsychological perspectives

According to Rapaport (1951a,b), Freud viewed consciousness as a matter of the distribution of attention cathexis,[40] a perspective that remains in vogue. As we have already noted, Gedo (1996a) suggests that when traumatic disorganization occurs during the first year of life, a clouding of consciousness may appear during adult psychoanalytic regression, a phenomenon that otherwise is extremely rare. The subject of consciousness has been reviewed by Olds (1992) for psychoanalysis and by Posner (1994), Shallice (1988), and Bridgeman (1996) for neuropsychology. Olds credits Peterfreund (1971), Basch (1976), and Rosenblatt and Thickstun (1977) for the early impetus to recast psychoanalytic theory based on neuropsychological understandings of attention and information processing. To this list I would add Shevrin (1973, 1992; Shevrin, Bond, Brakel, Hertel, & Williams, 1996; see also Levin, 1980, 1987; Levin & Vuckovich, 1983).

Shallice's (1988) review of consciousness research concerns itself with phenomena related to attentional mechanisms: blindsight, knowledge without awareness, the split brain, and dual consciousness. His conclusion is that *consciousness maps onto four interactive neural control systems that track various brain processes: the overall supervisory system, the language system, contention scheduling, and episodic memory.* Unfortunately, Shallice makes no further specification regarding why consciousness is necessary (other than self-tracking).

Posner (1994) goes further than anyone in specifying the neurophysiology of consciousness. In a nutshell, for him attentional networks of the brain bring together current sensory information and ideas stored in memory while maintaining a state of alertness in real time (p. 7398). Posner does not believe these particular functions constitute consciousness itself, "just as DNA is not 'life,'" but he holds that "an understanding of consciousness must rest on a appreciation of the brain networks that subserve attention, in much the same way as scientific analysis of life without consideration of the structure of DNA would be vacuous" (*ibid.*).

Consciousness is essentially an emergent property of the brain's attentional networks, especially the anterior cingulate cortex (Posner, 1994). What is perhaps more crucial is that *many important emergent functions of mind and brain, which I call hypercomplex (see below), appear to require attentional amplification (consciousness) for their realization on-line.* In fact, this amplification seems to be one of the key functions of consciousness, and it also seems a property of explicit memory systems (Levin, 1991). Without the anterior cingulate attentional system creating sufficient attention in real time, the brain's executive system (Posner, 1994, p. 7400) would be out of business; even working memory requires not only the lateral prefrontal cortex (p. 7401), but also the anterior cingulate part of the attentional system, or it would become more or less useless for maintaining the rapid utilization of the brain's databases.

In this regard, Shevrin (1992) has an important suggestion, namely, that consciousness tags (i.e., categorizes) experience according to whether it reflects a perception, sensation, dream, thought, or a memory of any such form of cognition, and thus reliably distinguishes these types of experience from one another. Unquestionably, *by means of any such a categorization (or tagging) of mental events, consciousness shapes the organization of mind–brain and provides a mechanism for rapid retrieval from databases.*

Olds (1992) describes the brain as an information processor, citing Shannon's information theory to indicate that any information system tends to degrade. Olds believes that one of the key functions of consciousness is to prevent information degradation. This, he reasons, is accomplished by the frequent "re-representation" of data from the long-term memory system into itself (pp. 423–424). To support his theorizing, Olds cites the work of Winson (1985) on off-line processing and the evolution of REM sleep. For Olds, dreams are possibly the earliest example of re-representation off-line, "a phylogenetic line of self-consciousness-like phenomena" (p. 433).

My view (1988a) is that *reentry further allows the brain to create more abstract perspectives* by comparing and then downloading (that is, sharing) data points between differing memory systems (in a manner similar to how the brain uses binocularity to create three-dimensional vision). This might, in fact, help explain the advantage to the brain's alternating REM (comparing) and non-REM (downloading) periods, namely, it allows for adding complexity/dimensionality to knowledge bases (Levin, 1988a, 1991).

As do Olds and I, Rosenblatt and Thickstun (1994) emphasize re-representation. They support their conclusion with the insights of Edelman (1987, 1989) on reentry and categorization and those of Margolis (1987) on pattern recognition (p. 697). *Basch (1976) also believed the brain's major activity to be the ordering (and I would add the reordering) of experience.* Rosenblatt and Thickstun (1994) conclude that by reentrant mechanisms "conscious understanding makes possible more adaptive decisions" (p. 703)—in other words, consciousness is involved in certain complex kinds of recycling of data within mind–brain.

A more speculative effort by Baars (1988), the "global workspace theory" (reviewed in Bridgeman, 1996), imagines consciousness as the product of competing modules (an idea similar to Shallice's) which serially provides for context setting, learning, editing, debugging, reflection, and decision making functions (Bridgeman, 1996, p. 4).

In order to proceed under the condition of diverging theories and limited knowledge, we are going to need to speculate some about why consciousness is designed into our brains. For this purpose let us now return to the subject of human functioning at the most abstract level, which earlier I characterized as *hypercomplex*. Essentially, I am referring to phenomena that are the subject of daily psychoanalytic clinical work, but which are unusual in the sense that no other field has undertaken their systematic study, neither the neurosciences nor philosophy. Using Searle's perspectives, I claim that no field other than psychoanalysis could provide data comparing complex mental states over extended periods of time.

In my opinion, evolution has indeed provided for particular brain modularity, which creates consciousness as a step in our cognitive–affective processing, and as an emergent function of the attentional system. A major first step, however, in linking consciousness to adaptation lies in explaining more exactly what consciousness provides the mental apparatus.

Let us speculate in a way that seems consistent with Rosenblatt and Thickstun, and with Shevrin. *Assume that all of the variable functions I am labeling hypercomplex require consciousness for their successful on-line instantiation* (that is, for categorization, restoration, etc.). Let us speculate further that *the ability to experience hypercomplexity conferred survival value on our anthropoid ancestors.* To assist your judging whether these assumptions seem reasonable, let me give some examples of what I mean by hypercomplex variables: human affectivity, the sense of self, empathic observational ability, introspective ability, psychological-mindedness, insightfulness, creativity, semiotic capacity (communication skill), transference and countertransference potential, advanced psychological development, object relatedness, cohesiveness of self, advanced learning capacity, the capacity to love, the capacity to establish and utilize human value and goal hierarchies, sense of humor, acceptance of mortality, etc.

Whereas many motoric, sensory, and cognitive processes require only nonconscious processing, these *hypercomplex functions clearly require a combination of nonconscious (automatic) and conscious (self-reflective) data processing.* Thus, what proves decisive about the human variety of mentation is its on-line integration of explicit and implicit memory systems. To imagine operating without such an integration, one need only think of performing an Internet search with a blank computer screen. This is clearly impossible, precisely because it would exclude the modulating input we call selective attention. To put it differently, *the human pattern of mentation appears to be much more efficient in problem solving than would an entirely automatic system that would require a nonconscious equivalent of selective attention* (more about this in Chapters Fourteen and Fifteen).

I am asserting that consciousness enables a variety of functions at different levels within the brain. *At a lower level,* memories are in all likelihood categorized, stored, and restored by largely but not completely nonconscious mechanisms that essentially provide re-representation or reentry. In computer terms, this allows for such things as the dumping of cache files and other kinds of automatic cleanup and editing, thus making room for newer and more accurate input. It also helps the system avoid confusional states. *At an intermediate level,* the degree of consciousness (attention) is allowed to fluctuate in a never-ending interaction (dialectic) between the brain's search for specific goal-related input and the priming effects of input on the brain's goal system (for example, just recall the mind–brain model presented in Chapter Four). *At the highest level,* however, conscious mechanisms prevail and provide the decisive input for the hypercomplex on-line functioning without which humans would not be very human. That is, consciousness represents a high level of attention that readily and rapidly feeds back into various brain systems, providing the simultaneity required for the formation of sufficiently enlarged systems to process hypercomplex mentation on line.[41]

Consciousness thus helps create, maintain, expand, and tap complex databases of mind and brain in real time. Rapid hypercomplex functionality could not be provided by nonconscious mechanisms, because *previous experience tagged as conscious most probably requires consciousness for its retrieval, just as the computer software that creates a file is always needed for its retrieval.*

As Posner (1994) puts it, consciousness, whose source is in the "activations in the cingulate–hippocampal system," makes use of attention, just as Freud thought, "which is the increase in neural activity within brain areas currently of the organism's concern" (p. 7401). For the purpose of ordering its data, the brain has a well-defined attentional system that is not a philosophical mystery but an anatomical fact. This attentional system essentially recruits a large enough network to get the job done, and consciousness is a necessary part of the machinery that facilitates certain choices with the requisite speed and accuracy.

Let me end with a brief vignette providing evidence for the early appearance of hypercomplex functions in our anthropoid ancestors. On the Laetoli Plain near Lake Turkana in Kenya, Mary Leakey discovered footprints made over three million years ago by hominids who walked erect. A female walked first, through earth covered with fallout from a recent volcanic eruption. A male followed closely behind. But exactly within one of these sets of footprints a third individual walked, a fact determined by Leakey's discovery of one print with the sudden appearance of two big toes! The third individual, it seems, had *purposely* walked in one of the other's tracks.

Was he or she afraid? Were they playing? We do not know, but such behavior is not characteristic of earlier simians; it is already an expression of a conscious act in a class by itself. The human capacity to make interesting conscious decisions was a decisive development at our beginning and is worth our further investigation.

CHAPTER EIGHT

Subtle is the Lord: the relationship between consciousness, the unconscious, and the executive control network (ECN) of the brain

Fred Levin and Colwyn Trevarthen

"All the life in the body is the life of the individual cells. There are thus millions upon millions of centres of life in each animal body. So what needs to be explained is . . . unifying control, by reason of which we not only have unified behaviour, which can be observed by others, but also consciousness of a unified experience"

(Alfred North Whitehead, 1929, p. 108)

"The conclusion of the first century of psychoanalytic work that may be of the greatest relevance for a theory of behavior regulation is the realization that a predictable series of regulatory modes succeed each other in the course of onto-genesis. These modes . . . constitute an epigenetic sequence [such that] each mode persists as a potentiality throughout the life cycle and may be called upon whenever it offers the opportunity for optimal adaptation"

(John E. Gedo, 1993b)

---

* This paper was presented October 18, 1997 to The Fusion of Science, Art, and Humanism: The Festschrift Symposium in Honor of John E. Gedo, Chicago, Illinois. It was published as Levin and Trevarthen, 2000.

Introduction

G edo's developmental hierarchical model, which he and Goldberg originated (Gedo & Goldberg, 1973) and which he has continued to refine (Gedo, 1993a), offers clinicians and researchers alike remarkable assistance in organizing their thinking about the patterns and control mechanisms of mind–brain. Most interesting to this monograph, Gedo has employed his model to explore consciousness, a subject on the boundary between the psychological and the biological (1988, 1991a,b).

Gedo's (1996a) recent writing on consciousness has already been introduced (Chapter Two, p. 64, and Chapter Six, p. 227); now it is time to go into substantially more detail in order to begin to sort out conscious and unconscious relations. Gedo reviews his lifetime of analytic work reporting upon three of his sixty-two patients who demonstrated altered states of consciousness sometime during their analysis. The clouding of consciousness in such adult patients is understood by Gedo and others (e.g., Brenner, 1996) as reflecting a lack of autonomy, secondary to the circumstance of early, severe, and continuing trauma. In fact, all three patients suffered similar kinds of emotional trauma starting during their first twelve months of life and thus can be considered victims of post traumatic stress disorder (PTSD).

The general importance of consciousness to psychoanalysis can be illustrated most easily by Shevrin's (1992) observation that within analytic treatment *mere understanding is rarely enough to change anyone's behavior*. Rather, what repeatedly proves decisive in clinical psychoanalysis is a raising of the level of the patient's consciousness, particularly consciousness of feelings within the transference, so that awareness of various hidden wishes, fears, conflicts, and complex mental states can occur in a manner that leads to a sense of conviction, understanding, working through, and lasting change (Gedo, 1995; Levin, 1997b; Shevrin, 1992).

Definitions of consciousness

Sperry (1983) defines consciousness as "the highest level organizing principle of the mind." Trevarthen (1979) contrasts three strands of consciousness in the following way. First *"conscious intentionality* is knowing what one is . . . [intending], and why." Second, *"conscious awareness* is being perceptive of . . . what is being seen, heard, touched, etc." Third, *"conscious sharing* of knowledge and personal feelings is having intimacy with the consciousness of others and awareness of affectional and moral responsibility to them" (p. 189).

From an internal observer perspective, conscious aspects of the ECN contribute decisively to the felt experience of self-cohesion, intentionality, and autonomy. From an external observer perspective, however, the ensuing discussion makes clear that *consciousness can also be conceptualized as that self experience which corresponds with the activities of the brain's ECN* (Posner, 1994, p. 7400). This anatomically localizes the suite of conscious-related functions.

A number of factors complicate the study and add ambiguity to the discussion of consciousness. Since only a small portion of the objective actions of the ECN are capable of becoming conscious, the understanding and description of such a complex system requires patience and effort to tease out exactly what consciousness itself might be contributing. Adding to our confusion, a multiplicity of terms has historically been used more or less synonymously within cognitive psychology and neuroscience: Along with the phrases "executive control network", "attentional system", and "executive attentional network" popularized by Posner (1994, p. 7400) there are references to "the supervisory system" by Shallice (1988), and to "neural control" by Niwa (1989), Ito (1984a,b, 1985a,b, 1988, 1993), and Levin (1991). Within psychoanalysis we have reference to "neural control" (Levin, 1991), and to "self regulation" (Emde, 1988; Gedo, 1979; Lichtenberg, 1989a,b; Wilson, Passik, & Faude, 1990) and a host of others.

Consciousness and the community of others

It will help to place consciousness in social context. Imaginative consciousness takes place in a community of understanding (Trevarthen, 1990; Vygotsky, 1956; Wittgenstein, 1953). Although we are individuals, and analysis investigates our uniqueness, we are, happily or unhappily, part of a nexus of intersubjective relationships which shape, value, and add meaning to our lives.

Intersubjective relationships play a particularly important role in the early development of our self-confidence, knowledge and skills—in infancy and throughout childhood. Somehow, this consciousness with and of others depends on the way we pursue purposes in awareness, and with or without feelings or emotions. Our conscious perceptions are not passively received but rather the results of active searches for particular experience. Sharing conscious experience is also an actively determined primary human motivation.

Planned actions are themselves motivated and guided by specific conscious motor images which neuroscience has long been interested in, but which are still at the margins of psychological theory (Ingvar, 1994; Jeannerod, 1994; Sperry, 1950, 1952). Yet in spite of limited knowledge, as Posner puts it, there is

> surprising evidence for a central executive attentional network involved in a wide range of tasks . . . as different as detecting visual targets, controlling verbal working memory, noting errors, generating associations and resisting conflict. . . . And all [show] activity within a strip of tissue along the central midline, mostly within the anterior cingulate gyrus . . . [Posner, 1996, p. 82]

Here Posner is attempting to identify a nexus in brain networks where intentions enhance experience by way of selective attention.

An interesting, and possibly novel, characteristic of the human variety of conscious experience is that *we humans are ordinarily capable of tracking multiple trains of thought simultaneously, generating polyrhythms of purpose and experience, with branching or overlapping chains of foci for consciousness.* Freud's early theorizing (1910e) revolves around the coexistence of antithetical thoughts, a necessary basis for any conflict psychology. Less well known, however, is evidence that such parallel processing starts early in life (Trevarthen, 1997). Multiple tracks of awareness and thinking are products of a mind that has gained freedom through gestures, narrative mimesis, and language.

Especially helpful are Posner and Rothbart's efforts summarizing their data on the onset of the appearance of attentional control. Very young infants have simpler and less reliable strategies for orienting their awareness, whereas a year or so later in life aspects of attention such as conflict and error detection in children can be measured that are more clearly related to confident executive control (Posner, 1997, personal communication).

More fascinating still is evidence that the patterning of our mental life with each other is largely genetically predetermined or constrained, although often environmentally released. Inner genetic blueprints and epigenetic schedules for a purposeful and conscious life sympathetic to the motives of others like ourselves start unfolding before birth in embryo and fetus, and continue to express themselves throughout the life cycle. This preprogramming includes the expectable stages in Gedo and Goldberg's hierarchical developmental model. For example, a trait as basic as our inclination to imitate each other, and the complementary pleasure in being imitated, are inborn characteristics of our species, capacities we can manifest within hours of birth (Trevarthen, 1985).

Baby and mother—two consciousnesses resonating as one: the sharing of executive control

Communication between mother and baby starts, for the mother, at the very least any time after the awareness that conception has occurred. It culminates in Winnicott's *primary maternal preoccupation* (Winnicott, 1969). We do not know exactly when baby actively joins in the real dialogue, but evidence supports the view that *some form of embryonic consciousness and sympathetic response to the mother's messages actually starts before birth* through the baby's listening to sounds of the mother's voice, and its awareness of her movements and of other sensations such as mother's touch. There are also the baby's responses in the form of movements which the mother can detect, thus locking the two into an early motor dialogue.

Shortly after birth the newborn can be ready to engage in "proto-conversations" with its mother and to imitate mother's facial expressions and hand movements, something which could not possibly have been learned (Trevarthen, 1985, 1989, 1995). A newborn baby, whose heartbeat accelerates with excitement when imitating, can voluntarily give back the imitated gesture to "provoke" a reply from a watching and waiting partner, and the baby's heart slows as a response is waited for expectantly (Nagy & Molnar, 1994).

Both mother and infant actively choose to engage in such inter-subjective experiences, while over time the baby's semiotic reper-toire extends from first messages communicated via affects in gestures and concrete signals directed towards objects and events, to verbal inter-change which gradually acquires a grammatically coded syntax, and ultimately to the creation and communication of shared representational and motivated narratives (Gedo, 1996b, p. 95; Levin, 1991). The felt sense of a conscious, autonomous self thus clearly builds through modes or stages in intimate companionship with the states of other minds.

Various particular kinds of mapping of diverse fields of reality also occur in the baby over time: the baby explores his or her body parts and their relationship to each other; he or she locates self-related purposes in a personal space, and can fill this with real, concrete experiences of intentional looking, reaching to touch, or listening; and all such sensory experiences map his or her self-conscious place in a community of human relationships, identify-ing individuals as family or strangers.

Cultures define normative expectations for role relationships, ambitions and values, which are themselves gradually internalized and recognized by the newborn, but the generation of this learning is within the social curiosity of the infant (i.e., an innate intersub-jectivity). The baby's intuition for human life is matched by the mother's willing offer of expressive play and concern for both the physical and mental aspects of life.

When the time is right to communicate with and interpret her willing infant, a happy mother does not need to learn *motherese* from her culture; she is born with an intuitive fluency of vocal expression for conversation, offered with appropriate feeling and richly embellished by gestures and postures, and she uses it (Trevarthen, 1989, 1997).

The voices and movements of mother and baby are continu-ously alive with feelings, and even with their later use of gram-matical language, the very sounds and movements of mouth, tongue, and lips often continue to imitate the meanings intended, as noted by Fónagy (1971, 1987). For example, the speaker who is angry, in almost every language, throttles his threats and curses. And affectionate words like "kiss" veritably ooze with sentiment. This human skill for representation of meaning in bodily gesture and "tone" of movement has been called "mimesis" by Donald (1991), who considers it the indispensable phylogenetic precursor of language (see also, Levin, 1991, Chapter 11).

Sympathetic, unreasoned consciousness of emotions identifies what is salient for learning (Levin, 1991, 1997a), for establishing goals and values as well as for consolidating interpersonal bonds (Trevarthen, 1979, 1993). Writing from an evolutionary perspective, Langer (1967, p. 444) notes that "value exists only where there is [a shared sense of] consciousness. Where nothing is [consciously] felt, nothing matters." *Consciousness is equated with feeling, which can only mean that it derives from purposes.*

Shared emotions and values enable us to better understand each other as individuals and as members of a particular family, societal group, and culture. Engagement with others neatly doubles, as well as acting as a prototype, for internal organization of thoughts in the conversation mode (Vygotsky, 1956; Wittgenstein, 1953), and also for the evolution of a defined, cohesive, and autonomous sense of self (Gedo, 1993b; Kohut, 1971; Winnicott, 1969).

But what really does this rich, varied and fundamentally innate consciousness in companionship consist of in terms of the mind–brain? In what follows, we explore this question in more depth, elaborating upon bottom-up, then top-down theorizing. Where appropriate, we offer speculations towards further understanding of Gedo's three traumatized patients.

Neuropsychological studies of consciousness

The bottom-up

"The bottom-up approach . . . look[s] at the physiological components and infer[s] from a knowledge of them how the whole system must work" (Crook, 1988, p. 350). To understand consciousness in bottom-up terms, hypothesizing motivational mechanisms, Posner and his collaborators focus upon selective attention within the visual system, which we shall briefly review again here. They identify anterior and posterior attentional systems that show significantly different characteristics (Bachtereva, Abdullaev, & Medvedev, 1992; Posner, 1988, 1994, 1995; Posner, Abdullaev, McCandliss, & Sereno, 1992; Posner & Raichle, 1994).

> The anterior attention system (composed of anterior cingulate gyrus and basal ganglia) serves executive functions and is involved in attentional recruitment and control of brain areas to perform complex cognitive tasks; the posterior attention system (composed of superior parietal cortex, pulvinar and superior colliculus) is largely responsible for selecting one stimulus location among many and for shifting from one stimulus to the next. [Stablum, Mogentale, & Umiltà, 1996, p. 263]

Dehaene, Posner, and Tucker (1994) have also confirmed the importance of the anterior cingulate cortex in monitoring performance and compensating for errors, what they call *attention for action* (p. 304). The picture which emerges is that of different modules involved in executive decisions, target selection, zooming in, and detaching from objects of interest (Posner & Raichle, 1994).

Damage to the ECN provides information about mind–brain correlations. For example, damage to the anterior cingulate disturbs the entire array of ECN functions, including such activities (of psychoanalytic interest) as error correction, associating, and dealing with conflicts (Posner, 1996).

In PTSD the anterior cingulate (along with amygdalar circuits) has been shown to "play a role in the pathological response of combat veterans . . . to mental images of combat-related scenes" but not in the responses of control subjects to the same stimuli (Shin et al., 1997). In autism and the related condition Asberger's Syndrome decreased metabolic activity has been found in the cingulate gyrus on PET scan (Minshew, 1992, cited in Aronowitz et al., 1997). As Posner points out, establishing ties between the PET work on infants and various kinds of developmental pathology would be extremely important for understanding brain mechanisms (Posner, 1997, personal communication).

In contrast to the case of damage to the anterior attentional system, damage to the parietal lobe (part of the posterior attention system) typically interferes with the ability to detach gaze from objects of interest (Posner, 1996). Thus, although we cannot be certain, it seems unlikely that the posterior attentional system plays any role in the problems of Gedo's traumatized patients. More likely, the clouding of their consciousness relates to traumatically induced changes in either the anterior portion of the ECN, its

"extensions" (which we will describe shortly), or the system relationships between the ECN and its "extensions".

Posner and colleagues' research has stimulated detailed investigation of various aspects of control of the visual and other sensory systems (Mattingly, Davis, & Driver, 1997; Posner, Abdullaev,
McCandliss, & Sereno, 1992; Rees, Frackowiak, & Frith, 1997). Visual
control bears a clear relationship to our "subjective experience of
awareness" (Posner & Raichle, 1994, p. 178), judging from the fact
that the anterior cingulate activates when subjects detect visual
targets and becomes quiescent when thoughts are cleared (p. 179).
The research of Posner and his colleagues has also spawned
clinical tests for identifying and even quantifying subtle but significant evidence of closed head injury to the ECN, based upon
performance on visual tracking paradigms (Stablum, Mogentale, &
Umiltà, 1996). Such examination of Gedo's three analysands would
effectively rule out covert neurological injury and would further
localize which portion of the attentional system is involved in their
consciousness disturbances.

The ECN's extensions[42]

Let us take stock briefly. We are suggesting that the ECN includes
a core and a variety of ECN extensions. The *core structures* are the
anterior cingulate, basal ganglia, posterior parietal cortex, pulvinar,
and superior colliculus. The *extensions* are the reticular activating
system (RAS), orbital frontal and selective other cortex, the amygdalar and hippocampal systems, corpus callosum and cerebellum.
We will now comment on these extensions.

We begin with the RAS and the orbital frontal cortex. The RAS
plays a well known role in general arousal (see Levin, 1991). The
orbital frontal cortex acts to inhibit, and sometimes produce amnesia for, impulsive and dangerous behavior. For example, tumors in
this area can produce homicidal acts carried out without apparent
conscious control (Relkin, Plum, Mattis, Eidelberg, & Tranel, 1996;
Damasio, Grabowski, Frank, Galaburda, & Damasio, 1994). Hadley
(2000) extensively discusses the orbital frontal cortex from the
perspective of Schore's (1994) study of self and brain. Schore speculates that during development in an optimal human environment

dopadrenergic midbrain neurons migrate upwards and forwards into the orbitalfrontal cortex, contributing decisively to self regulation (Pally, 1997; Schore, 1994). We may ask if this migration is part of what early PTSD alters? Later, we will note other effects of PTSD on the brain.

The next extension is the lateral prefrontal cortex which "... appear[s] to hold the relevant information [for conscious tasks] online ..." for the cingulate cortex (Posner, 1994, p. 7401), "a process known as working memory", a function currently without absolutely agreed upon boundaries (Rao, Rainer, & Miller, 1997, p. 821; Baddeley, 1986).

The cerebellum, which we are considering an ECN extension, influences a variety of sensory, motor, attentional, and cognitive systems "... in order to accomplish its prime function which is to learn to predict and prepare for imminent information acquisition, analysis, and action" (Allen, Buxton, Wong, & Corchesne, 1997, p. 1942; Levin, 1991; Levin & Vuckovich, 1983). In this way, "through its connections with attentional systems [the cerebellum] influences the speed and accuracy of ... attentional changes" (Allen, Buxton, Wong, & Corchesne, 1997, p. 1943; also see Trevarthen, 1990, p. 54).

Consider also as ECN extension the amygdalar and hippocampal systems. As noted earlier in this monograph, the hippocampus is responsible for creating and modifying the databases of mind–brain (Palombo, 1998).

The amygdalar and hippocampal systems show an interesting double dissociation affecting consciousness that has been identified by Damasio's group at Iowa (Bechara et al., 1995; Levin, 1997f). Specifically, bilateral damage to the amygdala prevents learning aversive responses, yet allows one nevertheless to learn the special circumstances associated with the appearance of pain (i.e., it damages semantic memory). In contrast, bilateral hippocampal damage allows aversive response learning to proceed normally but interferes with learning the associated specific circumstances (i.e., it damages episodic memory). This dissociation is what leads Hadley (2000) to call the hippocampal module a system for *belief* (we prefer *concern*) and the amygdalar module a system for *knowledge*. You might wish to think of the amygdala, also, as the fast circuit for reporting emergencies to higher centers, for rapid response.

In a separate study of selective focal hippocampal damage early in life (Vargha-Khadem et al., 1997), there is evidence that although episodic and semantic memory seem at least partially dissociable, "only the episodic component [seems] fully dependent upon the hippocampus" (p. 376), which fits with the work of the Damasio group already noted. Incidentally, such hippocampal damage is known to occur in PTSD secondary to the effect of stress-related chronically high blood levels of corticosteroids, and has been correlated with the patient's difficulty, once this condition begins, in properly analyzing stress and choosing adaptive responses to it; instead, the subject reacts in a uniformly reflexive manner (Van der Kolk, 1997).

Returning to Gedo's three traumatized patients, it seems that although psychoanalysis could be used to attempt to understand what these subjects originally experienced that was traumatic for them, and thus eventually acquire knowledge of the circumstances of their trauma,[43] this might be difficult precisely because any association or recollection within such treatment would itself depend to some degree upon the function of damaged hippocampuses (whose function it is to organize mind–brain databases). This is, in fact, why skilled analysts do not rely entirely on the patient's associations or memories, but also examine carefully their complex (transferential) affective and behavioral patterns in the treatment.

Commisurotomy

The final ECN extension is the corpus callosum, which interconnects the hemispheres and is itself associative cortex. This subject is sufficiently convoluted that it is best considered in a separate section. The psychological effects of callosal transection have been studied extensively (Sperry & Zaidel, 1977; Trevarthen, 1975, 1979, 1990). Basically, commisurotomy, in "test" circumstances where deployment of purposes and attentions is constrained, "detaches the two cortical memory stores so they operate as independent associative systems" (Trevarthen, 1990, p. 74).

Commisurotomy, usually done to stop otherwise uncontrollable epilepsy, can cause abnormally unstable attention and lead to fluctuating neglect, loss of vigilance, unconstrained perceptual completion of image building, mutism, and transient apraxias. However, perhaps unexpectedly, commisurotomy patients are *not* as troubled as normals are when presented with conflicting perceptual tasks. In fact, under such circumstances they actually show enhanced perceptual processing in the sense of readily holding within perception completely incompatible data sets.

Let us linger here to observe that the neurological concept of separate (incompatible) consciousnesses in split-brain patients coincides quite well with the Freudian concept of incompatible ideas existing within the normal mind. Our reading, from an interdisciplinary perspective, is that in this isomorphism we catch a glimpse of some critical design features of the normal human brain. Let me elaborate.

If under ordinary circumstances two or more separate and distinct consciousnesses can occur in one mind, as Freud noted, and as split-brain subjects readily demonstrate, then this can only mean that *the mind often behaves as if a true integration of incompatibilities exists when this in fact is not the case* (Bogen, 1990; Trevarthen, 1990; also see Rao, Rainer, & Miller, 1997, for an interesting example of research on the integration of sensory data in the prefrontal cortex). But how and for what reason is the appearance of integration accomplished, from either an experience-near or distant perspective?

One way would be for there to be frequent control decisions made by the mind–brain in order to switch mental processing between low level, routine, automatic attentional mechanisms (which might potentially get us into trouble by inviting awareness of incompatible impulses, thoughts, and feelings) and high level, selective, attentional mechanisms (which would have the capacity to mix and match the complex machinery of mind–brain in ways that could safeguard mental life). We are, of course, essentially describing here the well known psychological defense mechanisms which the mind–brain uses to deal with conflict or its mere appearance. But we are also describing what would appear to be a known operation of the ECN.

We are arguing, on a logical basis that the very same control structures of the mind–brain that create consciousness also create the dynamic unconscious. Thus, *the anterior cingulate cortex, by making high level decisions to selectively expand or shrink the ECN (by including or excluding extensions from a neural network), is using its capacity for selectivity of attention (i.e., consciousness) to protect unconscious thoughts, goals, and aims.*[44] For example, by eliminating or at least dampening cerebellar input to the ECN temporarily, the anterior cingulate can render "invisible" evidences of discrepancies between real and expected input, the kind of discrepancies that would otherwise invite awareness of unconscious motives. Later, when the ECN estimates that such discrepancies can be dealt with effectively, the cerebellar "gating" could be halted to allow for an analysis of what was "left out" in one's thinking or problem solving.

If we now switch back from a psychoanalytic to a cognitive neuroscience perspective, there is good evidence accumulating that the coordination of what are commonly the strikingly different viewpoints of the two cerebral hemispheres ordinarily falls to the ECN and its "extensions" as a group. This has been examined exhaustively by Shallice, and will be covered in the next section. The bottom line, however, is that "consciousness in the hemispheres may be profoundly changed by lateralized activation of the cortex. Such 'metacontrol' can further lead to poor cognitive performance . . . [for example] if allocation of activity is to a hemisphere ill-equipped for a given task" (Trevarthen, 1990, p. 75).

Incidentally, the term *metacontrol* was coined by Jerre Levy and Colwyn Trevarthen (1976), and derives from experimental data that suggest mental activity involving a supervisory system or ECN whose decisions essentially match hemisphere with current cognitive task. Clearly, in the present discussion we are extending the meaning of metacontrol significantly to include a defensive/adaptive function (used for protecting the self or other from seeing and/or experiencing evidence of conflict).

As noted, Posner and colleagues' research assigns metacontrol to the anterior cingulate gyrus, which issues orders to executive control modules within the prefrontal cortex, basal ganglia, corpus callosum and/or cerebellum to take over, in various combinations and permutations, in order to optimize processing for a given situation (Levin, 1991; Rees, Frackowiak, & Firth, 1997; Trevarthen, 1990). Such higher-level *special handling*, as it were, requires moment to moment consciousness (or, at least, monitoring) of vast amounts of information. Consciousness would thus appear to be a critical design feature of mind–brain.

Let us briefly reconsider Gedo's patients in light of the above considerations. It is possible to imagine that during and after traumatic overload states (i.e., as a consequence), metacontrol is what actually becomes disrupted, so that these patients end up matching various cognitive tasks to the wrong cognitive module, that is, one not well suited for the particular task at hand. This might show up as a momentary confusional state of altered consciousness as the self discovers un-anticipated difficulty in task completion. Anxiety and quick responses without forethought would be expected in this situation.

Summarizing this difficult section may help. We are proposing that what collosal transection eliminates is the highest hierarchical level of commissural links, the one "providing flexible choice of behavioral sets and orientations" (Trevarthen, 1990, p. 77). At times of complex problem solving, high risks befall the mind when the ECN decides to follow routine, low level, inflexible, contingency planning rather than high level organizing principles.

In our scenario, the anterior cingulate itself is what consciously tracks ongoing system events, creates and deploys focal attention to actively search for needed data, and most importantly, recruits and coordinates more of the mind–brain's controlling machinery for a variety of adaptive purposes, according to the anterior cingulate's best current judgments about the shifting requirements, nature, and importance of the task at hand.[45]

Top-down approaches to consciousness: the functions of consciousness

Top-down "means looking at the design features of elaborate performance and then inferring the sorts of components that could process the performance" (Crook, 1988, p. 350).

Shallice (1988) has inferred much about how the mind–brain works from his review of such partially functional states as so-called blind sight, knowledge without awareness,[46] and dual consciousness in the split brain. His conclusions are much the same as our own. According to Shallice, consciousness is essentially an emergent property of four interactive neural control systems: what he calls the overall supervisory system (which employs consciousness to monitor external and internal states and determines special handling for high priority mental operations), the language system (which responds to word-linked triggers with shifts in mental set), contention scheduling (which controls patterns for the more usual and customary low level operations), and episodic memory (which contributes its vast store of personal associations to cognitive processing). As noted above, some of the same research has also been described under the rubric of "working memory".

Employing the perspective of Shallice, Gedo's three analysands with disturbed consciousness suffer from knowledge without awareness. The problem analytically is how to begin to help them identify that there exists significant episodic, i.e. procedural memory (of trauma) which they are not conscious of possessing. Although most often this insight is accomplished in analysis by interpreting transferences, in the case of these patients, it may be more crucial sometimes for the psychoanalyst to recognize that a significant portion of the patient's important affective intensity seems not transferential at all. In somewhat different words, in Gedo's patients we meet some instances where it would be easy to conflate the cognitive non-conscious with the Freudian unconscious.

Shevrin (1992) reasons that for the rapid retrieval of brain databases to work, the different varieties of experience must have been properly distinguished from each other in memory. With this aim in mind, Shevrin believes that consciousness functions principally to tag (that is, to categorize) experience according to whether, or not, it is the recollection of a perception, a sensation, a dream, a thought, a wish, etc. His own empirical research (Shevrin, Bond, Brakel, Hertel, & Williams, 1996), distinguishing analytic and electroencephalographic markers of unconscious versus conscious events has lead him to this viewpoint. In other words, if one believes in a dynamic unconscious, it follows logically that some experiences are known and categorized by one system (the *system unconscious*, for example) but not by the *conscious system*. It seems a short step from this thought to recognizing that even within a single system (such as the system conscious) retrieval might well require a categorization tag to distinguish the various types of experiential memories from each other.

Shevrin's perspective appears in the neuropsychological literature under the rubric of procedural–implicit vs. semantic–explicit memory. Posner and Rothbart (1994a, p. 48–49) similarly tie the neurology and psychology of consciousness together when they describe, in the case of the anterior attentional system, how explicit learning is blocked by distraction whereas, in the posterior attentional system, implicit learning cannot be so easily blocked. However, this seems not to be the same dissociability of memory that we noted earlier regarding the amygdalar and hippocampal systems. Rather here, explicit learning is being localized anatomically within the ECN while procedural (i.e., implicit) learning is given no such localization.

The importance of such work on learning dissociation is as follows: within the first four months of life, and certainly by one year, infants learn who and what to attend to, and this relatively non-distractible, procedural kind of learning helps them with all further learning by focusing them on information their culture values (Posner & Raichle, 1994). The work on dissociation also helps us appreciate the complexity of the problem of our understanding circumstances where patients know things which they are not aware of knowing; that is, our subtle Lord has created, in our brains, multiple memory systems with an adaptive redundancy that sometimes appears to run amok!

Using Shevrin's insights, one must conclude that Gedo's patients have, through their early trauma, failed to properly tag or categorize critical memories, thus interfering with memory retrieval. When experiences without such tags necessarily manifest themselves (primed by experiences in the here and now) their confusing origin and unexpected nature cannot fail to tip such individuals into a temporary clouding, or a fragmentation of consciousness. These disturbed states express the patient's painful objectless confusion; they also serve as markers of the trauma and history of the deployment of primitive protection against pain by means of the mechanism of non-registration.

Olds (1992), in company with the majority of cognitive scientists, sees the brain primarily as an information processing machine. Reasoning from Shannon's information theory that any information system tends to degrade, Olds believes the key function of consciousness must be to prevent information degradation. Olds is supported by the generator-in-randomness thinking of Rosenblatt and Thickstun (1994), Edelman (1989), Margolis (1987), and the late

Michael Basch (1976). Applied to the example of Gedo's patients, Olds' reasoning seems as follows: One can imagine that as the patient's awareness of the true significance of their episodes of disturbed consciousness grows in treatment, the patient will attempt to hold on to this new, now correctly labeled and valued information by repeatedly feeding their partial insights into various memory systems. However, in the process they will generate a number of duplicate memories, each with somewhat different tags, and this will produce some further temporary confusion at times, but should ultimately lead to improved retrieval and a basic self reorganization around the reclassification of memory tags (which will include a new category, namely, *not categorized!*).

Attention requires instructions from the prefrontal cortex, that part of the brain most traditionally connected with working memory (Crick & Koch, 1992; also see Barinaga, 1997). Gedo's patients necessarily activate their working memories in order to expand their knowledge because it is only within working memory that memories become capable of reinterpretation by the self. Based upon the research of Posner (1995) and of Lassen (1994a), Levin (1997a,b) suggests that *one reason engaging the transference is often crucial for psychoanalytic learning is that the free association and spontaneity associated with transferences activate specific blocks of working memory.*

The philosopher Searle (1995c) raises thoughtful philosophical objections to the various propositions of top-down theorists. However, the downside of his own efforts is that along with Eccles (1973) Searle believes consciousness to be fundamentally mysterious, by which he means, unknowable. This, of course, puts consciousness research outside the reach of science, but safely within the bounds of philosophy. Additionally, Eccles asserts that *only* the left hemisphere has consciousness. We believe with Sperry (1977), however, that a more plausible and parsimonious conclusion is that *both* hemispheres are capable of consciousness, but that the left hemisphere particularly communicates its experience in words.

Finally, we mention Czikzentmihalyi's (1975) proposal that one phase of conscious experience (not further specified neurophysiologically but apparently associated with focused attention) tends to coexist with relaxation, joy, energy, and self confirmation, something which he colorfully denotes as *flow* (see also Crook, 1988, p. 355). We link *flow* to the (non-verbal) self-evaluating role of consciousness, a function most neuropsychologists would locate more with the right hemisphere (Damasio, Grabowski, Frank, Galaburda, & Damasio, 1994; Schore, 1994).

Czikzentmihalyi believes that disrupted flow can interfere with at least the quality of consciousness. This fits well with our sense that *consciousness is the experiential aspect of successful ECN activity*. In other words, optimal ECN functioning coincides with pleasurable feelings of self cohesion, intentionality, autonomy, and privacy. Non-optimal ECN activity coincides with temporary disruptions of consciousness, and secondary disturbances in mood (not uncommonly including shame).

Synthesis and summary

We have discussed consciousness and its relationship to the ECN, suggesting that the set of functions of the anterior cingulate gyrus shows a key relationship to both conscious and unconscious processing. In doing so, we appreciate fully that we run a risk of confusing some readers, by appearing to confound the cognitive non-conscious with the Freudian unconscious. From our perspective, however, these are clearly related but different domains which will require a separate treatment (see Chapters Fourteen and Fifteen).

What follows summarizes our discussion of consciousness, the ECN, and our various speculations about Gedo's clinical experience with those rare analysands who suffer disturbances of consciousness.

Although no consensus exists, Levin (1997a,d) believes that there are significant areas of agreement about the likely functions of consciousness. At the lowest level of brain activity, memories are in all likelihood categorized, stored, and maintained by both conscious and non-conscious means. In effect, this resembles what for computers is the dumping of old "cache" files, performing other cleanup and editing, and otherwise making room for new information while maintaining old information in retrievable format. It makes sense that the conscious component of this level of control is for the purpose of categorization, just as Shevrin suggests, so that the databases of mind and brain are usable on-line.

At an intermediate level of motivated and investigative activity, consciousness (as attention) is allowed to fluctuate in a never ending dialectic between the brain's purposeful search for specific goal-related input and the priming effects of input on the brain's goal system. Levin and Kent's (1995) cybernetic model of brain accounts for such activities and requires an executive or supervisory system with two inputs: (1) goal priorities and (2) feedback about motor output and current states. Such a conscious or executive control system seems closest to that described above as "attention for action" (Dehaene, Posner, & Tucker, 1994, p. 304).

Finally, at the highest level of organization, conscious mechanisms appear to prevail as the sine qua non for the on-line functioning of human hypercomplexity. *Hypercomplexity* here refers to the complicated, inborn facets of human mental life such as psychological defense, affectivity, and the autonomous sense of agency. Each of these functions requires the recruitment of networks (of specialized groups of brain cells) of varying size depending upon the scope of the task. Such activity necessarily demands not only rapid (on-line) access to the most sophisticated databases of mind–brain (e.g., working memory); it also requires a subtle kind of concerned decision making that only consciousness of the human variety has evolved to accomplish.

In presenting information about the ECN we have delineated current research bearing upon the question of what brain mechanisms seem responsible for the central organization of human mental functioning, including what analysts call the dynamic unconscious. Together with the work of Gedo and other psychoanalysts, Posner and his colleagues clarify that trauma early in life can result in decisive changes in cognitive development affecting later abilities to perform such mental activities as error correction, association of memory, and management of conflicts. A logical corollary seems to be that proper ECN functioning results in a quality of individual consciousness which, when shared with others, becomes a decisive part of the glue in relationships in general. In the end, of course, consciousness of community and optimal emotional and cognitive development influence each other (Levin, 1991). However, *when our inner conflicts remain largely unresolved, we each merely simulate the appearance of integration, but without its substance, and largely unconscious issues determine the subsequent patterning of our life.*

Because untimely emotional stress can create such conditions as PTSD through its decisive effect on the machinery of mind and brain (especially the all important hippocampus which organizes mind–brain databases), psychoanalysts, along with many other kinds of scientific specialists, have a need to investigate and help restore normal functioning (Pally, 1997). For reviews of PTSD, we have referred the reader to the work of Van der Kolk (1997).

We thus offer the following set of explanations for the fluctuations in consciousness that Gedo observed in three of his sixty-seven patients: (1) Gedo's sense that such patients lack autonomy secondary to their trauma (i.e., PTSD); (2) Levy and Trevarthen's view of metacontrol problems (Levy & Trevarthen, 1976), meaning trauma damages metacontrol; (3) Posner's conception of specific damage to the anterior or posterior attentional systems, or to the cingulate gyrus itself; (4) Shevrin's suggestion of disturbed tagging of memories with resulting difficulties in memory retrieval; and (5) Levin and Trevarthen's consideration of difficulties in the various extensions of the ECN (including damage to the hippocampus especially), and their associated memory systems, and (6) problems associated with inflexible (low level) vs. flexible (higher level) patterns of analysis. It should be clear that points (3), (4), (5), and (6) could also be seen as attempts to specify precisely the nature of metacontrol alterations in PTSD.

Of course, in highlighting primarily neurocognitive factors, we know that we will certainly appear to diminish the importance of traditional psychoanalytic perspectives (Gedo, 1995; Wilson, Passik, & Faude, 1990). In fact, however, we are rather attempting to explore more deeply into the factors behind the uncontrolled alterations in the levels of consciousness.

By describing details of the ECN we also hope to assist analysts in better identifying the relationship between the felt experience and the patterning of particular cognitive functions. The functions involved include attaching, zooming, detaching, associating, error detection, and scanning mind–brain databases. If looked for clinically, these patterns might be identifiable, leading to additional empirical knowledge about how best to facilitate their operation psychoanalytically.

Finally, as Einstein said: The most incomprehensible thing about the universe is that it is comprehensible! In this very sense we are surprised and pleased that our delineation of some of the design features of mind–brain that bear upon the uncontrolled clouding of consciousness in patients with PTSD seems comprehensible in terms of intelligent shifts between conscious and unconscious systems under the control of a precisely specifiable executive control network. In Chapters Nine and Ten details of conscious/ unconscious relations are further explored.

CHAPTER NINE

The conundrum of conscious and unconscious relations: Part 1—Ito's evolutionary model of brain and the role of the cerebellum[47]

Fred Levin, John Gedo, Masao Ito, and Colwyn Trevarthen

Introduction

T his chapter addresses the relationship between conscious and unconscious systems from the perspective of Ito's evolutionary model of the brain and what is known about the role of the cerebellum. The following chapter utilizes earlier discussions of Shevrin's research on memory tagging and the functions of consciousness, and Posner's work on the ECN,[48] and exploits these for further insights into the conscious–unconscious relationship.

In a recent major contribution, Ito (1998) discusses consciousness from the viewpoint of the evolution of mind–brain, considering psychoanalytic and neuropsychological perspectives without privileging either discipline. In what follows, we elaborate upon Ito's model, which we find compelling, concentrating primarily on the relationship between the conscious and non-conscious systems (or as Ito expresses it, the neurophysiology of emotional dynamics, cognition and "will").

Ito's Evolutionary Model will be described in detail; however, some definitions and disclaimers will help to clarify what we intend to consider, and what is beyond our purview. First, by unconscious we are referring only to the Freudian or so-called dynamic unconscious. For categories other than conscious and unconscious systems we shall use the term non-conscious, by which we refer to all activity in the brain that occurs outside of awareness. *The strictly non-conscious is thus a category which includes the dynamic unconscious, but which is obviously larger*. In our estimate most brain activity is non-conscious. *The extent of the Freudian unconscious is of course unknown, but it probably represents a small yet significant fraction of the non-conscious system*. Below, we provide further refinements of the unconscious–non-conscious distinction.

As for the disclaimers: this paper does *not* elaborate upon the non-conscious system *per se*. In addition, we are *not* principally debating what consciousness is about, a question for which there is nothing approaching a consensus, although we do take a position on this question.

Essentially, it is our belief that contemporary disagreements over the nature of consciousness will take a considerable time to resolve; therefore, we should not let the debate delay our examination of conscious–unconscious relations. We posit that new considerations about these relations might actually help to resolve the problems that have frustrated consciousness researchers for years.

It will help to note what some of these durable problems are, even if they are not a significant part of this chapter. They would appear to involve at least the following.

1. Understanding consciousness in terms of Freud's metapsychology, as well as from a complex philosophical perspective, including resolving disagreements about what is strictly knowable in a Kantian/Freudian sense (versus that which is merely inferred), and what is causally connected (versus what is merely *correlated*). Readers interested in this are referred to Solms, 1997; also see Baars, 1994, 1997, pp. 710–711, including the works of Searle, Dretske, Flanagan, and Chalmers, whom Baars cites on pp. 710–711.
2. Sorting out the complex relationships between consciousness, perception, memory, and cognition (see Olds, 1992, 1994, 1997).
3. Explaining the limited-capacity paradox, *viz.* the observation that consciousness "... is marked by a surprisingly limited

capacity" (Baars, 1997, p. 709) whereas the non-conscious seems virtually without limit.

4. Clarifying the conditions required for consciousness in terms of basic neuroanatomy and physiology (see Baars, 1997, p. 713).
5. Comprehensively relating motivation, affective organization (feelings), wishes, drives, and consciousness to each other (see especially Shevrin, 1997a,b).
6. Explaining why consciousness is a necessary design feature of mind–brain, i.e. what it does at various levels of organization (see Chapter Seven).
7. Relating consciousness to subliminal perception, etc.

How then can we address conscious–unconscious systems? First, we propose to review generally the current contributions to consciousness research. Necessarily, though we touch upon some of the subjects noted in the preceding paragraph (and chapters), our core area of interest is, as noted, the narrow inquiry into conscious–unconscious relations. To this end, we consider four closely connected areas of interdisciplinary research relevant to Ito's novel approach. These have already been introduced in Section III, and are connected with each of the authors of this chapter (plus H. Shevrin and M. Posner).[49]

The remainder of this chapter is organized as follows: after definitions of important terms there is a general background on problems relating to consciousness research and a summary of Ito's evolutionary model of brain. The latter includes a delineation of the complex role of the cerebellum. Finally, we preview our central argument in Chapter Ten (Part 2).

Some definitional problems

As the reader will appreciate, no discussion of mind–brain can occur without definitional difficulties, given our subject's inherent complexity.[50] Efforts to clarify definitions and sort out mind–brain relationships seem critical because of the great importance of such knowledge both clinically and theoretically. Through various definitions and footnotes we hope to clarify our meanings in this difficult terrain.

To begin, we believe, as Ito argues, *that the functions of mind are indeed founded on neural systems* that represent the body as a coherent, mobile and sensitive entity, and that movements in subject space set the tasks in motion for reception of information from the environment (i.e., for perception). In addition, we are generally in agreement with the standard definitions of consciousness Ito employs (see the next paragraph), although there is little doubt that these definitions are not intended to be either comprehensive or independent of each other.

Traditionally, consciousness has been considered to be a reflection of one of the following: (1) wakefulness (i.e., the level of or capacity for intake), (2) perceptual awareness (referring to the general content of perceptions), or (3) self-awareness (usually meaning the comprehension, in real time, of intentions, purposes, beliefs, etc.—presumably generated from our thoughts and feelings, that is, either from memory, or in immediate reaction to sensory events) (Zeman, Grayling, & Lowey, 1997).

Nor do definitional problems entirely disappear with the helpful step of redefining consciousness as relating to attention (as did Freud, in his *Interpretation of Dreams*, 1900a, p. 544, cited in Rapaport 1951a, p. 335). For example, Sereno (1996) writes

> over the years it has become clear in the cognitive [psychological] literature that 'attention' is not a very precise or unambiguous term. [For] when we use the term 'attention,' do we mean arousal, vigilance, orienting, search, selection, or shift? (p. 424).[51]

It is also possible that some cultures give too much weight to the critical examination of self awareness, that is, to the notion of the self as an isolated center of awareness. *What tends to get overlooked when thinking about consciousness only as self awareness is that consciousness could alternatively (or, if you will, simultaneously) be defined as the awareness of the self experience of others* (Levin & Trevarthen, 1997; Trevarthen, 1993, 1995, 1997; see also Chapter Eight).

Put differently, *self-consciousness is invariably socially qualified action, modified by culture and verbal description.* In this sense, what is usually called consciousness as awareness of one's inner experience, in isolation, could be seen as a dispensable artifact. That is, self-consciousness could not exist except in the context of internalized human relationships and associated feeling states and interpersonal goals.[52] Thus we disagree with Gallup's (1985) criteria for self-awareness; they strike us as having too much to do with self-grooming (i.e., acting on the self as if it were a social partner)—actions which seem to us as strange and potentially embarrassing as shaving in public (cf. Harpo Marx with Margaret Dumont in *A Night at the Opera*)!

Yet the subject of selective attention cannot ignore the fact that of course, under the right circumstances, attention becomes focused exclusively on the individual's current performance. But tasks of supreme difficulty may even lead not only to a loss of awareness of the external world, but even to lack of consciousness of one's own person. Examples would include a mathematician working seventy-two hours on research uninterruptedly, followed by not knowing even if he had eaten, or gone to the bathroom, and an artist waking up at the foot of his easel, having done much work on the canvas for which he had no conscious awareness (Gedo, 1996b, Epilogue).

Selective attention can thus lead to the scotomatization of internal processes (which psychological defenses such as repression and disavowal contribute to), or to the actual alteration of consciousness as a pathological symptom or even a psychological defense (Gedo, 1996a; Levin & Vuckovich, 1983, 1987; Levin & Trevarthen, 1997, see Chapter Thirteen).[53] For this reason the reader will appreciate our attempt to find a definition of consciousness which respects the complexity of the various phenomenal categories, but which is also in keeping with at least one modern trend within psychoanalysis, namely, the attempt to generally understand human feelings and behavior in terms of interactions and intersubjectivity (Fosshage, 1997).

An additional problem in delimiting and defining consciousness is deciding how to take into account the well-known relationship between CNS activity and perception. The very idea of a pure reflex reaction, triggered by a stimulus in a passive mechanism, seems sufficiently unnatural to render it potentially maladaptive. What we wish to emphasize here is that *no animal reaction to sensory events (excitations of sense cells) is likely to occur without prior orientation in terms of a hierarchy of motives (forms of relating to the world) and ulterior adaptive goals.* Of course, this is the core of what Freud referred to in his conception of the dynamic unconscious. But since this is even true of insect-catching plants, whose effectors "expect" insects (recall Chapter Five), how could it be any less true of humans? Thus, any thoroughgoing approach to mind–brain integration must come to grips with the idea of an active, goal-oriented perspective on consciousness.[54]

On the basis of the foregoing considerations, we wish to shift the conception of consciousness in Ito's model away from the implication of isolated associative activity and move it toward associative states *in linkage to a motivational schema* (i.e., in relation to interpersonal goals, and to relationships with important others). We make this suggestion because the commonly held belief that associative activity represents the pinnacle of CNS function misleadingly suggests that higher intelligence is constructed by merely combining lower level integrative functions, and nothing more. It seems to us more accurate to say that although higher intelligence obviously can and does employ simultaneously many more of the organism's provisional patterns of cognition, which in turn commit the organism to a greater diversity of motivated acts, what is decisive about such deployment is not the mere enlargement of the neural network involved. Rather, it is the fact that *when the organism employs a more complex system (rather than using a routine one) it is doing so because it already has decided that the goal being aimed it is an important one (recall Chapter Eight).* This will become clearer when we review the research of Shevrin and of Posner (and that of Levin and Trevarthen) in the following chapter.

In other words, doing more means having to perceive and anticipate more, which is aided by remembering more. Yet the overall principles of purposeful action and the way the body (with its symmetries and polarity) is coordinated to carry them out are not essentially changed in evolution between fish and man. A fundamentally homologous organization for psychological action is made evident throughout the vertebrates by the remarkable conservation of a polarized segmental CNS design, and by the homeobox-containing genes which regulate its formation, structure, and function. Most significantly, the genetic structure leads to biological drives that are expressible through behavior, though often disguised by the perpetrator's unconscious mind.

Still another matter complicates the study of consciousness, and this is the multiplicity of subtle qualities that enter into conscious experience. For example, we have not yet even mentioned the well-known distinctions between (1) attention for tracking the *presence* of the object (i.e., the brain's spatial, *where*, or dorsal system, involving the superior parietal lobule), versus (2) tracking the object's *identity* (i.e., the brain's form/figure, *what*, or ventral system, involving the inferior temporal lobe). Moreover, to complement the so-called *what* and the *where* pathways for visual attention one needs to observe that (3) attention also uniquely specifies the object's *potentiality for fulfilling sought-after goals*, i.e., largely concerned with interpersonal values (Gedo, 1991a,b, 1993a,b, 1996a,b, 1997; Iwata, 1996; Levin & Kent, 1994, 1995; Posner & Raichle, 1994, pp. 168–169).

Obviously, if our intuition would be correct, we need to clarify in some simple way the various ambiguities about attentional/conscious processes, and, as noted above, be careful not to neglect the complex motivational aspects of consciousness. Motivational systems are instantiated in the magnificent complexity of the mind–brain. On the one hand, just as Winnicott (1960) asserted that there can be no infant without mother, so there could be no consciousness without motivation and social context. On the other, when fulfilled behaviorally, the underlying drives are often concealed by nonconscious processes that relegate them to the dynamic unconscious (see below).

Ito's model of brain evolution: the brain–mind

Ito's model builds up from three core functional brain systems: (1) *reflexes* (of the spinal cord), (2) *compound movements* (spread from spinal cord to medulla oblongata and midbrain), and (3) *innate behavior* (involving the hypothalamus and rostral end of the brain stem).

To ensure survival, four additional regulatory structures appear:

(a) the *limbic system* (an evolutionarily old part of the cerebrum which modifies innate behaviors by appropriate + or − rein-forcement);

(b) the *basal ganglia* (which may serve to settle conflicts between brainstem and spinal cord, by suppressing or selecting desired functions);

(c) the *cerebellum* (a critical learning element driven by error signals and a unique kind of plasticity, discovered by Ito, called LTD for long-term depression);

(d) the *brainstem sleep-wakefulness centers* (which allow well-timed switches between these two states, for rest and recovery, and off-line processing).

Thus, the three functional systems (1–3) act with the four regulatory structures (a–d), to produce all possible lower vertebrate behavior.

If we next consider the CNS of lower mammals (for example, rats, cats, and dogs) we must add additional functional systems—the sensory and perisensory areas of the neocortex *and* the underlying thalamus (all of which are represented in the parieto–latero–occipital lobe). These provide sensory input for the functional systems, including decisive input for command signals to initiate motor output. Ito correctly assumes that the regulatory structures interact with the fifth, or associational system in the same way that the earlier functional systems did with the original regulatory structures.

Finally, the evolution of primates involves the appearance of the association cortex, which makes up two thirds of the entire neocortex. Images, concepts, and ideas are generated from the various parietolateral areas (surrounded by sensory cortex) which integrate that which is stored (in memory) with current sensory input. The prefrontal cortex sends command signals to the sensorimotor cortex, affecting attention, and the results of the previous operations of attention alter the parameters of future searches.

One key seems to be that the prefrontal and parietolateral cortices are interconnected (they form a loop), so that arguably these connections "represent the process of thought" (Ito, 1998, p. 193). We believe it is also important that since feedback is built-in to any such thinking process, it helps to account for what we appreciate psychologically as the dialectical quality of some thought; in other words, thought involves output, yet this output becomes input to the same system which alters further output (recall the mind–brain model presented in Chapter Four). It seems likely that the latest system to evolve (i.e., the associative cortex) also comes under the influence of the regulatory structures noted above.

The notion of feedback is critical for our thesis, since *consciousness allows one to focus upon particular elements of any experience, and it does so in a manner that re-presents selective material to the experiencing subject for reconsideration or modification* (Olds, 1994, 1996). This re-presentation (or sign function) gives us the capacity to adjust our actions or line of thinking in real time; without it, as we shall argue below, our higher mental functioning (symbolic processing) begins to fail because of undue delays or errors in thinking.

Ito surveys what underlies consciousness neuro-physiologically. First, describing wakefulness, Ito highlights the research of Urade et al. (1993) on the choroid plexus as an essential link in the brain pathway that leads to sleep induction. He readily admits, however, that no one yet fully understands what turns sleep on or off in the brainstem, or, for that matter, what controls attention.

Second, regarding consciousness as awareness (i.e., selective attention), Ito understands its prime target to be what is going on in the external world. Here we wish to introduce an important qualification, however. Although conscious attention is indeed frequently focused upon the external world, there are, nonetheless, critical times when conscious attention targets aspects of the inner world which then come into focus, thus permitting symbolic processing on an abstract level.[55] Put differently, *conscious attention seems most important when it is put in the service of adjusting, that is, changing the current register of databases of the nonconscious mind.* We like using the word "learning" for this kind of mind–brain activity. More about this later.

Ito also reminds us of the need to explain what Crick and Koch call *binding*[56] (i.e., how, for example, in the visual system, sensory input features such as form, color, and movement, become unified into a composite image). This question is important for a number of reasons. For one, if we have a theory of mind–brain action, then we need to ask ourselves how, from an engineering perspective, the mind–brain could actually accomplish its various functions. If the postulated mechanisms are theoretically possible, then this makes our theorizing at least credible, though not necessarily correct. A second reason why "binding" is important is that unless we understand how things actually happen in the brain, it is harder to imagine how mind–brain processes might be explicated through a single hypothesis (see Rubinstein, 1997).

Still a third consideration is that the "shape" of binding may bear a relationship to the parallel processes in which either (1) the various component sensory aspects of experience are brought together in the mind–brain into a unity, or (2) the way that thinking occurs when ideas are mentally decomposed and then recomposed creatively (cf. Levin, 1983; also Levin, 1991, Chapter One).

Ito makes two suggestions for explaining "binding": resonance (i.e., some frequency of oscillation that connects—that is, synchronizes cells into a time-controlled system) or a "convergence" of anatomical pathways.[57] Ito then raises a third consideration: Is self-consciousness essentially the same or different from self-monitoring? Here he relies on Gallup's work on self reflection in chimpanzees (i.e., the study of activity which humans and chimps appear to share), and this kind of thinking leads Ito to the idea that self-consciousness is essentially a consequence of a well-developed associative cortex (Stuss, Picton, & Alexander, 2001). In other words, *self-awareness, for Ito, is built up from rich associations in memory which give the self meaning. If the awareness of self would include that of the individuality of others, then we are entirely in agreement* with Ito here. His view does not answer, however, how associative cortex relates to the joining of conscious and non-conscious (especially unconscious) systems, something about which we will comment shortly.

Bridging to Freud

Ito attempts to build bridges to Freud's structural model. From this classical analytic perspective he connects id drives with hypothalamus and limbic system; the ego with the neocortex, both sensorimotor and associative; and the superego (a representation of cultural givens) with systems lead by the associative cortex "and the regulatory systems attached to it" (Ito, 1998, p. 194; also see Olds, 1994). The role of the amygdala includes but is not limited to determining whether stimuli are favorable or not, and thus inducing either hypothalamic pleasant emotions associated with approach, or unpleasant emotions connected with fight or flight.[58] The prefrontal area is postulated to have a modulating role for ego and id, presumably via its judgments about social appropriateness.

Despite our general agreement with Ito's insights, however, we need to point out that Ito's goal of understanding consciousness is somewhat vitiated by his choice of focus (in view of the widespread disillusionment within psychoanalysis with structural theory—as a tool for dealing with anything beyond neurotic conflict—and its epistemological shortcomings).

However, Ito's phylogenetic approach to CNS organization clarifies the difficulty of thinking of consciousness as anything other than a set of (synergistic) functions that are more usefully studied separately,[59]—as we point out below, drawing upon the vast psychoanalytic literature and clinical experience. In fact, this is one reason we believe that psychoanalysis is and will remain in a position to provide observational data of relevance to studies attempting to clarify the complex phenomena imbedded within consciousness.

What we are asserting, succinctly, is that ". . . *the psychoanalytic unconscious is centrally affective and motivational [in nature] and . . . this is what psychoanalysis has to teach . . . cognitive [and neuro-] scientists"* (our italics) (Weinberger & Weiss, 1997, cited in Barry, 1998, p. 9). Put differently, the unconscious is a system of mentation from which a well-developed capacity for higher-order consciousness has been withheld, for defensive (adaptive) reasons. Thus, before such a capacity develops and comes on-line for individuals (i.e., before symbolization has sufficiently developed) there is only one system: non-consciousness. Hence the unconscious part of the non-conscious operates on the basis of a symbolic system characteristic of the right brain (primary process, more or less).

We know that self-awareness does *not* depend on wakefulness (for dreamers may be fully aware that they are dreaming); that there are various degrees of wakefulness (from the hypnoid states already noted by Breuer, through hypnogogic and hypnopompic conditions, the states of people under hypnosis, and so on); that sleep may even heighten awareness of the emotional world and that a state of hyper-alertness (say in the face of external threats) may actually shut off self-awareness; etc. We also have observations which show that perceptual awareness of the external world has to pass through an associative filter to become available for symbolic processing (*viz.* negative hallucination; denial of reality; disavowal of meaning; and isolation of affect). Such anxiety-producing data often receive attention only in the form of traumatic dreams.

Ito is particularly illuminating about the (nonrepressive) operations that Hartmann (1939) called "automatization". Ito's postulation of cerebellar maps, which permit adaptive behavior without explicit awareness, gives support to his cerebellum-based model of self-in-the-world, which is that *non-symbolic self-organization is the probable core of human personality* (Ito, cited in Levin, 1991, and in Levin and Vuckovich, 1983, 1987; also see Gedo, 1991a,b, 1996a,b, 1997). A developmental neurophysiology that spells out the evolution of this module of the CNS would provide the necessary foundation for a biologically valid psychoanalytic model of the mind.[60]

The cerebellum

The sections of Ito's paper dealing with neural control and so-called "will" we conceptualize herein under the rubric of motivation (Gedo, 1993a,b). For Ito, the role of the cerebellum takes on special importance; this has long been one of his research interests. *Reflex control* involves a reflex center acting as a controller upon a control object such as the skeleto-muscular system. More complicated *compound movements* require a function generator (e.g., a rhythm generator) as well. *Innate behaviors* are still more complex and further require an internal program. Ito sees the cerebellum as involved in all three levels of function, although he is most tentative regarding the cerebellum's possible role in innate behavior.

Cerebellar control does not require feedback; rather feedforward control is accomplished whenever the controller has dynamics inversely equal to the dynamics of its control object. Another way Ito puts this is that there might be "... two stages of motor learning: first, the control is made feedforward using a cerebellar model of the skeletalmuscular system, and second, it is performed [non-consciously] by passing the motor cortex through the cerebellar model" (Ito, 1998, p. 195).[61] Since this is seen in Purkinje cell activity (ventral paraflocculus) during eye movements, the cerebellum must contain inverse dynamics for such movements. In contrast, reflexive eye movements are driven by visual signals processed cortically.

The cerebellum, in connection with the fourth and fifth functional systems (i.e., with the cortex—both sensorimotor and associative, and with the thalamus as well) can provide internal models.[62] In essence, the cerebellum copies some other system by receiving input from the system to be copied, and uses error signals (discrepancies between its early model and the actual system as modeled) to self-reorganize its neural network until the signal transfer characteristics of the cerebellar unit (read here as "model") are a perfect copy.

Practically, according to Ito, such modeling results from the loop existing between the motor area and paravermal cortex (i.e., cortex and cerebellum). The command signals for voluntary movements are also sent to a model of the musculoskeletal system in the cerebellum, the output of which is returned to the motor cortex. This loop is most interesting in that it allows the performance of movements without using external sensory feedback, but instead by relying upon the internal feedback through a model in the cerebellum. This cerebellar modeling via the cerebrocerebellar loop may explain dysmetria, which results from damage to the cerebellar modeling circuits. Since, however, the cerebellar hemispheres are connected to the cerebral cortex in parallel rather than in a loop, as in the paravermis, we can propose the following control system scheme for the operation of the cerebellar hemispheres. The cerebellum may form a model to replace the motor cortex, the controller: thereafter, any voluntary movement will be preformed "without conscious efforts to operate the motor cortex" (Ito, 1998, p. 195). That is, it will flow from non-conscious cerebellar models of self-in-the-world, as noted above. This helps to explain the well known research finding that mental imagery of movement is fully equivalent to actual movement in its effects on learning (see Roland & Friberg, 1985, cited in Levin, 1991; see also Roland, 1981 cited in Ito, 1998).

Ito notes that the prefrontal cortex acts as a controller for the manipulation of images, concepts, and ideas (represented in the parietolateral cortex), and that the cerebellar model can replace either the prefrontal or parietolateral cortex in this function. Therefore, cerebellar models exist for the automatised manipulation of thoughts (cf. Hartmann, 1939) just as the coordination of movements, thinking, and learning as noted above (Levin & Vuckovich, 1987). As Ito says, in the same way that we move our arms and legs, we move images, concepts, and ideas in our mind (i.e., such control systems share similar principles and have wide applications).

That is, it is based upon non-conscious cerebellar models of self-in-the-world, as noted above. This helps to explain the well known research finding that mental imagery of movement is fully equivalent to actual movement in its effects on learning (see Roland and Friberg, 1985, cited in Levin, 1991; see also Roland, 1981 cited in Ito, 1998). Cerebellar modeling also explains dysmetria, which results from damage to the cerebellar modeling circuits.

Ito notes that the prefrontal cortex acts as a controller for the manipulation of images, concepts, and ideas, and that the cerebellar model can replace the prefrontal cortex in this function. Therefore, *cerebellar models exist for the automatised manipulation of thoughts (cf. Hartmann, 1939) just as for the coordination of movements, thinking, learning* as noted above (Levin & Vuckovich, 1987).

Addressing the question of *will*, which we have adumbrated under the rubric of *motivation*, Ito concludes that its anatomical localization remains unclear. However, reasoning from his considerable experience with control systems, he addresses the problem starting from the need for instruction signals to initiate action (and thus, instantiate will). Ito sees will as a positive aspect of consciousness, by which he means an active, self-organizing aspect. Premotor and supplementary motor areas send instructions of this sort to the motor area. The supplementary area is a source of a readiness potential (cf. our comments in Part 2 of this essay, regarding the work of Shevrin) that "arises prior to the onset of a voluntary movement" (Ito, 1998, p. 195, citing Deeke, Scheid, & Kornhuber, 1969).[63] Ito's collaborator, Sir John Eccles, thought this supplementary area is actually the source of will.[64] The problem is that other areas are known to drive the supplementary motor area.[65] Finally, Ito notes additional input to this area, namely, input ". . . from sensory association areas and cingulate gyrus . . ." (1998, p. 195), concluding that "it appears that sensory and emotional signals are integrated in the supplementary area as instruction signals for voluntary movement"[66] (*ibid.*).

Neural plasticity allows the brain to change with experience; that is, the Hebbian neural network changes its loadings over time.

Ito describes research on various so-called Perceptrons: simple and multilayered computational devices ("neurocomputers"). The only area where some details of neural control have been worked out, however, concerns the cerebellum (both adaptive and internal-model-based control).

It is tempting to tie in the basal ganglia (with what Ito calls its winner-takes-all principle) but currently too little is understood about this area. Perceptrons also fail in some computations because they apparently operate on the back propagation of error signals, which Ito believes does not apply to mechanisms of the neocortex. Rounding out this subject, according to Ito other possible ways of explaining basic brain computations are as follows: *molecular mechanisms* of computation (nothing yet); *large scale neural systems* (this would explain the occurrence of event-related potentials, such as the readiness potential Ito mentions, but the details have not been worked out within neuroscience[67]); *oscillatory networks* underlying thinking (see Sasaki, Tsujimoto, Nambu, Matsuzaki, & Kyuhou, 1994; but the details here also are far from being understood and will require more research).

Two of Ito's notions deserve special attention: (1) that cerebellar-related systems (which include the anterior cingulate) move ideas (cognition) just as they coordinate our limbs, eyes and ears, and are thus very likely related to consciousness, and (2) that consciousness is initiated when we act purposefully. This hypothesis of Ito's is simpler than that of Eccles, who explains "will" in terms of a divine mover. However, to understand more exactly how conscious and unconscious systems function and relate to each other we need to review the research of Shevrin, of Posner, and their collaborators, which is taken up in Part 2.

Summary

In Part 1 we have noted the principal debates within consciousness research that have complicated understanding how conscious and unconscious systems relate to each other. We have presented Ito's evolutionary model of brain (and his effort to apply it to psychoanalytic theory, including especially the role of the cerebellum).

We have also laid the background for understanding the unique contribution of the conscious, non-conscious, and specifically dynamically unconscious into an overarching system. The system conscious provides selective control of the level of processing in real time based upon what is currently deemed important as a goal. This includes awareness of the consciousness of others as critical input for mind–brain. The dynamic unconscious system provides for the defensive preservation and the privacy of mental life. Together, the system of cs/ucs provides creative learning (adaptation) in the context of human relationships.

In Part 2 (Chapter Ten) we plan to extend our conclusions by focusing on the following: Shevrin and colleagues' work on memory tagging; Posner and colleagues' research on the executive control network, and its extensions; Gedo and Levin's efforts to establish a unified theory of mind–brain; and Trevarthen and Levin's efforts to integrate the work of Shevrin, Posner, Gedo, and Shallice.

The conundrum of conscious and unconscious relations: Part 2— The tagging of memory, the dynamic unconscious, and the executive control network (ECN)

Fred Levin, John Gedo, Masao Ito, and Colwyn Trevarthen[68]

Introduction

I n Part 1 of this essay (Chapter Nine), we introduced our central subject of conscious–unconscious relations; now we wish to build upon what we have already discussed. We made clear the complicated history of research in this area, including some difficulties in defining terms.

Having provided background for our initial discussion, most of our effort was to introduce the original ideas of Ito (1998) by way of his evolutionary model of brain, and his efforts to bridge to the Freud of the structural model. We elaborated upon the role of the cerebellum because this area of Ito's work is particularly refined, and because it appears to us to lend itself to making some better approaches to understanding our central subject.

We believe that we can now provide a suitable synthesis of Parts 1 and 2 (the previous and current Chapters) in which we identify what conscious, non-conscious, and unconscious modules seem designed to provide to the overall system. However, to accomplish this we first need to consider the research of Shevrin and of Posner, which follows immediately.

Searching for the functions of
conscious and unconscious systems

Shevrin and colleagues' interest is in differentiating the conscious system from Freud's dynamic unconscious system. The central experiment is as follows (Levin, 1997c; Shevrin, Bond, Brakel, Hertel, & Williams, 1996). First, experimental subjects (whom we will call patients) are selected. They suffer from a variety of illnesses, especially phobias, some grief reactions, and neurotic conflicts. These patients are then interviewed by experts in psychoanalysis who are part of the research team. Over time, a psychodynamic formulation is achieved, in great detail, describing the patient's presumed inner conflicts. In the process the various analytic diagnostic interviews and their conclusions are discussed by the interviewing team, to reach a consensus, and to follow up with more interviewing for those patients for whom diagnostic information is felt to be missing. Finally, the team of interviewers and the rest of the assessment team together select, for each of the patients in the experiment, separate word lists that represent the patients' putative core conscious and core unconscious dynamics. Lists are also carefully constructed of two other word clusters of positively and negatively valenced ordinary words, for purposes of comparison and as controls.

The patients are then shown individual words from each word list both subliminally and supraliminally by tachistoscopic means while simultaneously each patient is monitored by EEG. The EEG is later evaluated using a time frequency analysis of evoked response potential, and the EEG data are then refined using various complex algorithms to make further distinctions. The computer is used to analyze the EEG data in a variety of creative ways.

Remarkably, as the result of the EEG analysis, *various "tunes" or "signatures" of unconscious conflictual brain activity become readily identifiable.* The key word here is reliable: that is, *Shevrin and colleagues have developed a method that can blindly pick out the unconscious conflictual material and distinguish it from the conscious material directly off the EEG tapes!*

The ability to make such a discrimination moves us closer to the ability to employ these "signatures of conscious and unconscious conflictual activity" to delineate exactly which brain subsystems in what time order are involved in conscious and unconscious activity. Shevrin's work should eventually serve as a kind of Rosetta stone for the activity of mind (which is frequently out of awareness, in a dynamic unconscious sense) and other activity of brain (conscious, or simply non-conscious).

Let us now turn to Shevrin's ideas about what consciousness might be accomplishing. We begin with his statements regarding what Shevrin calls the Freud–Rapaport solution (Shevrin, 1997a, p. 750, 1997b, 1998b) and with the work of Opatow (1998), whom he cites. According to Freud (1900a) and David Rapaport (1951a), the key to understanding consciousness is attention (in Freudian terms, the distribution of attention cathexis, where cathexis, however, means what currently in psychology is called "activation"). In short, Shevrin (1997a) believes, along with Freud, that under certain circumstances attention is what confers consciousness.

Shevrin (1997a,b) describes two major pathways into memory, only one of which involves consciousness:

1. If the critical attentional threshold is surpassed, then something becomes conscious, and enters memory.
2. If the critical threshold for consciousness is *not* exceeded, even though there will be no conscious experience, a subliminal perception can and often does occur and this subliminal activity leaves a memory trace in and influences memory (including the unconscious mind). Thus both conscious input and subliminal perceptions can and do effect memory and the unconscious.[69]

Two further considerations. First, Shevrin postulates that what consciousness confers is an indication of reality in the form of a tag to the memory of the original perception. In this manner those mental activities which respond to things in the world outside and are taken in through the primary sense modalities are usually identified and labeled in memory as specific kinds of perceptual experience. In brief, all *experiences are tagged differently according to their original experiential mode.* Another way of putting this is that perception and other conscious mental activities are distinguishable on the basis of the postulated tagging process associated with consciousness.[70]

What does this tagging accomplish? We believe, under ordinary circumstances, it helps us to discriminate between *real events which are internal* but independent of perception (say imagining, wishing, thinking, dreaming, or fantasizing) from the revival of memories of *real events that are the immediate consequence of external stimuli* (i.e., sensory input). As we noted above, however, there are times when such distinctions may be obscured, as when memories are formed on the basis on subliminal perception, which occurs (as noted) without any tagging of memory.

Another consideration: Shevrin (1998b) suggests that a second function of consciousness is to usefully organize our internal and external world models by virtue of the series of tags noted above.[71] One might think of such memory tags as helping to order our mental processing or the databases of mind–brain.[72] The importance of database re-organization is that any such re-organization constitutes learning and is adaptive. Otherwise, memories would remain constant, experience would not help us to avoid the endless repetition of behavior, and we would be relentlessly subject to the influence of whatever patterns of behavior are hard-wired into the CNS (i.e., our drives). Database re-organization (learning) is thus a momentous achievement for any organization (not just mankind).

We wish to recall the third function of consciousness, which we briefly mentioned in Part 1 of this essay. This is its role as a sign function (Olds, 1992, 1997). By this we mean that it re-presents material to the experiencing self in a manner that allows for adjusting our ongoing behavior or for changing the data of thinking and remembering in accord with a variety of aims. In our judgment, each of these three closely related functions of consciousness are critical for the connection of consciousness with unconscious activity; and it is the connection of these systems that allows for successful adaptation in general.

Let us make two different attempts to explicate more thoroughly the forgoing conclusions. First: we consider Shevrin's hypothesis; in the next section, that of Posner, Shallice, Levin, and Trevarthen. Relying on his own work as well as that of Opatow (1998), Shevrin rounds out his view of what the unconscious and conscious systems are doing in relation to each other. He conceives of the situation of the infant that Freud once discussed, feeding at mother's breast, at times imagining doing so again (which Freud called "hallucinatory wish fulfillment", a process we feel can be explained more clearly in a different manner—see below). Let us imagine that the infant is feeling hungry, and therefore, associating to the source of food, softness, and comfort in the arms of mother. However, the pleasure in the imagery of being at mother's breast does not, in itself, satisfy; that is, it is not the same as really being there. After a short time of imagining pleasure frustration ensues, and the famil-iar distress signals of the hungry infant tune the mother in to the infant's need to have an actual feeding.[73]

If these cycles are repeated sufficiently, Opatow argues that at some point a momentous decision is made by the infant develop-mentally: *it negates the entire mental mode of wish fulfillment, not simply individual instances of doing so.* Shevrin (1992) and Opatow (1998) believe that "at this juncture both consciousness and the unconscious are born" (p. 11). The unconscious thus begins as a mental set asso-ciated with a shift in cognitive mode, yet still guided by what Freud called the pleasure principle.[74] In contrast, consciousness continues under what Freud called the reality principle. Shevrin believes the conscious and unconscious mental domains are not clearly demar-cated at the outset, and remain mixed to partial degrees forever, with dynamically unconscious elements continually influencing behavior via transference. In other words, wishes are more or less constantly at variance with reality and thus the unconscious always seeks out satisfaction with appropriate disguises (Gedo, 1993b).

The executive control network (ECN)

Posner (1994, Posner & Raichle, 1994) has studied the relationship between brain anatomy (circuitry) and high level skills, including attention. Using EEG, functional MRI, PET, and other scanning technologies he has made it possible to identify, during the neuro-cognitive testing of normal and injured individuals, how the mind–brain works to solve various tasks. In essence, focusing largely on tasks about word usage and visual attention, Posner has described what he calls the executive control network (ECN), which is made up of anterior and posterior attentional systems.

The anterior system, composed of the anterior cingulate and basal ganglia, provides for selective attention and control of the executive control network itself. The posterior system is composed of the superior parietal cortex, pulvinar, and superior colliculus; it appears critical for the function of attending to and detaching from objects of interest. The anterior and posterior attentional systems also combine with several other brain systems to extend the executive control network according to various contingencies.[75] This last point will become critical for our argument (below) about what the linkage of conscious and unconscious processing likely entails.

The distributed areas (of the ECN) include the corpus callosum (which is true associative cortex; it does not merely connect the hemispheres), the bilateral amygdalar and hippocampal systems (which access critical memories and allow such things as learning aversive responses and their associated circumstances), the orbital frontal cortex[76] (which contributes to working memory), and the cerebellum (which also anticipates incoming information,[77] responds with alertness when expectations are not met, influences the accuracy and speed of changes in attention, and also forms and utilizes various models of self-in-the-world).

The anterior cingulate[78] is required for the experience of consciousness (Posner, 1994). For example, it is activated when subjects become suddenly aware of having made a mistake. Children who are in distress activate their anterior cingulate (which receives major input from the limbic system), whereas this activation ceases when these same children are distracted by attention to new objects which temporarily eliminate their behavior evidencing distress.

Levin and Trevarthen (1997, see Chapter Thirteen) contend that the knowledge Posner and colleagues are accumulating about the ECN can provide a conceptual basis for understanding consciousness[79] and exploiting in particular attentional shifts within clinical psychoanalysis. As noted, they have related the workings of Posner's ECN to the necessary shifts between high versus low level processing of the mind–brain. The recognition of these changes in cognitive processing builds on the contribution of Shallice (1988) on contingency planning; it also owes a debt to the Russian neuropsychologist Luria. Shifts in level of processing provide an adaptation through which the CNS may choose the most economical method for information processing. This involves using the most complex and powerful cognitive systems only when they are deemed necessary for particularly challenging or important tasks, and otherwise employing low level contingency planning (routine or reflex, simplified and smaller networks) for less challenging or relatively unimportant situations.

Levin and Trevarthen (1997; see Chapter Thirteen) believe the developing young mind employs mostly low level reflex type attentional mechanisms (cf. Shallice, 1988) when tasks are judged to be routine or relatively unimportant. However, in order to satisfy its important goals, and to minimize their frustration, there begins to occur a decisive shift: the infant taps a built-in genetic potential for learning how to shift the attentional system away from low level contingency planning to high level executive control, especially when dealing with novelty and/or difficulty. This is accomplished by briefly expanding the activity of the ECN.

What evolves during such shifts is the distinction between conscious and unconscious systems, but we believe that it would be prudent to conceptualize the first steps involved as gradual. We hesitate to assert that the Freudian unconscious comes into existence during the first year, because we believe that the part of the non-conscious which is dynamically unconscious most likely requires further cognitive development, which itself does not seem to appear until later (Barry, 1987, 2000). However, for descriptive purposes, the reader can easily appreciate that whether non-conscious or unconscious, we are describing the infant's activities in matching inner needs and wishes with outer realities.

Consciousness is required for its capacity to tap our genetically built-in potential for employing sensory data and modifying that data in accordance with various complex motivations, especially when operating in difficult or novel situation modes that require some fine tuning to succeed using higher-level processing. *Non-consciousness* enables the economy of ordinary low-level contingency planning for most activities. The *dynamic unconscious*, however, has special utility in properly expressing yet protecting hidden wishes and needs, so that they are taken into account in the final compromise of behavior, yet remain private. *The beneficial ability to change back and forth between these various modes of information processing gradually comes under the control of the individual through development* (Gedo, 1997).

We believe this explanation for the conscious–unconscious distinction is a viable alternative to that postulated by Opatow, but one which does not rely on Freud's notion of hallucinatory wish fulfillment. Clearly, conflicts of all sorts are a part of life, and require an adaptive repertoire fulfilled by all subsequent personality development. In addition, what the infant learns (and continues to perfect over time) is how best to bring together information from its various sources in perception and memory, to continue to learn from insight. *In other words, the modes of conscious, non-conscious, and unconscious activity appear to be part of the biological plan for making timely shifts in the mode of processing information (which encourage learning) and the striving towards important goals, while protecting the individual's privacy.*[80]

A reasonable conclusion would appear to be that the behavioral repertoire and the rhythm of the changes[81] which individuals learn to employ when problem solving uniquely characterizes their personality. Moreover, as we have attempted to show, we are describing three phenomena simultaneously: the effect of motivation (i.e., biological need gratification) on behavior and thought; the nature of the learning that accrues from experience (i.e., the importance of continuous database updating, in other words, the formation of expert systems); and the relationship between motivation and learning in terms of interactive systems (i.e., conscious, non-conscious, and unconscious activity).

The concept of *cognitive rhythm* suggested above obviously is much more complicated than it seems. Let us suggest, for example, that the cerebellar module (described in Chapter Nine) contributes in some unique ways to cognition, by its control over the pattern of shifts between conscious and unconscious systems, or, if the reader would prefer, between simple and enlarged systems of executive control. *Solving problems also depends on their decomposition and recomposition in advantageous ways that lead to novel solutions* in their own right. In this sense, all of us require the availability of an ECN which is quite flexible. If such is not the case, and we attempt to solve too many problems at once, or with the "wrong" machinery, cognitive efforts may fail, but not as the result of any pathological need to achieve, narcissistic sense of omnipotence, or a deep seated masochistic impulse (Levin, 1997e).

Further discussion

When Ito describes the cerebellum as a locus for motor and thought models that can operate in parallel with other brain loci, he is indicating a brain-centered approach to information processing with which we concur (cf. Olds, 1992). The approach of Olds sees consciousness essentially as a sign system: "... a system in which *cellular events in the consciousness system re-present cellular events that have recorded information in the [non-conscious] brain*" (Olds, 1992, p. 425, original emphasis). In short, Olds believes (and we agree) that consciousness provides feedback through input that allows for various kinds of real-time correction and adjustment of memory. This same function is provided by the digital readout on our phones that tells us whether we have dialed correctly. Such feedback loops are critical adaptive mechanisms in biological systems.

Our discussion of the work of Shevrin and Posner can therefore be described in the following overview. Essentially, consciousness is, a critical element in the mind–brain's general system for adaptive change and learning. Under routine operating conditions, where tasks are not particularly important, novel, or demanding, ordinary non-conscious contention scheduling (i.e., routine procedures) and minimal attentional networks are sufficient. In contrast, more complex and critical tasks require feedback with conscious review mechanisms that allow for moment-to-moment creative adjustments. In this manner, the repertoire of possible adaptive responses grows. (Our summary of the function of the unconscious system appears below.)

We have attempted to characterize the origin (evolution and development) and functionality of conscious, non-conscious and unconscious systems. Our conjectures, based on available evidence, have identified the following features.

1. The tagging of conscious memories according to the state in which they are first experienced.
2. The continuous re-organization of data-bases of mind–brain (by the hippocampus) based upon such memory tags. This includes the creative decomposition and recomposition of thoughts, with a parallel process occurring as experiences in different sensory modalities are "bound" into a unified experience.

3. Utilization of the feedback or sign function of consciousness to correct or adjust memories in real-time (whether conscious, non-conscious, or unconscious) to shift behavioral adaptations as required by circumstances.

4. The utilization of input from subliminal perception to selectively update memories.

5. A running dialectic between the conscious and non-conscious systems, wherein directives from conscious and non-conscious goal systems influence what is searched for in the outside world, and the impact of the outside world effects the goal-directed or motivational system, whether conscious, merely non-conscious, or unconscious.

6. Adaptive shifts between high (conscious) vs. low-level (non-conscious) processing networks, depending upon what is judged to be the complexity or novelty of the task, the importance of the goal, and the optimal machinery for solution. Overall, creativity, adaptation, personality development (as the pattern or rhythm of changes in information processing), and learning are greatly favored by linkage into a smoothly functioning conscious–non-conscious super-system.

Regarding the Freudian unconscious system we have posited that its key importance is to maintain privacy (disguise) while influencing goal satisfaction and coloring thoughts in desirable ways. Without such protection there could be no true or private self (Modell, 1993; Winnicott, 1960); *and without the coloring, there could be no sense of aliveness.*

With regard to a further analysis of consciousness *per se*, Ito's discussion of will and its relationship to the readiness potential is a subject about which Shevrin and colleagues are accumulating more data. Using a conditioning model, Shevrin and colleagues have shown that a readiness potential can be obtained entirely unconsciously. In that study an unpleasant face was conditioned to a mild shock supraliminally. When the face was presented subliminally thereafter, a readiness potential appeared in the ERP about 200 msec before the shock had been administered in the supraliminal conditioning series (Wong, Shevrin, & Williams, 1994). Ito's ideas about the oscillatory nature of thought appear quite close to Shevrin's thinking, especially regarding findings on time-frequency features and conscious and unconscious processing.

Some final comments. Ito's distinction between awareness (which he identifies with sensory events from the external world) and consciousness (which he identifies with attention directed towards our internal world) is similar to what PET studies have shown to be a posterior orienting form of attention to sensory events vs. the activity of an anterior network involved when we generate ideas from memory (Posner, 1994, Posner & Raichle, 1994; Posner & Rothbart, 1997). The cingulate-based system (for focal attention) appears to integrate both emotional (limbic) as well as cognitive (frontal) areas. Posner and Rothbart (1997) show how ECN develops in relation to self regulation of emotion and then gets involved in cognitive regulation in the third year of life.[82]

Understanding the nature and time frame of these emotional and intellectual developments is critical for understanding the subject of this essay, for clearly there are various levels of individual consciousness: for example, primary vs. higher levels (see Edelman, 1998; also Levin, 1998). But in addition, one wishes that there were more empirical studies that would permit the comparison of such developments within humans, as well as across species. In addition, since the human form of encoding input involves symbolic representation, studying ECN development requires special patience in identifying exactly what distinctions are made, by what parts of the mind–brain. All that can be concluded at present, however, is that the cerebellum, the anterior cingulate, and the basal ganglia play a critical role in these attentional networks, and that the elucidation of their exact role in such matters will eventually solve many important problems in conscious–unconscious research.

Summary and conclusions

Ito's model of brain evolution has important implications for understanding mind. We have focused particularly upon consciousness and made a number of suggestions regarding how to understand it, especially in relationship to the Freudian unconscious system. Along the way we have necessarily updated Freudian theory, as one would expect of any science such as psychoanalysis.

We have also hopefully reduced some of the ambiguity inherent in extant definitions of consciousness. But naturally we are far from completely resolving the many difficult problems relating to understanding conscious–unconscious relations.

We have suggested that the definition of consciousness needs to be expanded to include the ability to know and learn together from the inner experience of others (Trevarthen, 1975, 1979, 1989, 1990, 1993, 1995, 1997). We have also reviewed the research of Shevrin on identifying an EEG "signature" of unconscious activity, as well as his suggestions regarding the tagging role of consciousness, and its provision of a reality sense.[83]

From Posner's research we have accepted his clarification of the executive control network (ECN):

> ... attention [is defined as] a brain function of three interrelated systems: Alertness or arousal providing tonic attention, dependent on the mesencephalic reticular activating system and its connections; the posterior attention or attention of perceptive selectivity that depends on zones of the right posterior parietal cortex and its connections; and, anterior attention or supervisory attention that regulates deliberate attention, and [is further] supported by zones of the anterior cingulate and lateral prefrontal cortex and the connections of [these] zones. [Estevez-Gonzalez, Garcia-Sanchez, & Junque, 1997, p. 1989]

Building largely on the insights of Ito, Shallice, Shevrin, Posner, Gedo, Levin, and Trevarthen, we have supported the conjecture of Olds (1992) about the role of consciousness in re-presenting information stored in parts of the brain that are essentially non-conscious (Olds, 1992); we have also identified other associated functions concerning the manner in which conscious circuits affect how memories are accurately stored, retrieved, updated and applied (i.e., that bear on the question of learning). Moreover, it feels correct to assume that the system non-conscious accomplishes the above overall functions while protecting the privacy of our inner world of wishes, needs, fantasies, fears, motivations, and our core sense of an affectively alive (true) self in relation to others. Here we are also grateful for the insights of Modell and of Winnicott.

It should be obvious that we see the conscious and unconscious–non-conscious systems as operating in parallel, and suspect their connection and coordination guarantees that we not only observe our environs and our feeling states consciously, but we simultaneously take into account our deepest level affective life, which addresses our deeper motivations (Olds, 1992; Roose, 1994). Motivations determine what we look for and find in the world outside; what we find outside in turn effects our motivational (goal-seeking) system in a never-ending private dialectic (Levin, 1997a). In this manner, learning (both mental contents, and mental procedures) is facilitated; without such an arrangement mankind would not generally benefit from experience, life would merely repeat itself endlessly without progress or creativity, and we would remain completely under the control of our impulses (i.e., biological drives) or sensory input.

Our conclusions are in keeping with Ito's model, and extend his insights beyond any narrowly based conflict-psychology (i.e., the useful but now dated structural model of Freud[84]) to include the core of the self as non-symbolic self-organization (Gedo, 1991a,b, 1993a,b, 1996a,b; Gedo and Goldberg, 1973, p. 63). In other words, what gets created over time is a usable cerebellar-based self-in-the-world model (see Ito, cited in Levin, 1987, 1991) that through resonance or convergence feeds into larger systems with two-way communication with the cerebellum and basal ganglia.

In this way, we have strengthened some tentative links between modern cognitive neuroscience and contemporary updated psychoanalysis. In other words, we are refining our understandings of details of a brain-centered informational approach to conscious and non-conscious systems (Levin, 1991; Olds, 1992) that have an enormous input on our decisions.

We are, of course, also pointing out some of the details as to why psychoanalytic insight is insufficient in itself for psychoanalytic progress; namely, for learning to occur there must always be genuine changes in the way the mind–brain processes information (Gedo, 1997). For example, we believe sometimes this will be a function of decisive shifts in the pattern or rhythm, and level of the shifts between the conscious and non-conscious systems. These rhythms, of course, will need further investigation. But we already know clearly many basic details of how they reflect the mind–brain's ability to compose and decompose intellectual and emotional problems in creative ways, a process which we believe is directed, just as Ito has stated, principally by the cerebellar module,[85] together with contributions from the basal ganglia and anterior cingulate cortex. That is, disturbances in the functioning of the ECN alter system relationships within the brain, and need to be differentiated from or correlated with what are usually called psychological difficulties. Alternatively, one could imagine that the neurophysiology we have been examining may eventually turn out to be the brain activity "behind" specific psychological (mind) patterning.

SECTION IV

PSYCHOANALYSIS
AND CHAOS THEORY

CHAPTER ELEVEN

The paradigm of bifurcation:
Priel and Schreiber on chaos theory*

Fred Levin

A s noted in Chapter Five, it is possible to significantly expand our understanding of subjects such as the psycho-analytic transference if one considers it from both analytic and extrapsychoanalytic perspectives. Priel and Schreiber's work was mentioned, but a discussion of chaos theory was deferred until now. Chapters Eleven and Twelve elaborate the exciting possibilities that derive from bridging psychoanalysis and chaos theory.

Priel and Schreiber's (1994) article is a good place to begin because their concise article invites one to consider several complex psychological variables in relation to non-linear dynamics (catastrophe theory, chaos theory, bifurcation theory), a branch of mathematics that covers phenomena that appear random but are actually deterministic. When the equations which describe behavior can be discovered, the behavior can be modeled. This kind of modeling "... has been made possible only recently, thanks to the high computational power of today's computers" (Ekeberg, 1995).

This chapter reviews Priel and Schreiber's (1994) paper "On psychoanalysis: The paradigm of bifurcation" and two short discussions published along with their original article, the first by Denman (1994), and the second by Gardner (1994). An earlier version of my review of these three articles was published as Levin, 1996b.

Consequently, much of the terminology and imagery presented in Priel and Schreibers' article deals in part with geometric diagrams, a subject not commonly seen in psychological journals.

Priel and Schreiber begin with *bifurcation points*, also called rapid doubling) which they define as those points on a Feigenbaum diagram which "designate the emergence of several new and stable solutions . . ." (p. 212). They introduce a Feigenbaum diagram, Figure 5 (see also Peitgen, Jürgens, & Saupe, 1992, pp. 586–592, for

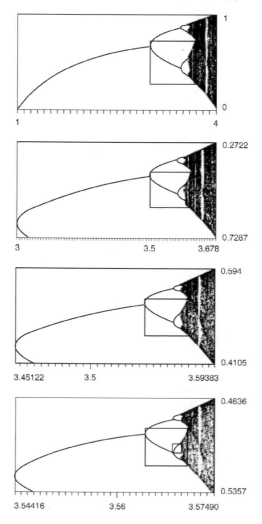

Figure 5.

further background on the significance of the diagram), which demonstrates how the frequency of some oscillatory phenomenon is doubling rapidly, meaning the system is shifting into so-called "chaos". The authors are highlighting this critical time period (also technically called a phase state shift) because this "moment", involving the evolution of so-called chaos, is something about which experts in chaos theory generally agree. That is, from a strictly mathematical perspective "universal" principles and mathematical constants characterize the changes apparently independently of the nature of the system involved, whether it be laser, heart, brain, electronic circuit, weather, or whatever (an idea elaborated upon below when we further explain the Feigenbaum constant). Although chaos (and its graphical representation) can indeed be esthetically beautiful, the subject remains at times dauntingly difficult, nevertheless, and finding mathematical solutions to chaos related functions is sometimes impossible at the present time. Naturally, there will be questions about whether and how to apply this specialty knowledge to psychoanalysis.

Within chaotic systems in general, initial conditions can prove decisive, making a difference, for example, regarding which direction the chaotic system takes. This is called the "butterfly effect", as per the example in which the presence or absence of a single butterfly somewhere in the world can allegedly determine whether or not such events as a hurricane ultimately develops at another particular time and place somewhere else. (For more details on the importance of shifts between qualitative and quantitative states, see Galatzer-Levy, 1988, and Guckenheimer, 1994.)

Priel and Schreiber assert the applicability of chaos theory to psychoanalysis for a variety of reasons. They point out that Freud's historical description of logical chains of associations involving "two or more threads of associations meeting and thereafter proceeding as one" (Breuer & Freud, 1895d, p. 290) can be seen as neatly overlapping the mathematical perspective of a bifurcation point topographically, but one "where one of the ramifications have been suppressed" (p. 212). They also make a number of other assertions as well, which support their claims even better about both the utility of chaos theory not merely as a metaphor, but its specific relevance to psychoanalysis far beyond mere metaphor.

One advantage of chaos theory for them is that it smoothly takes into account the surprise and complexity that invariably plays a crucial role in clinical psychoanalysis proper. A second advantage is that such moments of surprise, from the perspective of chaos theory, represent "... a process of destabilization—a transition to a non-linear, far-from-equilibrium stage—that allows for bifurcation points to occur" (p. 213). What they really mean here is that *chaos theory appears robust in capturing or depicting psychological change in development, based upon its "enhanced sensitivity in perceiving the [local] environment ..." (p. 213) as well as its ability to formally express with mathematical accuracy "a multiplicity of solutions" to a complex equation (ibid.).*

Most interestingly, *the authors suggest that variables such as the psychoanalytic transference phenomenon itself might be better illuminated when seen in relation to the behavior of the "attractors" of chaos theory* (p. 214). In a nutshell (in terms of chaos theory) transferences might then be considered "transitions from [non chaotic] 'limit cycles' to strange [chaotic] attractors through bifurcation ..." (*ibid.*). (More about this follows immediately, as we begin to define our terms, and pull things together.)

Attractors are "... geometric forms that describe the long-term behavior of a [complex] ... system" (*ibid.*). That is, "... an attractor is what the behaviour [*sic*] of the system settles down to, or is attracted to ..." (*ibid.*) such as the example of a pendulum's movement over time towards a fixed point of rest. This rest point is described as an attractor because it is as though the point attracts the pendulum. But strange attractors describe still more complex patterns; for example, they can represent the inception of chaotic patterns, and are one of four basic kinds of attractor classifications. The authors cited above can only provide tidbits or hints regarding the many details of chaos theory relevant to psychoanalysis, but we will attempt to extend their discussion in this and the following chapter.

Lest the reader find himself or herself disturbed and/or confused by the arcaneness of the subject or the "strange" terminology (forgive and enjoy the pun) and begin to doubt the relevance of the subject to psychoanalysis, it should be noted that we are aware that a number of scholarly U.S. psychoanalysts, notably David Forrest (1991a,b), Robert Galatzer-Levy (1978, 1995, 1997), Stanley Palombo (1998), and Vann Spruiell (1993) have made similar valuable efforts to alert the psychoanalytic community to chaos theory. Although none of this American work is cited by Priel and Schreiber, this is not surprising given how rarely American authors cite British scholars, at least that's our impression.

A larger problem seems to be that the Priel and Schreiber have condensed their article too much so that there is only a bare minimum of illustrations of their ideas and documentation of previous work in their own interdisciplinary field. Also, although a few diagrams do appear (such as the classical Feigenbaum diagram, shown in Figure 5) they are generally inadequate to the task. Therefore, most readers will benefit from more detailed explanations, which it is our intention to provide (in this and the following chapters).

For example, it would have helped considerably to illustrate that if one analyzes the Feigenbaum diagram one can show that as one proceeds from left to right the bifurcation points double at junctures with a certain regularity, namely, approximately $1/4.5$ of the previous interval of time is required for the next doubling to occur. The denominator of this fraction is called the Feigenbaum constant. It turns out to be $4.6692\ldots$ and is a constant in nature just like the number "e", the base of natural logarithms, or the number Pi = $3.14159\ldots$ Moreover, if one would enlarge any portion of the right-hand side of the Fiegenbaum diagram, one can readily show that virtually any enlargement, *ad infinitum*, exactly repeats the pattern of the original from which it is selected as a part, so in this way the fractal quality of chaotic phenomena is readily demonstrable.

The writing of the American psychoanalysts cited above (along with the works of mathematicians and interdisciplinary scholars such as Çambel, 1993; Devaney, 1989, 1990; Guckenheimer & Holmes, 1983; Gulick, 1992; Hale & Kocak, 1991; Jackson, 1989; Peitgen, Jürgens, & Saupe, 1992) might also be usefully consulted for readers who wish a better understanding of what is being bravely asserted by Priel and Schreiber. For example, Vann Spruill's summary article helps with verbal explanations of the nature of non-linear dynamics and its specific application to psychoanalysis; also, Galatzer-Levy's articles provide helpful visual metaphors (of topological folding) as a means of making the subject still more comprehensible, while David Forrest's work provides the best general overview of integrating psychological and mathematical approaches that we are aware of.

The above difficulties or complexities in Priel and Schreiber's presentation are especially unfortunate, because it means that some excellent points by the authors are given their weakest possible supporting arguments. However, the deficiencies should not detract from the fact that *Priel and Schreibers' article is an important, valuable and unique original contribution to the application of chaos theory towards understanding specific psychological complexity.*

All of us have a great interest in understanding mind–brain, surely the most complex subject ever examined by mankind, and any technology that might organize or simplify this study should at least potentially be valuable to us. Moreover, other medical sciences have attempted to exploit chaos theory, so psychoanalysis is also entitled to test out its utility.

For example, epilepsy experts, trying to better understand and control seizures, are monitoring the EEG with non-linear dynamical analysis. In terms of treatment, their hope is to precisely time and spatially allocate doses of electrical stimulation to the patient's brain so as to bring the complex electrical system of the patient's brain under better control (Schiff et al., 1994). Similarly, cardiologists are attempting to control cardiac arrhythmias by precisely timing and placing an electrical stimulation into the patient's heart, while monitoring the patient using non-linear dynamical maps of the heart's conducting system activity (Garfinkel, Spano, Ditto, & Weiss, 1992). These efforts are aimed at describing, predicting, and exploiting our knowledge of complex systems. It should therefore not surprise the reader that mathematically inclined psychoanalysts are thus very interested in chaos theory and its applications.

In my opinion, the best part of the paper of Priel and Schreiber deals with the application of chaos theory specifically to transference. The idea is basically as follows: (1) certain transferential moments represent on the one hand possibilities of structural change in the mind–brain, and on the other hand bifurcation points with creative potential; (2) ". . . bifurcation potentially creates information . . . [that is,] . . . space symmetry breaking [to be defined below] is the necessary prerequisite without which the possibility of constructing an information processor simply would not exist" (Nicolis & Prigogine, 1989, cited on p. 213); and (3) chaos can be useful to communicate or carry information (as in Shannon's theory of communication, viz., the amount of information conveyed by any communication varies indirectly with our ability to predict what will be said).

In other words, the authors cited are asserting that it is possible that the mind–brain of the transference experiencing subject in psychoanalysis may at times be undergoing specific states that involve learning readiness ("windows"), and these states would seem to coincide with the onset of chaos, as understood mathematically. What the chaos involves is a kind of *"freedom" to form bifurcation points in one's thinking, and analyzing, thus reorganizing critical databases of mind and brain.*

Denman's comments on Priel and Schreiber

In the volume in which Priel and Schreiber publish their original article there are two attached commentaries (one we discuss here, the other follows in the next paragraph). I will comment upon these to round out my introduction to chaos theory and psychoanalysis. Denman's criticism of the idea of usefully applying chaos theory to psychoanalysis is seen in his disparaging remarks about Lacan's interest in knot theory, Matte Blanco's application of set theory, and Jewish mystical (Cabalistic) interest in calculating the numerical values of certain words, all of which, unfortunately, he lumps into the same bag of useless endeavors. He sees the authors as humanizing mechanisms and mechanizing humans, objecting in particular to seeing human psychology in terms of watch mechanisms (p. 220). His principle objection to applying chaos theory to psychoanalysis is that ". . . psychoanalysis has not yet conclusively been shown to be efficacious . . ." (p. 220), which is both beside the point and uninformed (see Bachrach, Galatzer-Levy, Skolnikoff, & Waldron, 1991). In other words, Denman does not take seriously any of the possibilities inherent in Priel and Schreiber (for an integration with psychoanalysis).

The comments of Sebastian Gardner

Gardner's approach is that of a philosopher, and he is understandably more cautious about criticizing Priel and Schreiber except in the area of his own expertise. Thus he holds Priel and Schreiber's work to be "methodologically sound" regarding their claim of "... the pervasiveness of certain basic (mathematical) forms in nature ..." (p. 223), but wonders still if the level of psychoanalytic discourse and that of chaos theory are "logically on a par" (p. 223). He continues:

> ... there is a powerful reason ... for thinking that Priel and Schreiber are mistaken in supposing that the absence of predictability-securing lawful causal connections in psychoanalytic explanation is logically on a par with the non-predictability of non-linear systems. Psychoanalytic explanation, although it is indeed causal, does not employ causal laws. It operates in a different way which hinges on the identification of connections of representational content between mental states ... [and] interpretation, and not inductively grounded causal laws, provides the lens through which mental causation is discerned in psychoanalysis. [pp. 224–225]

[Thus he concludes that] the similarity between the unconscious mind's activity and non-linear systems "is an illusion" (p. 225); consequently, Priel and Schreiber's contribution is reduced to providing naught but an interesting metaphor. What is unfortunate here is the misperception of psychoanalysis as exclusively based upon inference from an "interpretative framework" of associations or "representational content between mental states" (p. 225).

If psychoanalysis were reducible to this and nothing more, then Gardner would be entirely correct; however, clinical psychoanalysis is dynamic and as such it has developed considerably over time from the dated methodology Gardner associates with psychoanalysis. Current practice is based upon multiple methods, models, and strategies (Gedo, 1986, 1988, 1991a,b, 1993a,b). We combine empathy (vicarious introspection) and observations (as in any scientific field, say physics or mathematics), and we think equally important the patient's words, thoughts, affects, actions, and the referential contact between these variables. Our theories are also becoming more complex, and we shall need interdisciplinary input to advance our theory and practice.

In summary, although I disagree almost completely with the commentators on Priel and Schreiber's work in the *British Journal of Medical Psychology*, I believe that all of us are enriched by their efforts. Let us now proceed with Chapter Twelve, and build on this introduction to chaos theory.

Learning, development, and psychopathology: applying chaos theory to psychoanalysis*

Fred Levin

> "Nothing in nature is random . . . A thing appears random only through the incompleteness of our knowledge"
>
> (Baruch Spinoza, cited in Gray & Davisson, 2004)

> "Our job is not to penetrate . . . the essence of things, the meaning of which we . . . [cannot perfectly] know anyway, but rather to develop concepts which allow us to talk in a productive way about phenomena in nature"
>
> (Niels Bohr, cited in Nielsen, 1977)

Introduction

This chapter assumes the reader's knowledge of Priel and Schreiber's work (as covered in Chapter Eleven). It begins with a review of the pioneering contributions regarding how

---

* An earlier version of this paper was presented as the discussion of Robert Galatzer-Levy's lecture on chaos theory to the Chicago Psychoanalytic Society, October 28, 1997 (Galatzer-Levy, 1997). This current paper appears as Levin, 2000b.

best to apply chaos theory to psychoanalysis. However, in spite of the increasing number of publications on the subject, there remains an urgent need to make this difficult subject more readily understandable by individuals (read here, psychoanalysts) not trained specifically in mathematics.

A lone American reviewer (Levenson, 1994), and both of the British reviewers mentioned in Chapter Eleven, Gardner and Denman, are quite skeptical that anything useful for psychoanalysis will ever come from chaos theory. However, the majority of the authors covered strongly disagrees and sees great potential for chaos theory benefiting our field: In the United States Galatzer-Levy (1978, 1995, 1997) and Moran (1991) describe the utility of chaos theory in explicating development, quantitative to qualitative shifts, and the importance of recognizing fractal-like *signatures* in psychoanalytic clinical material; Levin (1996a, 1997a,b) believes chaos theory offers a unique vocabulary and perspective which can further our understanding of learning, development, and psychopathology; Forrest (1991a,b, 1995, 1996a) explores the vast domain of artificial intelligence and chaos theory, finding much that can be positively applied to developmental psychology and psychopathology; Gleick (1987), Moran (1991), and Spruiell (1993) explain nonlinear dynamics (another name for chaos theory), raising a broad range of theoretical issues; Sashin (1985) and Sashin and Callahan (1990) demonstrate stunning but generally as yet unappreciated results[86] employing unique affective response models, and these need amplification; and Moran (1991) and Galatzer-Levy (1995, 1997) have each made thoughtful integrations, the most important of which appears to be the idea that *psychoanalytic process reduces psychopathology by adding complexity to mental functioning.* In this regard, Palombo (1998), writing about *coevolution,*[87] sees dreaming as "the edge of chaos" (p. 261), resulting in nothing less than the adaptive reorganization of memory (i.e., learning), just as we have indicated seems a reasonable conclusion from the experimental literature.

Outside this country fine papers on chaos and psychoanalysis have appeared in France (Quinidoz, 1997), Israel (Priel & Schreiber, 1994), and South America (Matte Blanco, 1986, 1989).[88] These have significantly added to our knowledge of what chaos might be accomplishing, and seem to comprise two related notions: that *chaos facilitates learning by means of symmetry breaking (elaborated upon below), and that chaos plays a role in transference as well* (Levin, 1996a, 1997a; see also the Priel and Schreiber 1994 work, and the previous chapter).

We wish to clarify what appears most salient in the oeuvre on chaos theory, so that our readers can better form their own opinions about such matters. Let us begin with a discussion of the idea that chaos theory offers a descriptive vocabulary for and a better way of framing psychological development.

Development

In discussing developmental theories, Galatzer-Levy (1997) specifically critiques the idea that proper development in children essentially correlates with reaching age-typical norms. Paraphrasing Anna Freud, he notes that when development is progressing, even if it deviates from the norm, the child has nevertheless engaged the major psychological task of childhood. Yet, we may ask, if different individuals follow different pathways, what exactly is normative about development and how are we to understand variations in the process?[89] It seems clear that at present we have too many developmental theories and too little agreement among them to begin to reliably answer such questions. Moreover, each of the current coterie of developmental theories cannot be correct because their assumptions seem quite different if not mutually exclusive.

Such are the difficulties in improving the situation of finding an overarching theory of development. Moreover, the problem becomes even more complicated if seen in relation to the goal of eventually creating a developmental model that is self generative, that is, which builds itself up from basic starting conditions. At present no psychoanalytic model of development meets this requirement perfectly, although Gedo's hierarchical model comes quite close. Yet this is where chaos theory appears to offer something exceedingly useful to psychoanalysis: *chaos theory shows a robust capacity to portray the evolution of systems, making it a natural candidate for solving the modeling problem.* More about this below when we will discuss so-called *attractors.*

Chaos theory (also known as catastrophe theory, bifurcation theory, or nonlinear dynamics) is an outgrowth of work early in this century by Poincaré (1916–1954), and in more modern times by René Thom (1975). The terms fractal and chaos were actually coined in 1971. *The advent of the modern desktop computer is the* single *decisive discovery which permitted widespread experimentation with complex chaotic systems and thus the accurate solution to otherwise intractable problems in differential equations.*[90]

In what follows, we shall briefly describe in more detail chaos theory and its history, then explain why it is a clear choice for helping psychoanalysis in its search for fundamental mechanisms in development, learning, and psychopathology.

Basics of chaos theory: the Feigenbaum diagram and constants [FML1]

Although we have already introduced the Feigenbaum diagram in Chapter Eleven, in this brief section we will reintroduce the subject in more usable detail.

The core idea of chaos theory can be demonstrated most simply by reference to a Feigenbaum diagram (see Figure 5, Chapter Eleven, p. 176), which represents the graphing of an equation, called the quadratic iterator,[91] which reads as follows: $x_{n+1} = ax_n (1 - x_n)$, where n=0,1,2,... In Chapter Eleven, the various values of "x" appear on the y-axis, while the x-axis denotes time (that is, the number of iterations). For values of "a" below 2, the value of "x" slowly increases. For values of "a" between 2 and 3, "x" bounces back and forth between two relatively fixed values. But if "a" is larger than 3, especially as it approaches 3.5699456..., then "x" begins to fluctuate first between 2 values, then 4 values, etc. in a cascade of *rapid doubling* (also called *bifurcation*). Such rapid doubling of the value of "x" is, by definition, the onset of mathematical chaos.

The onset of chaos always occurs at a point (along the x or horizontal axis) of 3.5699456 ... which is now known as the *Feigenbaum point*. Moreover, the time of each interval of doubling, divided by the subsequent interval of doubling, is also a constant, 4.669206 ... which is known as the *Feigenbaum number* (also called sigma). In other words, rapid doubling (chaos onset) occurs 4.6692016... times faster with each doubling event.[92]

What is most interesting, however, is that each of these numbers (the Feigenbaum number and Feigenbaum point) are constants in nature, like "π" (3.14159 . . .), or "e" the base of natural logarithms. Whether "x" is the rate of firing of a brain cell, or water dripping from a sink, or an oscillation in a electromechanical system, the graphing of chaos in nature always produces exactly the same Feigenbaum diagram, characterized by the Feigenbaum point at chaos onset and the Feigenbaum number relating to the rapid acceleration of periods of doubling.

One other issue is important. If any portion of the chaotic pattern of the Feigenbaum diagram is enlarged, it will reproduce the entire original Feigenbaum diagram. This can be repeated as many times as one likes, always with the same result, and it represents the so-called fractal[93] quality of nonlinear dynamical systems. More about this later.

Applying mathematics to psychoanalysis

A brief word about the history of attempts to bridge psychoanalysis and mathematics is in order. The pioneer modern psychoanalyst polymaths are Robert Galatzer-Levy and the late Jerry Sashin (who died in 1990 before he could complete his important contributions to bridging psychoanalysis and mathematics).

Let us quote briefly from Jerry Sashin to further explain our subject and also elaborate on the relation of chaos theory to neuroscience, as follows:

> Catastrophe theory models form a bridge between the psychology and the corresponding neurology. I'll try to explain how. When you study the dynamics of systems involving oscillators, you discover that coupled oscillators show behaviors which are described (modeled) by catastrophe theory models. What this suggests (since many localized regions of the brain can be characterized as oscillators) is that . . . *affect-response is determined neurologically by [the following]:* the coupling of the regions of the brain having to do with fantasizing, with language, [and] with containment[94] [meaning the container function] and [with] emotion. Since emotion is probably in the limbic-hypothalamic region, [visual] fantasizing . . . the occipital area, language . . . the left [hemispheric] cortex, and

containment . . . the prefrontal region (all of this being greatly over-
simplified and now out-date [of course]), what we are dealing with
is not just linkage between left and right [hemispheres] as proposed
by Sifneos, Hoppe and others, but also up/down (cortical/limbic
[cerebellar]) and anterior/posterior linkage as well. [Personal
communication]

Early on, Sashin pursued his research at René Thom's institute
in Paris, Thom being one of the guiding geniuses of chaos theory.
Parenthetically, the Japanese (especially Professor Utena of Tokyo
University) were simultaneously pursuing similar models (for
example, Utena's so-called Kabuki model, named after the move-
able stage in Kabuki plays, to connote the idea that our brain's
connectivity runs in all directions, not just integrating left with right
hemisphere, and that emphasizes that this complexity is critical for
the integration of cognition and emotions).

Development and growth: the edge of chaos

Galatzer-Levy's (1997) core idea is that the mind is a complex
system on the edge of chaos, that is, with sudden lurches of change
rather than smooth progression. This novel perspective seems quite
important to me, as I will attempt to explain shortly. A good example, outside of the realm of psychology will help the reader understand better what is intended here. Consider the seemingly simple
subject of how humans grow in height. Medical schools teach that
height growth is continuous, that is, a smooth curve; many of us
remember the smooth growth curves for infants and children in
texts and hospital charts. This is all well and good, except we now
know that this view of smooth linear growth in height is absolutely
wrong!

In reality, human beings spend most of their youthful lives, over
99% of it, not growing at all! What happens, rather, is that possibly
one evening a month there are massive growth spurts during which
all of the growth occurs for that month. Such growth spurts represents a very small percentage of the overall time of one's life, in
between which there is actually zero growth. *It's just as our mothers
always said: Boy, you grew several inches last night!*

The subject of growth is important to this discussion because chaos theory neatly describes developmental patterns, whether the growth of trees, snowflakes, brains or minds. Most such processes involve the repetition of self-similar patterns at decreasing scale (cf. fractals), and are thus expertly modeled with computers.

Galatzer-Levy (1997) further suggests that when analysts observe in their patients sudden dramatic episodes of psychological growth that we should not be so quick to dismiss these as events of unlikely or exaggerated significance.[95] He describes the case of a Mrs. R., a women who changed suddenly and dramatically around the time of seeing a particular movie scene, that is, in response to only very slight changes in her ordinary mental state. *Here he chooses his words very carefully in order to introduce an isomorphism between chaos theory and psychoanalysis, namely, the potential in each domain for small changes in initial conditions to profoundly effect the outcome of complex systems, the so-called "butterfly effect".*[96]

An example of such sensitivity to initial conditions has already been presented, in fact, in the case of the Feigenbaum diagram, which, as you will remember, is dependent upon the fact that changing the initial value of "a" only slightly in our equation resulted in radically different outcomes, only one of which leads to the onset of chaos, characterized by periods of rapid doubling.

Let us consider a second example of rapid change, a clinical vignette taken from an article by Wolf (1990) to illustrate this same sensitivity to initial conditions, but this time within a specific psychoanalysis. Franz Alexander was very frustrated with a certain male patient, who seemed narcissistically entitled. One day he came into Alexander's office with mud caked on his feet and dirtied the analytic couch. Alexander screamed at his patient to get his feet off the couch! This change in initial conditions proved to be *the* decisive moment in this young man's treatment, after which things really improved.

Alexander attempted to explain the change as follows: The analysand's father had always indulged him, but now his analyst, in a father transference, was not indulging him. However, what was more interesting was that this time the angry analyst-as-father was seen by the patient as nevertheless remaining essentially on the patient's side. Alexander felt that it was the patient's experience of this discrepancy between the historical father and the person of the analyst (especially around how they each handled real situations) that lead to insight and sudden, that is, unexpected growth.

Although we would all surely differ over what actually changed in Alexander, his patient, or their analytic work together that allowed the patient to finally see Alexander as a good but angry father figure, we might nevertheless agree that we are very much in need of a more productive way of communicating about the phenomenon of change, especially sudden change such as occurred in this case. *Chaos theory offers a special terminology for communicating about such change; but it also offers a unique way of thinking about the conditions associated with such change.*

For example, chaos theory allows us to talk of such things as transitions into chaos, where the time intervals of doubling shorten according to determined rate (for example, 1/Feigenbaum's constant), and where the emerging patterns demonstrate a beautiful orderliness, as seen in fractal qualities (as is true of the Feigenbaum diagram and a related figure, the so-called Mandelbrot[97] set).

What makes these factors relevant to psychoanalysis is the notion that arguably, each patient shows a consistent *signature* in their pattern of being (see Galatzer-Levy, 1997). This signature is fractal-like in that it re-appears at various levels of "magnification" in the patient's behavior and thinking. In other words, such patterns of thinking or associating can be observed in the patient's grossest behaviors over years of time, or seen to emerge repeatedly over periods of months or weeks of analytical sessions, or found repeating themselves in a single session.

Although there is no time to consider all such details in a brief essay, chaos theory further allows or invites one to actually quantify the amount of chaos (change) in a given system.[98] Finally, there are so-called *strange attractors*, which are specifically what depicts the exact temporal and spatial trajectory of chaos. Let us explain further.

Attractors in general are ". . . geometric forms that describe the long-term behavior of . . . [nonlinear] systems" (Priel & Schreiber, 1994, p. 214), that is, systems where the output is not proportional to the input.[99] More specifically, ". . . an attractor is what the behaviour of the system settles down to, or is [conceived of being] attracted to . . ." (*ibid.*) such as a pendulum's movement over time towards a fixed point of rest. This rest point is described as a *simple attractor* because it is as though the single simple rest point "attracts" the pendulum. *Limit cycles* are a second intermediate type of attractor; these have trajectories that reach, as a limit, the contour of a closed loop, that is, they do not settle down to a simple point but rather to a loop. An example of such a limit cycle would be the repetitive movement of a clock pendulum following a more or less constant loop trajectory, without slowing down from friction because the system has an external source of power. Finally, there are *strange attractors* that show the most complex trajectories of all, such as are seen in chaotic systems. An example is the famous Lorenz attractor, which loops back and forth, first inside one cluster of concentric elliptical shapes, then inside a companion cluster.

All of these attractors express the dynamics of a variety of forces, some of which expand and others which serve to contract, brake or condense trajectories within phase space[99] (Quinodoz, 1997). Most interesting, the trajectory of strange attractors is self repeating on smaller and smaller scales, so that in the case of strange attractors fractal qualities are always the rule. Quinodoz, under the influence of French–Swiss culture, sees these attractors as constructed much like French pastry or bread, with multiple inner foldings or, you might say, layers of self-sameness.[100]

The very novelty of the terminology of chaos theory, of course, is poten-tially confusing, but the ideas expressed can be useful to psychoanalysis exactly because they capture change in a universal language; moreover, they (like the differential equations which lie behind them) wrestle with the precise nature of change, that is, with its geometry and timing. Mathematicians think of such qualities of attractors, mapped onto a multidimensional *phase space*, as reflecting the various identifiable factors whose alteration changes the trajectory of their overarching system.

So we see that chaos theory constitutes a very precise way of denoting change qualitatively and quantitatively while simultane-ously noting the role of specific factors producing the change. *Galatzer-Levy believes such mathematical descriptions enhance our understanding of development by adducing the mathematical rules result-ing in complex outcomes.* This is reflected in Mitchell Feigenbaum's diagrams, and particularly in Feigenbaum's formulation of what he calls *universality*. This term refers to the following idea: the point in the Feigenbaum diagram where chaos starts (that is, the particular value of "a") logically contains within it all of the information that is manifested by all subsequent chaotic events.[101]

In addition, and this has been a surprise to everyone: the pattern of chaos depicted in the Feigenbaum diagram (Figure 5, Chapter Eleven, p. 176), appears to be *universal* in the sense that *virtually all chaotic phenomena studied in nature to this point appear to be structured identically*. This gives us a feeling that we are discovering a decisive orderliness in nature. Complex nonlinear behavior no longer seems random against the backdrop of our new knowledge of chaos.

Another interesting aside: the transitions zones from order into rapid doubling (and also back) are actually themselves neither orderly nor chaotic *per se* but something *sui generis*. Such *transitional zones* are perhaps the most interesting special states demanding scrutiny in this new science of chaos.

Psychopathology and complexity

Lest one conclude that all this mathematical gobbledygook is too arcane to be relevant to psychoanalysis, consider that our field has long been fixated on how seemingly small differences in initial conditions radically alter outcomes! In fact, this is why we pay special attention to the direction and time course of change and shifts in state of our patients. As in the case of Wolf's depiction of Alexander and his patient, part of every transference analysis involves attention to such details. Moreover, Freud's so-called genetic hypothesis, along with our general attempts as analysts to understand what particular experience means to a given patient, also rely on our analysis of the effects of subtle changes in initial conditions.

In fact, *one can argue that psychoanalysis has literally been built upon this question of understanding precisely the effect of subtle initial differences in personal meanings or interpretative responses or both, variables which fluctuate and interact in a lawful manner*. So we are each of us, without knowing it, from the mathematical perspective, already deeply involved with chaotic phenomena; therefore, it makes good sense to make use of chaos theory to shed further light on mental processing.

Let us now turn briefly to the issue of pathology, which involves special patterns of mental functioning. Here Galatzer-Levy, Levin, and Moran all agree that either extreme regularity or extreme disorganization are capable of leading to psychopathology, from the viewpoint of chaos theory. It will help, however, to clarify that the freely fluctuating states of chaos and regularity, which occur in complex nonlinear systems, are actually *normative* in the sense that they are expected properties of complex systems, that is, they obtain when such systems are working properly. So please, do not fall into the trap of connecting chaos itself with abnormality.

Rather, from the vantage point of chaos theory *abnormality occurs when the mind–brain gets locked into either chaotic or highly regular states, rather than shifting naturally between such states in a dynamically normal yet complex manner.* From this perspective, one crucial form of psychopathology is the lack of freedom. *Fixity, the aberration from the natural variable functioning of complex systems, is the real psychopathological culprit.* To think of fixity, just reflect on obsessive compulsive illness or any significant character disorder.

Utena (1996), whose Kabuki Model was touched upon above, has commented on the significance of freedom in exactly the sense implied earlier. He writes that we all need to be free in terms of three variables: freedom in the sense of having optimally functioning brains (which is where the various biologically oriented interventions come in); freedom in terms of mastering psychological development, which allows us to access the functional capabilities of our mind (which is where most psychotherapy and psychoanalysis enters in); and freedom to enjoy living within a community of other people (this is the important social domain which can sometimes be neglected in therapy). For Utena, normal development is that which supports or creates having choices. As analysts, we work hard to assist the actuation of each such freedom in our patients. In other words, imagine that mental freedom reflects the proper free functioning of chaotic systems in mind and brain. Or, as Moran puts it, some psychoanalytic interventions might essentially be working by means of their interference with nonlinear systems by adding complexity and thus interfering with fixity.

The case of learning

Let us now address the variable we call learning. Although there is as yet no generally accepted psychoanalytic theory of learning, there have been continuing efforts to apply interdisciplinary perspectives towards this purpose (Levin, 1991, 1997b; see especially Chapters 1–5 of this monograph). In what follows, we elaborate further on such a learning theory, but this time based upon Priel and Schreiber's implication that *shifts into chaos are important facilitators of learning.*

Priel and Schreiber make two decisive points. First, they highlight Freud's historical description that logical chains of associations invariably involve two or more threads of associations meeting and proceeding as one. They see this formation of associative chains as neatly overlapping the mathematical perspective of a series of bifurcation points topographically, but "where one [or more] of the ramifications has been suppressed" (p. 212). It should be noted that *these researchers are assuming, without exactly saying so, that the acquisition of knowledge (i.e., learning) accrues from the expansion and increasing depth of associative trees.*

Second, Priel and Schreiber state explicitly that the psychoanalytic transference phenomenon is illuminated when seen in relation to the behavior of the so-called *strange attractors* of chaos theory (p. 214) where transferences are "transitions from [non chaotic] "limit cycles" [i.e., intermediate attractors] to strange [that is, more complex chaotic] attractors through [the mechanism of] bifurcation . . ." (p. 214). In other words, these authors believe that ". . . *bifurcation potentially creates information . . . [through the mechanism of] space symmetry breaking*[102] . . ." which they see as ". . . *the necessary prerequisite without which the possibility of constructing an information processor simply would not exist*" (*ibid.*, my emphasis). (Incidentally, what Priel and Schreiber refer to as a shift in attractor seems to coincide with the previously mentioned shifts in the direction of complexity. Such complexity is an antidote to psychopathology, a point clarified further below.) But what exactly does symmetry breaking refer to? I shall take this up next.

Symmetry breaking

The term symmetry breaking appears in physics, computer and engineering science, cognitive neuroscience, and psychoanalysis.

Within cosmology, it refers to a creative phase in the origin of the macroscopic universe consequent to the so-called Big Bang, where the original symmetry (homogeneity) is broken and apparent local concentrations of matter settle out as the known subatomic particles, elements, and galaxies of the universe.[103] Within the related field of particle physics, it refers to deviations in the patterning of the *flavor* and *mass* in the expected variety of subatomic particles (such as quarks, leptons, muons, and so forth) (Chivukula, Cohen, Lane, & Simmons, 1997; Thomas, 1995).

Within computer science, symmetry breaking refers to special creative techniques for finding algorithmic and other mathematical solutions to complex network problems (Awerbuch, Cowen, & Smith, 1994). In cognitive neuroscience, symmetry breaking relates to the effects within neural networks of creatively shifting the loading of input variables and system relationships. For instance, the orientations of visual cortical cell columns in the brain are said to be regulated by "symmetry breaking [which alters] cortical feedback connections" (Dong, 1997). *It should be obvious that although none of these definitions of symmetry breaking is exactly the same, they nevertheless all share a common theme: the creation of qualitative change via reorganization.*

Finally, and most important for our discussion, within psychoanalysis we have the work of Matte Blanco (1986, 1989) which deals with his own unique version of symmetry breaking. I believe Priel and Schreiber have this in mind without exactly saying so.

Matte Blanco has developed a self-consistent theory depicting the mind–brain's so-called *bi-logic*, by which he means that the unconscious mind's (primary process) logic is always in stark contrast with the (secondary process) logic of the conscious mind. In applying his theories, Matte Blanco systematically incorporates the idea of symmetry breaking to explain shifts between belief systems that are seen on the one hand as symmetrical or asymmetrical, and on the other hand which appear associated with steps in psychological development stimulated by psychoanalytic interventions of various kinds. An example will help quickly explain how symmetry breaking is used by Matte Blanco.

Wolf's earlier discussion of Franz Alexander's patient is actually quite similar to one Matte Blanco (1989) discusses in detail from the perspective of symmetry breaking. Both of these patients begin treatment in a stage in which their memories of their father have been kept relatively frozen. Under the influence of creative psychoanalytic intervention, however, a stage (of symmetry) is entered wherein each patient sees his analyst not merely as similar to but literally identical with his father imago (and imbued with positive qualities). Next, these patients move into a treatment stage that is symmetrical in a different sense: now they see themselves and their analyst/father as similar[104] (while nevertheless retaining the positive valence of both images). Finally, these patients move into a decisive asymmetrical stage (which coincides with symmetry breaking) in which they see themselves as persons separate[105] from both their father and their analyst, but while still retaining a feeling of positivity about themselves.

Let us return now, briefly, to Priel and Schreiber, who quote Heisenberg (1971) as follows: "The same organizing forces that have created nature in all its forms, are responsible for the structure of the soul, and likewise, for our capacity to think" (p. 217). Their use of symmetry breaking, although not entirely unambiguous, relies on the work of Heisenberg (1971), of Nicolis and Prigogine (1981, 1989), and, I believe, on that of Matte Blanco, as we noted above. *The key is that each of these investigators believe that how we think, feel and behave derives from the variegated patterns of feed-forward and feedback (networking) processes which alter the chaotic mind–brain system we call our self, while simultaneously breaking new ground in creative acts designated as symmetry breaking, a term bathed in a rich network of associations that include the idea of self differentiation and growth in various natural settings.*

Let us attempt to further synthesize the various perspectives suggested in this and the previous section. *It seems logical to conclude that there is likely such a thing in humans as optimal chaos. This optimal chaos would seem to involve the "freedom" to form novel bifurcation points in one's thinking, thus decisively organizing and reorganizing mind–brain databases* (i.e., creating new connections, ideas, and more complex and usable memories). Such freedom could also be conceptualized as a consequence of increments in complexity in the nonlinear dynamical properties of mind–brain systems. In other words, the freedom to break symmetry and operate with mind–brain systems on the edge of chaos (rather than getting trapped in some rigid or fixed systems) optimizes learning, and may also make it much more accessible. This is a novel explanation for psychological change compared to the usual theoretical explanations given psychoanalytically (cf. Shevrin, 1998).[106]

Sashin and Callahan's discovery: the tunnel

Let us conclude this chapter by touching upon two additional novel perspectives. The first and most important comes from the work of Sashin and Callahan (1990), who developed a *double cusp model of the mind*. Putting their mathematical model through its paces, they discovered an unexpected topological shape, which they called the *tunnel*, the observation of a phenomenon that we find compelling. *Their "tunnel" coincides with those successful moments in every analysis where the patient is finally feeling the full intensity of private important affects, but where such emotion is now only modestly inclining the patient towards disruption* (i.e., where the experiencing patient essentially feels safely able to contain feelings which were previously enormously disturbing but are no longer so). Sashin and Callahan's conclusion follows from the way their exact variable loadings in the model are controlled.

Now the idea of a capacity shift is not new to psychoanalysis. It has been noted by Bion and many others. But *the tunnel, conceived by Sashin and Callahan in space–time, is also the virtual space where these two researchers conceptualize that mending occurs in the emotional container function. Most important here, the observation of a tunnel coinciding with an emotional container function is also, strictly speaking, an empirical finding which grew out of Sashin and Callahan's strictly mathematical analysis of affect responses to stressors in a chaos model within a ten dimensional space!*[107] Clinical research is, of course, needed to confirm their findings, but I believe this will be accomplished, if it has not already been.

In terms of the earlier notation of symmetry breaking, the *tunnel* would appear to represent a decisive configuration in space–time that allows for creative kinds of information processing associated with "freedom" in the exact sense also described by Utena (1996), whose work I discussed at length above, and in earlier chapters.

Chaos and higher mental functions

Second, we wish to report a highly speculative, as of yet unproved correlation of our own. During our writing of this chapter, we decided to see if we could find any independent general supportive evidence that the higher cognitive functions in man express patterns that might themselves be related to chaos. To do so, we reasoned that the EEG patterns associated with such higher mental functions might show a precise relationship to Feigenbaum's constants. What we have found is the following.

Duilio Giannitripani devoted himself to studying the EEG correlates of higher cognitive functions in the basement of Michael Reese Hospital (Psychosomatic and Psychiatric Institute) from 1966 to 1971, and elsewhere thereafter. Most interestingly, his monumental treatise of this subject shows that all the EEG frequencies associated with higher mental functions are themselves multiples of 3.5, something he calls Giannitripani's rule of 3.5. As you recall, Feigenbaum's point (where chaos begins) is invariably 3.5699456. . .), which is suggestively close to 3.5! Now, this possible correlation requires further research to confirm, because it could merely be accidental and of no deep significance.[108] Also, there are mathematical tests that need to be performed on EEG recordings to properly identify that which is in fact chaotic. We are currently in the process of evaluating whether Giannitripani's rule of 3.5 and Mitchell Feigenbaum's point are indeed significantly related in any deeper sense. We believe they are.

Summary

Chaos theory contributes a supremely useful terminology for and a way of thinking about development, learning, and psychopathology. In a nutshell, psychoanalysis invites learning by means of its effect on the hierarchical modes of the mind so that new levels of complexity are added to the ways these modes are actually utilized (i.e., instantiated in mind–brain). The consequence is that psychopathology based upon rigid or fixed mental functioning is reduced to a minimum, and instead new freedom of a biopsychosocial sort is created. In strict mathematical terms, *freedom is a signal property of nonlinear deterministic systems when they operate on the edge of chaos and the edge of fixity or regularity.*

Through the terminology of chaos theory we can better describe what we are observing clinically in terms of something more fundamental in nature that human minds and brains are, of course, a part of. From such a perspective, psychological development is merely one important example of the chaotic normalcy of the world. And psychopathology, in contrast, is the loss of freedom associated with fixity, when complex systems become too simple or disorganized and therefore are no longer resistant to minor irritants (just as posited by the significant number of psychoanalytic researchers who have been applying chaos theory to psychoanalysis), or when learning has relatively stopped (Levin, 1991).

Scholars of mathematics, neuroscience, psychology, and psychoanalysis have been experimenting with chaos theory in order to establish better models of developmental change, learning, and psychopathology. In particular, they awaken us to various kinds of symmetry breaking that appears to be a correlate of change. We need to credit the pioneer polymath psychoanalysts, such as Sashin, Galatzer-Levy, Moran, Forrest, Matte Blanco, and others, for their highly original work in this bridging area. But we need most of all to follow up on insights such as Sashin's and Callahan's regarding the *tunnel* and the *container function*, which would seem to epitomize in strict mathematical language what psychoanalysis has already adumbrated in a number of its theories: growth of our faculty to contain our most intense and precious emotions is a decisive element in learning and development, and its absence undoubtedly contributes to psychopathology.

SECTION V
CLINICAL CONSEQUENCES

Psychoanalytic operating principles: how they derive from understanding knowledge acquisition

Fred Levin

Introduction

This chapter[109] addresses knowledge acquisition in relationship to two closely connected topics: the workings of mind–brain, and the clinical situation of psychoanalysis. *If we understand how knowledge is acquired I believe it is then possible to outline a series of operating principles which can effectively guide our analytic work.*

Let us start with a discussion of the problems inherent in conceptualizing mind–brain theoretically in terms of so-called "internal representations". In its place I propose what I consider the more useful perspective of "expert systems". *Human learning is the result of brain plasticity and depends upon neural systems that change in relation to experience and the build-up of expertise. Any psychoanalytic theory of learning or personality must be consonant with what is known about learning, memory, and knowledge formation* from neuroscience (Cloninger, 1991; also see Chapter Four).

Of course, any comprehensive psychoanalytic theory of learning must also take into account what is known about the psychoanalytic transference (reviewed in Chapter Five). In what follows I therefore aim at further clarifying specific clinical recommendations that facilitate learning in general by both creating and exploiting learning readiness. *The psychoanalyst reader will especially appreciate the attempt to connect specific clinical recommendations with the neurophysiological principles upon which they rest.*

Each generation of theoreticians must ponder difficult questions regarding the nature of knowing and thinking, squaring their scientific theorizing with their religious/cultural beliefs (Chapter One). Since Kant's concentration on these issues two centuries ago, we have advanced in our understanding of the material universe, including many details about our brain and behavior (Chapter Two); yet in terms of sorting out which are the most useful "categories" to facilitate further scientific progress we still and always will face substantial challenges (Chapter Three). For example, consider the category designated by the word "representation," which is popular within neuroscience, cognitive psychology, and psychoanalysis. One can ask if we really understand the precise meaning of this term, or whether any substantial or useful part of its meaning is actually shared by these three disciplines.

Problems with the concept of internal representation

Neurologically, the body is conceptualized as being "represented" within the brain in various feature maps based upon the different sensory modalities. This is a relatively concrete, physiological meaning of the term "representation" in which the word indicates that some such experience is essentially being coded in memory. This neurological meaning appears to make sense, since there is evidence that at times our reasoning proceeds by way of a process of internal "imaging" and the manipulation of visual, perceptually near experience. Consider, for example, the circumstance of being asked to look at a geometrical figure and judge if it is the same or different from another figure drawn from a different perspective. The reaction time to accomplish this task seems to depend upon how much mental rotation is required of an assumed internal image.

However, although this concrete physiological definition of "representation" seems clear enough, the exact meaning in terms of brain function is not altogether unambiguous. For example, in his *On Aphasia* (1953 [1891]) Freud carefully describes how during the imaging process what one ends up with is not likely to be an exact point-for-point correspondence within the brain's cortical level, but rather a looser "representation" (*Vorstellung*) of the original sensory input, which has been essentially transferred across numerous synapses and finally becomes part of a rich network of meaningful mind–brain associations (Rizzuto, 1990; see also Reiser, 1984). Also, as I have noted with Vuckovich (1983), Freud's neurological speculations on language disturbance become a significant precursor to his later psychoanalytic conceptualizing. For example, as Rizzuto (1990) points out in elegant detail, Freud's views on the nature of brain "representation" are a cornerstone of his book *On Aphasia*. In any event, one can only conclude that even within neurology "representation" has a set of meanings rather than any single referent, although most of these are principally tied to the remembering and imaging processes, that is, to aspects of working memory.

The problem of defining representation becomes even more complex, however, when imprecise neurological concepts such as self- and object-representation are amalgamated with even vaguer psychological constructs such as "self" and "object," and imported into psychoanalysis, for example, by Sandler and Rosenblatt (1962). Although these scholars are careful in their evocation of a helpful metaphor, nevertheless, all subsequent theoreticians run the risk of working such original ideas into a reified web, seemingly explaining and contrasting in the process certain core psychoanalytic phenomena of even greater abstraction such as those subsumed under the rubrics of "introjection," "identification," and so-called "psychic structure."

An aside may help, since the reader will appreciate that in criticizing the use of the word "representation" in psychoanalysis I in no way intend to denigrate the efforts to understand and delineate such core psychoanalytic concepts as are covered by such terms as "introjection" and identification." In fact, I personally hold these ideas to be prescient psychological constructs on the road toward a meaningful interdisciplinary theory of knowledge acquisition. This I try to spell out later in this text, where I remind the reader of the pioneering work of Rapaport, who integrates the insights of Freud, Hartmann, and Piaget. Rather, in this chapter, I am addressing the danger of overusing the ambiguous term "representation" and thereby potentially avoiding acknowledgment of our general ignorance of how mind–brain actually works.

A second example of this linguistic trend in modern psychoanalytic conceptualizing is the work of Bucci (1985, 1993), who describes essentially three elements as internally represented: the nonverbal, the verbal, and correlations between the two (which she calls the referential).[110] Not unlike Bucci, I myself have written repeatedly of how the mind–brain represents different aspects of mentation, which can then be either isolated or integrated with various purposes in mind. For example, I have speculated that over the course of development we build a self-in-the-world model, the manipulation of which allows us to think without recourse to obvious sensory experience (that is, without apparent manipulation of the real world). In so doing I would seem to have obviously cast my lot with those within psychoanalysis who believe in "internal representations." Yet the more I have pondered over such terminology the more I have concluded that the very conceptualization of "internal representation" within psychoanalysis has lost some of its precision and utility, although the perspective may yet be important as a handy image to manipulate (that is, rather than anything correlatable with objective reality in the mind–brain). The problem here, as I see it, is that we are most unclear whether psychoanalytic internal "representations" are concrete sensory (reference) images for the brain to manipulate, the memory of such images, epiphenomena associated with remembering and/or information processing and working memory, mere metaphors (for "gedanken", i.e. thought experiments), each of these, or something else! Unfortunately, the ambiguity of the terminology can lead to considerable confusion and the mere illusion of insight. Most critically, the vagueness of the idea of representation sets an arbitrary conceptual limit on the amount of insight we are ever likely to achieve about mind–brain correlative mechanisms. It also reinforces our failure to look for the details of how mind–brain accomplishes its activities, because one does not look for what one believes one already has in his or her possession!

But cognitive psychology's conceptualizations of "representation" appears equally ambiguous; moreover they are primarily based upon a rapidly aging analogy between mind–brain and computer. Worse still, the psychological meanings of representation seem not only concrete but also subtly different from the meanings of "representation" as used in neurology and in psychoanalysis. First of all, computer memories are real, mechanical devices for storing and processing data. That they must actually function in ways unlike the brain–mind is not always appreciated. According to this view the computer has various types of memory (RAM, ROM, working memory, CD and hard disk drives etc.) and presumably such mechanical "memory" bears a relationship (albeit unspecified) to biological memory processes (sensory, short- and long-term, including long-term potentiations).

To add to the confusion, psychology has its own set of meanings for "representation," as is the case of such "representational constructs" as semantic nets, frames, and scripts. These abstract categories have been proposed and have their own attraction as theoretical tools, partly because, as noted, these words also refer to concrete, computer-related software with utility in its own right. But a danger remains. Because these borrowed computer concepts are the basis for useful mechanical devices, the unwary are lulled into believing that this is how mind–brain actually works. That is, because we respect computer technology we get drawn into believing the authority of neuroscientific and cognitive psychological pronouncements![111] Yet *neuroscience and cognitive psychology are no more authoritative on the workings of mind–brain than are many other fields that study the same phenomena* and no one in either neuroscience, cognitive psychology, or psychoanalysis knows definitively how all information is actually coded in the mind–brain! Moreover, even experts within artificial intelligence are likely to agree that *"complete theories of knowledge representation [either for computer or human intelligence] do not exist now"* (Salton, 1991, p. 977, my emphasis).

In summary, one must conclude that a major problem with the simultaneous reference to "representation"[112] (without further clarification) within neuroscience, psychology, and psychoanalysis is that these are three different sets of conceptions. Even if one argues that these meanings overlap, the net result of their combined usage can sometimes obfuscate rather than clarify things. In a nutshell, the brain remains "a consummate piece of combinatorial mathematics" (Max Born, quoted in Eisley, 1975, p. 258; also see Eisley, 1971). Where then do we go if representational terminology no longer enlightens us that much about mind–brain? The answer: expert systems, a subject I will take up momentarily, after a brief detour.

Connectionism and psychoanalysis

Before proceeding, a word about neural networks. Some may object that in my discussion to this point I have not sufficiently high-lighted a connectionist description of brain function (e.g., Palombo, 1998), and this may alter the apparent value of "representation." Connectionism, or neural net theory, poses a set of paradigms that are indeed useful to our understanding of mind–brain. For example, Olds (1994) points out how such theories describe brain as "less dependent on [the concept of] a central processor" (p. 581). While this statement is technically correct, the situation in the brain is actually much more complicated, as Olds is well aware. According to the research of Posner (1995) and Lassen (1994a,b), cognition involves the tying together of zones or brain cell modules that are both dispersed (i.e., function as neural networks) *and* highly specialized functionally (i.e., arguably different from neural networks). The key, apparently, is how specialized populations of neurons connect in time and space in order to accomplish given cognitive tasks in assembly-line fashion. This anatomical–physiological wrinkle renders ordinary forms of neural network theory or neural connectionism limited in their human application, since the idiosyncracies of specific brain architecture are rarely referenced.

However, for the purposes of this essay, the differences between a pure (i.e., simplified) connectionist approach and the more complex and sophisticated approach such as Palombo's, based upon co-evolution within systems, do not necessarily alter my conclusions about the problems inherent in the idea of internal representations. In fact, *had I chosen to highlight a connectionist approach it would actually make my argument against internal represen-tation even stronger* (also see Forrest, 1987; Anderson & Rosenfeld, 1989; Spruiell, 1993). Let me explain. This is because representation, in the sense of its usual meanings, has virtually no fixed relation-ship to how any task is accomplished by the network. In a nutshell, our task is to understand how things work in mind–brain, and neural network theory lacks the ability to clarify the "representational" process in any manner that convincingly mimics real minds and brains. The same point was highlighted in Chapter Seven when I considered Searles Chinese room argument (p. 114).

In order to obviate the problems inherent in the conception of "representation," this essay therefore presents an alternative approach. The remainder of the essay is thus organized as follows. First the question of expert knowledge is introduced. This leads to two important considerations: cognitive psychological research on judging similarity and transferring knowledge between content domains, and a discussion of what is known about the varieties of knowledge, their acquisition and retrieval (cf. Chapter Four).

We shall see that Rapaport's ideas of integrating Freud, Hartmann, and Piaget became the basis for the first systematic thinking of a psychoanalytic theory of learning, and how this was subsequently used as the foundation for outlining a modern learning theory and a hierarchical developmental model based upon integrating psychoanalytic and neuroscientific knowledge. Finally, there is a discussion of how these nonrepresentational conceptions and insights about the phenomenology of learning can be fashioned into practical means of evoking "learning windows" within the clinical psychoanalytic situation.

Comparing experts and novices: a step toward a psychoanalytic theory of learning

In *Mapping the Mind* (Levin, 1991) I suggest that at least one essence of memory is that each quantum of human experience infinitesimally changes the mind–brain; in other words, memory involves tapping the brain's plasticity to build databases of knowledge. Therefore, the process of remembering would seem to involve (exactly as Freud [1891, 1953 (1891)] argues on the subject of aphasia) the recreation of the mental–neural events connected with the original experience itself. Our best approach to understanding how learning works would thus appear to be to steer clear of older theories of representation and instead concern ourselves with how the mind–brain organizes knowledge.

Let us consider asking, for example, the following kind of question: *What is it that makes experts tend to solve problems more efficiently than novices?* Experts have the edge presumably because they are "more likely to have explicit, accessible [knowledge] of the relational structures of the content domain" (Gentner & Ratterman, 1991a, p. 36). Stated differently, experts are better able to recognize "similarity" between current and old problems and "transfer" the relevant knowledge (that is, apply the old solutions) to the current situation. What is especially useful about such a perspective is that it shifts attention from the ambiguous concept of "representation" to more precisely definable process categories (such as judging "similarity" and "transferring" knowledge), which can more easily become the subject of specific experimental manipulation and investigation.

In addition, although this may not appear obvious, it seems possible that what neuroscientists call priming and what psychoanalysts call transference might coincide with *what cognitive psychologists label judging similarity and transferring knowledge* (Chapter Four). If this proves correct, then to appreciate the phenomenon of priming mentioned earlier we need to study how we judge similarity, and how we transfer knowledge between content domains and in the psychoanalytic situation as well. Let me elaborate. Gentner and Ratterman point out (1991a,b) that research on very young children, infants, and primates shows that innate mechanisms allow for the apprehension of relational similarity. Moreover, if one examines language,

> the possession of names for relations, including [the words] *same* and *different* [as examples] may be [particularly] important for the appreciation of analogical similarity. This in turn suggests that the changes in knowledge that drive [the recognition of] changes in similarity do not simply consist of accretion of domain facts, but rather include the deepening and systematization of the [individual's] knowledge base. [1991b, p. 227; see also Chapter Four for an elaboration of some of these points]

This could mean that when in a psychoanalysis a patient's out-of-awareness feelings are named and correspondences (subtle similarities and differences) noted between their specific episodic experiences, then there is likely a simultaneous and significant deepening and systemization of the patient's knowledge bases in particular areas. Further, there is reason to wonder if this cognitive reorganization and consolidation of knowledge based upon judgments of "same/different" might not coincide with what analysts call increasing self-definition and/or cohesion. Clearly, psychoanalysis constitutes a virtual laboratory for learning about learning in individuals.

Varieties of knowing: some neuroscientific observations

Before presenting Rapaport's approach to learning theory, a few additional remarks seem in order on the mind–brain's systems or ways of knowing, each of which constitutes (to a degree) its own variety of intelligence, its own mode of using that intelligence, and its own worldview (or its own contribution to any overreaching worldview the brain can assemble as a whole). That humans have two cerebral hemispheres suggests we have no less than two different kinds of knowledge or knowing, just as Aristotle posited. The contribution of the left hemisphere appears to be via syntactical language and logic, references to famous people (i.e., appeals to authority), insight by means of temporal sequences, and a tendency to synthesize and explain.

In contrast, the right hemisphere seems to have a logic all its own, and operate more "timelessly," emotionally, socially, and intuitively (like Einstein and Poincare [1916–1954] did at certain points in the discovery phase of their work, say, on relativity theory; or perhaps more like a Zen mystic than a taxi driver). The consensus is that although knowledge usually refers to the category of learning depicted by the operation of the left hemisphere (formally called "declarative" or "explicit" knowledge), the right hemisphere's intuitive (i.e., emotional, personal) system also constitutes knowledge (formally called either "procedural," "implicit," or "episodic"). The left hemisphere is capable of rapidly searching through associative linkages or decision trees; the right contributes in a similarly rapid style that is both holistic and, perhaps more importantly, intelligently guided by feelings.

But one might consider other kinds of knowledge as well, based upon the contribution of integrating subsystems of the brain, for example, the cerebellum, the striatum, the amygdala(s), the hippocampuses and/or the thalamus (each of which contributes to so-called "procedural" knowledge in its own unique way, much like dialects uniquely reflect a mother tongue).[113]

Space does not permit an elaboration of how the qualities of these subsystems might differ, but one such example might be the interesting distinction Hadley (1985, 1987, 1989) makes between the hippocampuses as a knowledge system versus the amygdala as a belief system. According to Hadley, only a belief system has the power to impel action. The distinction between knowing and believing thus becomes important; although a full discussion of Hadley's distinction is beyond the scope of this brief essay, there is a possibility that "the hippocampus subserves the coding of the external context ([i.e.,] of sensory, temporal, spatial, and somatic response attributes [of experience]), while the amygdala subserves the coding of internal environmental context ([i.e.,] sensory, temporal, affect, and autonomic response attributes)" (Kesner, 1984, p. 112). Obviously, the brain operates as a whole, combining the unique contributions of all of its parts. The major effort remains in specifying exactly how coordination and synthesis between the various parts obtains and influences the results.

One final comment. For the distinction between "declarative" ("book learning") and "procedural" ("habits and behaviors") credit is due to Aristotle as well as Endel Tulving and the late Gilbert Ryle. Tulving does the most to differentiate these patterns in terms of cognitive psychology; but Ryle, as early as a 1945 address to the Aristotelian Society, and later (Ryle, 1949), notes the cardinal difference between "knowing that" (something is so) and "knowing how" (to do something) (White, 1982, p. 14). Specialists in other disciplines also employ this ancient differentiation, as in the distinction between physics and engineering: the former is said to deal with descriptions of how things "really are," the latter with the practical problems related to "how to do things" (Channel, 1991, pp. 573–574). Certainly there must be many other useful categories of knowing that have simply not yet been identified as such or named. Their specification will undoubtedly also involve "judging similarity" and "transferring knowledge" within and between domains.

Rapaport's contribution to a theory of knowledge acquisition: the integration of nature and nurture

There are naturally many interesting modern experiments on the relationship between nature and nurture.[114] However, the earliest integrated theory within psychoanalysis of how it is possible for humans to acquire knowledge is that of Rapaport (1951a,b) and can be summarized as follows. The theory synthesizes the ideas of many philosophers (see Gedo's discussion of Rapaport in Gedo, 1986, especially pp. 63–81), as well as contributions of Freud, Hartmann, and Piaget, and has been updated by modern researchers (Gedo & Goldberg, 1973; Gedo, 1986, 1989a,b, 1993a,b; Levin, 1991, pp. 43–82, 105–120, 195–200) into a hierarchical, developmental model. Such a model is much to be preferred over a representational schema approach, which fails to examine the details of how any such a model works (for example, how progressive and regressive developmental steps relate to each other).

According to Rapaport, the biological roots of humans involve the innate drive towards care giving objects, who are never given up in our unconscious life. Freud's primary contributions to a theory of learning include his descriptions of the dynamic unconscious and infantile sexuality (i.e., drive theory), phenomena which guarantee that all of our loving attachments will recapitulate our earliest love relationships, and that abandoned object cathexes will crystallize as internal structure. From Hartmann we add the notion that our egos are relatively autonomous from the drives on the one hand, and from the human environment on the other. This guarantees that learning is possible, but invariably difficult. And finally, from Piaget we have the description of hierarchical, developmental phases that are biologically determined, yet environmentally released. The philosophical implications of the Rapaport model are not discussed here but in Chapter Three.

As Rapaport puts these component theories together, learning occurs from the viewpoint of psychoanalysis in three crucial steps: the first involves "introjection," which he defines as that step in which the lost or unavailable object is recathected in memory (versus in perception). This step basically states that the individual subject involved is incipiently aware that someone exists in memory, who is or was felt to be worth knowing. The second step is "identification," which means that the ego or self is now altered by its knowledge of and feelings about the introjected person. The experiencing subject is now in a stage of encapsulating the qualities and knowledge identified with their relationship to the loved or revered person, but will initially do so *en bloc*. What remains is a third (unnamed) step[115] in which the knowledge connected with the identified but unavailable person becomes organized as one's own, so it can be thought about without thinking of the lost object *per se*, but rather by means of some identificatory "tags" that categorize the knowledge, for example, on the basis of similarities.

The sequence is thus of investing in or loving someone, feeling oneself "losing" them in some way, remembering the experience of them, and finally making specifically chosen, perceived qualities associated with our relationship with them our own. Although many subtle details have been added by modern psychoanalysts, this sequence remains basically the best answer we have to Aristotle's question about how humankind transforms perception into knowledge (the agent of change which he called "psyche"). The reader is referred to Chapter Three for further details. What we need to do now, however, is to fill in more scientific details regarding each step of knowledge acquisition, and this is increasingly complex for several reasons. For one, knowledge is no longer seen as a human monopoly![116]

A second complication in understanding knowledge acquisition is that cognitive development does not invariably proceed in a standard manner. For example, the neurocognitively impaired and multiply handicapped, including the blind, the deaf, the autistic, and the learning disabled, have much to show us about normal development. In each of these cases there are practical reasons why special modes of learning are at times required before an individual can proceed with learning in general. For instance, the deaf need first to learn sign language before they can optimally learn any other language; that is, they first need exposure to a language modality they can use and learn naturally. Similarly, the learning disabled often suffer from "imprisoned intelligence" unless properly helped to learn how better to learn (Orenstein, 1992; Pompian & Thum, 1988). This often involves learning first how to respect themselves and not always worry about how others judge our mental efforts.

One related conclusion is that all of us require optimal exposure to such things as our native language in order to develop properly such traits as the ability to use syntactical language correctly or in a helpful way. Optimal development of personality also seems to require exposure to and immersion in a normative cultural milieu. For example, mothers invite children to feel good about themselves by loving these same children and enjoying their children's affects and communications.

Principles for creating and utilizing "learning windows" and the principles which underlie them

In this section we will draw upon our earlier chapters on learning and on utilizing the transference. Optimal timing of input during development bears a direct relation to what are sometimes referred to as "learning windows," and would seem to involve priming of the nervous system. So far, not much is understood about what controls the timing of these critical periods of learning readiness. This knowledge would seem crucial, however, if we are to alter learning windows or reestablish them in the here-and-now for the benefit of sensorily deprived or emotionally traumatized (nonoptimally exposed) individuals. It seems to me that psychoanalysis (in collaboration with other fields) might play a significant role in this challenging task of discovering the control mechanisms for "windows," since analysts habitually concern themselves with remediating situations where learning has become arrested and behavior repetitive—that is, with the creation of learning readiness. In *Mapping the Mind* (1991) I discuss what is known about the relationship between learning and brain plasticity. In this book I wish to speculate more on some possible means of creating learning readiness and their possible mechanisms of action.

First, traditionally analysts have motivated learning by the proper timing of their interventions. Let me explain how this works. First, they center their attention upon *what the patient wants help with* at any given moment, as compared to what we as psychoanalysts might judge to be important (see Schwaber, 1983); this (patient-centered) orientation has a specific powerful impact on enhancing nuclear trust and confidence, but it also has specific effects in facilitating learning (see below; also recall Chapter Five).

Second, we have learned the importance of communicating our tentative understandings to patients in terms that are *experience-near*. Third, by respecting the patient's learning initiatives we help the patient build cognitive "bridges" upon the stronger foundation of what he or she already feels relatively successful at. In other words, learning "bridges" are best extended to new territory only after they are anchored, as it were, in *something the patient comfortably "owns"* or has a sense of mastery of. (In Chapter Five, I attempt to describe how such learning works, based upon the activation of working memory units for specific modalities related to what is remembered in the learning task.) Fourth, spontaneous activity on the patient's part usually expresses his or her intuitive understanding of what needs to be learned first, what second, and so on; that is, it involves an appreciation of the individual's own knowledge of how he or she learns best. Finally, my impression is that there is yet another reason for carefully respecting the patient's sense of what is important to the self. My conclusion is that it is the gentle introduction to new information and the gentle testing of new abilities that may be required to optimally help the mind–brain deal with the special kind of *novelty anxiety* relating to the effort to learn something new.

Let me explain what I mean by *novelty anxiety* by reminding the reader briefly of neglect syndromes in which previously mastered brain functions are lost owing to illness or injury. When a brain-injured patient encounters the existence of a lost function he or she first becomes alarmed and may refuse or be unable to recognize a new perceptual reality. In a similar way, when new functions are activated that have not yet been encountered and/or mastered, a normal individual learner may respond with anxiety to the novelty of the situation that resembles that of the brain-injured. During the period of practicing the new function it has been proven important *not to misinterpret the patient's hesitations as either resistance or defensiveness*, in the traditional psychoanalytic sense of these terms. I am convinced that this understanding is an important part of what has led some experienced Chicago psychoanalysts, such as George Moraitis and Lou Shapiro, to emphasize in their teaching the importance of generally not interpreting resistances and defenses directly, but rather to focus instead primarily upon engaging the hesitant or anxious patient in a process of gentle analytic inquiry (see Smaller, 1993), and learning. Such a perspective would seem to respect the patient's vulnerable feelings about what is novel and unknown, as well as what is known about knowledge acquisition from psychoanalysis, psychology, and neuroscience.

A slightly different way of summarizing some of the points made about learning is to relate learning in psychoanalysis to two elements: (1) Freud's free associative method, and (2) neuro-scientific research visualizing cognition. This will make it possible to understand simply why *free association is so decisive in creating learning "windows."* The key lies in the research of Lassen (1994a,b) and Posner (1995, 1996), which shows decisively that when people are spontaneous in their associating, they more successfully activate working memory for the associated material. This means that the patient's free associations are the place to start in learning, for *learning requires working-memory activation* (Levin, 1994). This approach, typical of analysis, is quite different from approaches that begin intervention at a point distant from what is central to a patient's current free associations and spontaneous interests, for then we can be sure working memory will not be activated, and consequently learning will necessarily increase in difficulty by several orders of magnitude.

The learning model employed, like that of Rapaport mentioned above, involves releasing functional capacities within the mind–brain on the basis of extending the patient's spontaneous outputs in a loop through the external world (meaning especially the world of the patient–analyst interaction), with input then returning to the patient. From an information-processing perspective, what appears particularly crucial to learning facilitation in this mode is that the output is from one part of the patient's brain, and the input that returns (from the loop through the world) comes back to a different part of the same mind–brain. In this manner *psychoanalysts facilitate a deepening and broadening of mind–brain communications and connections.* It is argued that when novelty anxiety occurs, the information outputted returns, but to the same rather than to a different part of the mind–brain. Another way of saying the same thing is that for learning to occur optimally a functionally enlarged neural circuit is required, and this probably requires that the level of anxiety be kept to a minimum, or at least be as much as possible under the patient's control.

A final word on the retrieval of knowledge and the psychoanalytic model of learning

Each form of knowledge would seem to have its own method for coding and its own mechanisms for reading and writing such codes. There is reason to believe that within the brain the coding process is related to multisensory mixing and/or integration phenomena involving the same critical parts of the major learning subsystems mentioned above. For example, the amygdala and hippocampus located on each side of the brain are a portion of the cortical hemispheric systems for knowledge acquisition. Most recently Squire and Zola-Morgan (1991) have further demonstrated that the medial temporal lobe memory system itself functions "to bind together the distributed storage sites in neocortex that represent a whole [declarative] memory" (p. 1380). Only after an initial processing period does a memory apparently become independent of this medial temporal lobe system, further explaining what Rapaport speculates about years ago when describing learning stages (see above).

This new set of observations is particularly exciting because the temporal lobe system includes the parahippocampal cortex, which has been implicated in panic attack syndrome. Also, I have already noted the crucial importance for learning of maintaining anxiety within tolerable levels. Thus there is a possibility that *panic attacks might themselves be a consequence of the brain's anticipation of danger in association with its own perceived failure to store useful (adaptive) information because of a disturbance in the (temporal lobe) memory-fixing system.* It is also possible that what anxiety then "accomplishes" is the prevention of certain long-term storage of painful experience.

We conclude that many brain systems are important in long-term memory and the recall of knowledge: the cerebellum, the central parietal cortex, the gyrus cinguli, the corpus striatum, the thalamus, the amygdalas, and hippocampuses. Not surprisingly, those areas of the brain involved in sensory integration also appear to be those most involved in memory and general synthetic activity (Levin, 1991).

In other words, remembering is not a function of any single subsystem, but rather a system property of very large arrays of neurons, working together in a particular and intricate manner. *Remembering* (the gerund) is a more evocative word than memory (the noun), since the verb form *implies a process in which something that happened within the brain is now happening again. Recalling past events is possible because the brain has been changed infinitesimally by each experience. Remembering is thus more like recreating a file than finding and opening a file that abstracts experience.* The proof resides in the various neglect syndromes. For example, when the visual subsystem for color V4 is damaged (in the occipital area) the subject not only can no longer see color (only shades of gray), but they also cannot even remember having previously seen color, nor understand the very concept of "color" (Zeki, 1992).

As I suggested at the outset, psychoanalysis can play a decisive role in the timely recovery of useful but seemingly unavailable information and/or skills. The revolution in facilitating the retrieval of lost memories is, of course, created by Freud with his monumental discovery that human beings have a tendency to repeat rather than to remember. (Or put differently, both repeating and remembering are really aspects of the same tendency of the brain to express itself through the recurrence of previous patterns of excitation.) Thus we do not need to know consciously about the knowledge we have in order for us to use it. This utilization of sometimes unconscious and personally unknown knowledge is at the core of the so-called "repetition compulsion," as Freud (1920g) discusses (see also Bornstein & Pittman, 1992, on perception without awareness). The psychoanalyst, because he knows the patient and has his or her confidence, is in a preferred position to comment constructively about possible novel meanings of such complex, recurrent mental patterns.

The additional useful strategy psychoanalysts have discovered is to concentrate on the patient's nonverbal experience and communication. In contrast to verbal experience, which is easier to code and therefore tends to be either conscious or preconscious, nonverbal experience can coincide with decisive, unconscious feelings. Only the total communication (Levin, 1991), however, carries the complete message. And the nonverbal component of the total communication is particularly overlooked, in my opinion, except by experienced therapists and intuitive beginners, because it is in-effable (that is, seemingly indescribable in words).

But the major approach to facilitating the recall of affective ex-perience is for the psychoanalyst not to be afraid at times to allow himself or herself some liberty in "priming" the patient's memories, as noted at the beginning. This means that, based upon our under-standing of so-called "procedural knowledge" (see above), if we allow ourselves to not just be a blank screen, but rather to manifest unobtrusively the compassion that we feel in resonance (attune-ment) with our patient (meaning reflecting back to him or her, verbally or otherwise, our own reactions to what he or she is communicating), then some patients (those who cannot proceed otherwise) will find that the analyst's free associations, sponta-neously given, will stimulate their own associations; that is, they will prime the patients' procedural memories. Among these memo-ries may be included some of the patients' most obscure but rele-vant nonverbal experiences. At times such experience may only be retrieved through the re-experience of something akin to the initial state in which the experience first occurred (as a consequence of being primed) and cannot be remembered by any questioning of a logical sort. Such is the case when, for example, the analyst whis-tles an interpretation to a patient in the form of a particular, precisely chosen classical tune. When this opens floodgates of memory in the patient, one cannot fail to wonder if such recall could have been tapped so richly by any other means.

Of course, I am suggesting a fundamental change in psycho-analytic technique, but only so far as it is usually described formally. I am convinced, however, that what I am advocating was often not only Freud's strategy but that of most experienced analysts, whether they say so in writing or not. For example, Roy Grinker Sr. (1940), notes that during his analysis with Freud, Freud made periodic spontaneous remarks about such things as the reac-tion of Freud's dog's to Dr. Grinker's associations! (Freud's dog was frequently in Freud's office during his analytic work with patients.) When the dog scratched to go out, Freud might say: The dog is very disappointed with you today! And when the dog returned, Freud commented: She has decided to give you another chance! The reason why Freud never mentions such priming comments as a matter of technique would seem to be that he took this kind of creative playfulness for granted. *Freud's real technique thus involves not only learning from "arbeiten und lieben" (work and love) but also from "spielen" (that is, play).* The key is that play is spontaneous, that is, self-initiated, and as such is often associated with the activation of working memory as noted above.

The point of the foregoing discussion is to clarify the importance of positively valenced affective involvement for learning phenomena, since affect is often most available when people are playfully involved (that is, when they are comfortable). Michael Vuckovich and I struggle repeatedly with the question of how a psychoanalyst might best facilitate the optimal internal communications between the various knowledge subsystems of the patient's brain (Levin, 1991, chapters 2 and 3). Of course, such communication optimalization is what free association accomplishes *par excellence.* In our papers (1983, 1987) Vuckovich and I first speculate that *the cerebellum plays a major role in learning in general and not merely in motor learning.* Since 1983 the occasional role of cerebellar pathology in infantile autism, schizophrenia, and other conditions has been reported upon, supporting our speculations about a decisive cerebellar role (Decety, Sjohlm, Ryding, Stenberg, & Ingvar, 1990; also see the work of Ito). The clinical significance of these comments is that *the analyst should tap his own playfulness;* that is, that priming is required at *times for the patient's optimal learning processes to occur.* Of course, it goes without saying that by playfulness here one does not mean anything that would lack tact or sensitivity to the patient's feelings. Rather, the emphasis should be on the importance of the analyst not forgetting his own spontaneity and humanity.

Optimal learning thus appears to require active interventions on the patient's part. Jeannerod (1985) suggests that every spontaneous action is also a test of a hypothesis about the world. Actions lead to continual modification of a putative model in our brain (possibly in the cerebellum and/or the basal ganglia) that has been designated the self-in-the-world model (Levin, 1991). Analysts might note that here I am talking about at least two kinds of nonconscious activity: one is the psychoanalytic *unconscious,* and relates to conflicts; the other deals with the normal out-of-awareness utilization of knowledge generally (see Bornstein and Pittman, 1992; and also Ito's work, and Levin, 2009, *Emotion and the Psychodynamics of the Cerebellum*).

To be more precise about the hypothetical learning mode I am employing, it seems that the major difference between children and adults regarding their behavior in exploring the world is that children appear to need sensory stimulation to think about things: they must mouth, look at, touch, smell, and taste their world, presumably because they are still building up the internal schema which they will later manipulate cognitively in lieu of active physical contact with things. In contrast, adults appear to make use of knowledge without the obvious manipulation of concrete objects. However, personal observations have led me to conclude recently that *this difference between adults and children may be more apparent than real.*[117]

Two final qualifications. First, I am not arguing that all thinking occurs by means of either the manipulation of concrete objects (the paradigmatic case of children) or the manipulation of concrete internal images as parts of models (the case of adults). I am merely suggesting that *problem-solving and exploratory behaviors appear to stimulate our need for strong sensory experience (that is, for "priming"), which is similarly required for the recall of learned information in both children and adults.* Unfortunately, we do not yet have sufficient information about learning and recall to appreciate what machinery the brain uses for such cueing (Gabriel, Voght, Kubota, Poremba, & Kang, 1991) and the resulting provision of refined neural control. One thing we can say, however, is that the insights of William James so long ago seem particularly apt: James surmised that the judging of similarity constitutes possibly the central element in mental organization (Leavy, 1992).

Second, it should be stated explicitly that some new knowledge results not from a new combination of the recall of old information, but from the facilitation of new operations altogether. In this sense, *some colorful interpretative metaphors invite activity in sensory–integrative systems of the mind–brain for the first time, making it possible to experience certain perspectives that are either intrinsically insightful or catalytic of synthetic activity.*

Conclusion

Armed with the certainty that our knowledge and theories of mind and brain are incomplete and likely to remain so, we are in the best position to interact with our patients as human beings and to frame experimental approaches that will eventually improve psychoanalytic knowledge, theory, and practice. New learning in treatment is most likely to occur through a combination of the following (all of which are the legacy of Freud): aiming at investigating rather than being therapeutic; collaborating (working and playing) with patients in a partnership of mutual respect; staying attuned to what the patient is curious about and associating to, and why; and being precise in our theoretical thinking about such psychoanalytic constructs as "representation," which may otherwise tend to be too ambiguous or misleading to be useful. This essay has considered some of the neuroscientific reasons these approaches make sense, while focusing particularly on problems inherent in the idea of "representations."

Regarding psychoanalytic practice, I have further described how remembering of unconscious elements is facilitated by free association, attention to "total communication" (especially its easily overlooked nonverbal component), and allowance for "priming." I have speculated that what neuroscientists call priming is the same phenomenon that psychoanalysts call transference and cognitive psychologists label judging similarity and transferring knowledge. In addition I have wondered if the process of deepening and systematization of such personal knowledge bases of mind and brain might not coincide with what analysts consider movement towards cohesion of the self. In this way I have tried to show the advantage of nonrepresentational models of learning.

Most importantly I have suggested why anxiety is antithetical to learning. All the strategies to facilitate learning readiness would seem to be effective because of their impact on the creation of enlarged circuits within the brain, and the consolidation of these circuits. Anxiety disrupts neural networks.

Eventually we will better understand what determines "learning windows" for certain kinds of learning and improve our ability to facilitate the acquisition of genuine knowledge. For the moment, however, there is a strong suspicion that the creation and recreation of concrete, sensory experiences within the context of a flexible psychoanalytic setting is not only important for the patient's discovery and experience of the phenomenon of transference and for feeling supported and/or understood, but also a decisive part of the mind–brain's method of tapping its knowledge and capacities for particular conceptual tasks. Learning always requires the activation of working memory. The psychoanalytic technique of free association greatly favors this activation of working memory. Such learning and development within psychoanalysis clearly also involves "judging similarity" and "transferring knowledge between content domains," mental processes we need to better understand if our problem-solving techniques are ever to improve.

CHAPTER FOURTEEN

What the amygdala, hippocampus, and ECN teach clinical psychoanalysis

Fred Levin

It seems appropriate, before delving into further psycho-analytical clinical recommendations, to review some recent research on the limbic system, particularly the amygdala and the hippocampus (and some closely related structures) since these appear to contribute decisively to our processing of emotions, a subject near and dear to psychoanalysis. One issue to be aware of, however, is that neuroscience scholars currently differ on what is properly included in the limbic system anatomically (Ledoux, 1996). Therefore many will wish to learn more about such details, as follows.

Let me begin with a fascinating article on Phineas Gage (Damasio, Grabowski, Frank, Galaburda, & Damasio, 1994), the colorful railroad worker of the last century who was unlucky enough to have a explosion blow a hole in his head and yet to survive! Since Gage's damaged skull was donated posthumously to Harvard Medical School, Damasio and colleagues used various means to study Gage's brain, and confirmed that Gage's injury most certainly involved damage to the ventral medial frontal lobe of his brain. This supports the view that it was ventral medial frontal lobe damage that played a role in Gage's post injury personality changes, including his trouble attending and his tendency towards socially inappropriate behavior. Such behavioral–anatomical correlations can prove decisive in verifying hypotheses regarding neurological functional units.

In separate articles, one in the *New York Times* (Blakeslee, December 18, 1994) reporting on work originally appearing in *Nature* by John Allman of the California Institute of Technology, and another in *Science* by the Damasio group, then of the University of Iowa (Bechara et al., 1995) patients are described who have sustained specific injuries to the amygdala and hippocampus. The amygdala and hippocampus are bilateral structures that connect to the ventral medial frontal lobe, and a problem has been to differentiate the functional contributions of the amygdala's and hippocampuses from that of the frontal lobe itself.

The *New York Times* (Blakeslee, 1994) report describes SM, an unusual woman patient who suffered bilateral damage to her amygdala and became unable to experience fear either on the faces of others or in herself. SM was also studied at Iowa by the Damasio group and is in fact one of the subjects in the *Science* article cited above (Bechara et al.). SM could recognize most feelings: happiness, surprise, sadness, and anger for example, but not fear. The contrast between SM's successful recognition of faces and her failure to identify their associated feeling states neatly demonstrates how facial analysis must involve multiple modules (cf. how the visual analysis system contains separate modules for analyzing form, color, and movement).

But even more fascinating is a particular "double dissociation of conditioning and declarative knowledge relative to the amygdala and hippocampus" (Bechara et al., p. 1115) which appears in the research studies on SM and other similarly injured patients. To quote the authors:

> A patient [SM] with selective bilateral damage to the amygdala did not acquire conditioned autonomic [fear] responses to visual or auditory stimuli, but did acquire declarative facts about which visual and auditory stimuli were paired with the unconditioned stimulus. By contrast, a [different] patient with selective bilateral damage to the hippocampus failed to acquire the facts but did acquire the conditioning. Finally, a [still different] patient with

bilateral damage to both amygdalas and hippocampal formations acquired neither the conditioning nor the facts. [Bechara et al., p. 1115]

This means that the amygdala is a critical part of the circuit for experiencing fear in others and identifying fear in ourselves. Without an intact amygdala bilaterally we retain only the dry factual information relating to particular scary experiences, but we do not learn (i.e., we do not become conditioned) to avoid these dangers in the future. In contrast, the hippocampus is a critical part of the circuit for acquiring the avoidance reaction (conditioning) to danger, but without a properly functioning hippocampus bilaterally we cannot preserve in memory the declarative facts associated with the danger situation. Thus, *the act of undergoing fear conditioning and the act of forming a memory of the circumstances that create a specific fear situation are dissociable from each other*. In other words, fear conditioning (aversive learning) and declarative memory for fear- laden experiences are handled by significantly different circuits.

As LeDoux (1996) puts it (1) the amygdala is wired as a rapid response/danger detection system (if you see a snake in the woods it is the amygdala that prompts you to escape from it as fast as you can), while (2) the hippocampus is wired to facilitate learning danger avoidance (that is, fear conditioning). Ultimately, both kinds of reaction patterns are required for successful adaptation; the conditioning (i.e., the formation of traumatizing memories), however, can also disrupt one's life at a later date (see below).

Still another way of describing these facts is to say the hippocampus relates to declarative (also called explicit or semantic) memory while the amygdala is responsible for procedural (also called implicit or episodic) memory. Let me elaborate on amygdala–hippocampal relations further by citing LeDoux (1996) a little more. According to LeDoux, the perirhinal cortex supplies the amygdala with some of its memories. The hippocampus sends input to the amygdala regarding context (for example, if seen in a zoo a snake is unlikely to represent danger, but if seen in the woods a snake might very well signify danger). The sensory cortex along with the sensory thalamus sends information to the amygdala regarding object identification. And the prefrontal cortex is responsible for sending extinction signals to the amygdala which allow for the possibility of aborting an initial reaction to what is judged to be a fearful situation.

Given the prefrontal cortical role in extinction signaling, it should be clear that if the prefrontal cortex is damaged and not functioning properly (as was the case with Phineas Gage after his accident) it may become difficult or impossible for a person to extinguish their initial reactions to many experiences and they may sometimes become trapped in perseveration or impulsiveness. There are thus potential causal relationships between disorders of the prefrontal cortex, parts of the limbic system, and a variety of illnesses seen psychoanalytically including anxiety states, phobia, impulsive disorder, obsessive–compulsive disorder (OCD), and other closely related conditions. Psychoanalytic and neuroscientific frameworks are thus potentially complementary in the following ways. First, psychoanalysis has the power to identify the connecting linkages that have gotten "lost" between affective (fear) responses and the situations which gave birth to them, thus facilitating the mastery of trauma. Second, neuroscience can specify the nature of the "memory" disturbance system involved in particular illnesses, giving important clues to the analyst regarding potentially useful insights and interventions. This latter perspective is elaborated upon in what follows.

Conditioning creates linkages that are held in association and capable of revival at later dates. Understanding implicit versus explicit memory systems becomes a specific critical goal for psychoanalysis as it attempts to approach the understanding and extinction of unconscious fears (involving the implicit–procedural–episodic memory system) and their conscious mastery (also see Siegel, 1995 and Gillett, 1996) usually through a discovery process that involves what is called working through. Interestingly, fear conditioning, according to LeDoux (1996), occurs at each level of the evolutionary ladder from fruit flies to fish to man. So far as we know, however, *only mankind has the capacity to exploit this knowledge of mind and brain and alter intentionally its patterns of conditioning.*

The topic of escaping from the unconscious consequences of painful memories is the subject of Daniel Alkon's book *Memory's Voice*, reviewed in the *Minneapolis Star-Tribune* by Jim Dawson (1993). Alkon writes both as head of the Neural Systems Laboratory at the National Institute of Health and as the childhood friend of a woman who committed suicide as a consequence of repeated child abuse. As analysts can affirm, Alkon comments that the "templates" formed from such early formative experiences can be very difficult to attenuate (Dawson, p. 5B). Such templates or scripts clearly involve the implicit or procedural memory systems mentioned above.

Before making some clinical suggestions, I wish to note one further area of neurocognitive research that bears indirectly on the subject of modifying unconscious memory "templates." Michael Posner and his collaborators (Posner & Raichle, 1994; Posner & Rothbart, 1994a,b), through their work on human attentional systems, describe some neural functions that psychoanalysis might conceivably exploit. According to Posner (Posner & Raichle, 1994), attention is controlled by an anterior and a posterior attentional system. The anterior system involves the frontal cortex and the anterior cingulate. The poster system involves the posterior parietal cortex, thalamus (pulvinar), and midbrain (superior colliculus).

Posner's research on attention has already been covered in Chapters Eight, Nine, and Ten, hence I will make only a small number of points. First, in Posner's opinion the anterior attentional system is essentially an explicit memory system, whereas the posterior attentional system is based upon implicit memory mechanisms. Therefore, my second point is that our goal of understanding implicit, that is, procedural memory further can be simplified by shifting our attention temporarily to Posner's description of the posterior attentional system.

So let us examine the posterior attentional system in somewhat more detail. This posterior system can be seen (in a simplified version) as accomplishing at least three fundamental operations. The first operation is "disengaging" from objects of interest, which is required for new objects of interest to come to our attention. For the "disengage" order the parietal cortex is crucial. The second operation is "cueing" and is based upon the superior colliculus. Cueing involves increased alertness to certain locations where objects are expected to occur. "Zooming" in on (also called "amplifying") new objects of interest involves the thalamus (pulvinar) most critically (Posner & Raichle, 1994, Posner & Rothbart, 1994a).

The anterior and posterior systems thus collaborate in a number of complex ways. For example, when handling match/mismatch processing (see Levin, 1991, 1995b), when there is a mismatch occurrence, the anterior system indirect pathway (from cortex via the striatum) tends to down-regulate the anterior system so the posterior system can function more optimally (Posner, 1988). It is further known that the activation of the anterior system increases as the number of "targets" (meaning interesting objects) presented to it increase in particular voluntary tasks (Posner, 1988).

This basically means that parietal lobe lesions create problems in disengaging attention. Injuries to the superior colliculus therefore prolong reaction times causing as well a loss of so-called "inhibition of return" (in which attention increases in the direction of gaze other than where gaze has moved, thus increasing the receptivity to novel stimuli). And pulvinar lesions create problems in engaging or locking onto objects of interest (Posner, 1988).

Psychoanalytic clinical considerations

It will help to now take what has been said about attention and apply it to our clinical work more specifically. Let us start with Posner's ideas. If "inhibition of return" turns out to be a more generalizable phenomenon than merely a property of the system controlling visual cueing switches (that is, if it involves imaging and other sensory modalities as well) then there is an interesting possibility psychoanalysts might be able to confirm: *that patients will be most receptive to novel stimuli immediately after they switch the direction of their "mental gaze."* Therefore, we should attempt to exploit such shifts to see if such events might mark unusual receptivity.

Taking the kinds of attentional system details noted above into account, it seems we might further subtly adjust the way in which we listen to our psychoanalytic patients so as to enhance our facilitating their learning from their own implicit memories. By this I mean that what the psychoanalyst ordinarily considers dynamically unconscious he might instead consider something that belongs to two classes simultaneously: "the dynamic unconscious" and "implicit memory." The latter term "implicit" here implies a particular structure for the unconscious, based upon the properties of the implicit memory system which neuroscience researchers are currently explicating, specifically how items are held in attention (or you might say, some forms of short-term memory).

Consider, for example, the following two additional possibilities noted in the next section, for usefully modifying our psychoanalytic thinking and technique: (1) *If we intentionally reduce the number of "target subjects" which we and the patient are tracking* in the treatment process at a given time, this should help the patient shift from the anterior to the posterior system and with this shift pay greater attention to content of the implicit (unconscious) memory system involved. In fact, reducing "targets" may be what the analytic setting accomplishes *par excellence*. (2) *If we pay more careful attention to the ways in which particular patients disengage, cue, and zoom in on subjects, we may be able to observe telltale clues when these processes are not shifting smoothly.*

In other words, it seems obvious that in general patients should fail to "disengage" their attention when psychological defenses are interfering with free association. Such "attentiveness" may initially invite the conclusion that the patient is deepening an insight-oriented process, but actually he or she may be doing exactly the opposite, burrowing in for the purpose of avoidance. In such circumstances *we can subtly interfere with this defense by reminding the patient of what they seemed headed towards when they fixed upon a partic- ular issue which they hesitate to leave* (but fail to experience emotion- ally or to deepen with insight).

Or consider a patient who engages a topic frequently but over time persistently fails to usefully zoom in on it. This could be evidence of a psychological defense against particular implicit (unconscious) memories connected with the thoughts and feelings the patient is circling; and it could also be evidence that *the patient either has not yet acquired the cognitive skill involved in penetrating a subject, or, this person may suffer from a neural (parietal lobe) deficit which makes zooming in difficult or impossible. He or she may thus require our help to zoom in.*

Elsewhere I have discussed novel yet subtle analytic inter- pretive viewpoints, for example, *the critical importance of sometimes "priming" the patient's (implicit) memories* (Levin, 1991, 1995a,b; see Chapter Two). In this neuroscience review I am essentially re- visiting the interesting subject of when and how to facilitate learn- ing within psychoanalysis. In both cases, however, I am suggesting that it is worth our while to understand as well as possible those neuropsychological mechanisms which pattern the cognition that overlies and conceals painful or traumatic implicit memories.

To do psychoanalytic work it helps to appreciate how conscious (cs) and unconscious (ucs) process connect to each other. Chapters Eight through Ten have covered this subject comprehensively. The essential new idea is that at a critical point in the life of the developing infant, an autonomous decision is made not to proceed along the path that Freud referred to as hallucinatory wish fulfillment, but instead to move towards a shift in mental operation that is a step in the development of the ucs–cs distinction.

This step occurs as the infant chooses signaling its state of thirst/hunger over indulging in memories of previous satisfaction. Shevrin and Opatow argue that although the inner distinction between cs and ucs process is never complete, it nevertheless becomes central for the management of conflict, since the conscious process leads to focusing on reality factors, whereas the ucs process favors pleasure and fantasy, and these two dimensions to experience always both require attention in human affairs.

But as we pointed out in Chapters Eight and Ten, the picture of the same events can also be understood from another perspective. In this view, the infant can be seen as primarily programmed to process experience on the basis of low level, routine attentional mechanisms (what the English neuropsychologist Shallice calls contention scheduling). However, at the time when fantasy is assumed to fail the infant (e.g., not bring the same level of satisfaction as that connected with a real satisfaction, say breast feeding), the infant makes a decisive shift toward higher level attentional mechanisms (according to Posner, it essentially recruits an enlarged attentional system, based around the organizing control of the anterior cingulate cortex[118]). In essence, the infant is dealing with conflict, and it uses the system of executive control, which is equivalent to Freud's system for unconscious versus conscious processing, for conflict resolution. Or one may say, it aims at satisfying its frustrations.

I would like to point out something which may not be so obvious, however, namely, that the same kind of developmental step which the infant makes to begin the cs–ucs differentiation, is continued thenceforth throughout life whenever similar conflicts appear which need to be resolved. In other words, the mind continues to rely upon the executive attentional system, so well described by Posner and his collaborators, to sort out and control behavior, which provides a powerful piece of evidence concerning what conscious and unconscious (in the Freudian sense) are doing. The Freudian cs and ucs are design features of the mind and brain, which exactly parallel the shifts in the executive control system between high and low level processing, and just as Freud thought, attention is one of the major keys to the overall process (Levin, 1997b).

CHAPTER FIFTEEN

What working with the neuropsychiatric patient teaches clinical psychoanalysis*

Fred Levin and Meyer S. Gunther

Introduction

W hat we have to say grows out of our work as clinicians, teachers, and researchers. Specifically, each of us has had the pleasure of working as a member of an interdisciplinary rehabilitation team, one (FML) with the MENDAC[119] Program for the Deaf, the other (MSG) with the Rehabilitation Institute of Chicago. What we have to say in this chapter, however, should complement previous discussions elsewhere in this monograph on specific approaches to psychoanalytic treatment based upon understanding the workings of mind–brain.

Kinds of illness

The literature on analytic approaches to neuropsychiatric cases is highly varied (Christensen, 1992; Forrest, 1994b; Kallert, 1993;

---

* An earlier version of this paper was presented to the International Conference on Neuropsychiatry: Restoring Brain Function, University of Illinois (Chicago), December 1, 1995. Published as Levin and Gunther, 1996.

Kaplan-DeNour & Bauman, 1980; Morozov, 1989a,b; Persinger, 1993; Sandin, Cifu, & Noll, 1994; Soderstrom, Fogelsjoo, Fujl-Meyer, & Stensson, 1988; Stablum, Leonardi, Massoldi, Umiltà, & Morra, 1994). Most rehabilitation cases requiring psychiatric consultation involve patients suffering from acute brain or spinal cord injury from accidents; the next largest group of patients suffers from strokes, malignancies, or neurodegenerative disorders (amyotrophic lateral sclerosis, multiple sclerosis, and the like). A third or miscellaneous group involves brain complications associated with burns or massive soft-tissue and bone trauma, and children and adults with congenital or developmental problems (including such things as deafness, blindness, autism, language or developmental delay, epilepsy, Tourette's Syndrome, etc.).

Our orientation focuses in particular upon two of the patients' experiences: (1) the alteration in capacity to perform the various role activities of daily living because of a deficit, and (2) the way in which conscious and unconscious meanings are attributed by patients to the deficit or its (therapeutic) consequences. One major point is that therapeutic needs, like the resultant psychopathology, generally evolve over time as patients pass from initial onset of symptoms to first stabilization, inevitable collapse, secondary stabilization, and finally chronic adaptation to injury or loss.

The brain injury patient's anxiety following upon their frightening experience of "I have changed catastrophically" is arguably the major clinical management problem in most of these cases. Anxiety often reaches profound levels and is usually associated with substantial disavowal and/or denial of the organic lesion and its significance. This should not surprise us, since the brain is the only organ responsible for protecting us through its vigilance; thus, whenever brain injury interferes with this protective function, it necessarily creates an awesome sense of vulnerability, helplessness, dismay, and confusion. The alteration of the brain also produces a general shift in perception (Iwata, 1996) that will require considerable adaptation.

Our second major approach as the team psychiatrist is assisting the care-givers who might have become enmeshed in unrecognized feeling and reaction patterns (countertransferences), which translate into counterproductive behavior with their patients. Staff (including the psychiatrist) can become impatient, angry, or make overly ambitious plans for the patient which the patient then frustrates.

On the one hand, we might also understand the angry component of this reaction to be a result of projective identification wherein the patient's profound anxiety, helplessness, slowness, or confusion potentially renders the staff temporarily helpless in dealing with the patient. On the other hand, we believe the overambitious component can best be understood as the staff's attempt to establish its own sense of control; that is, to defend against any outbreak of personal helplessness and anxiety evoked by their perception of the patient's illness.

Of course, under optimal circumstances the staff avoids extended immersion in countertransference feelings and behaviors and assumes instead a therapeutic mode of (empathic) listening with acceptance of and genuine appreciation for the patient's feelings about their plight. This acceptance of patient's feelings will always be facilitated by staff's conscious awareness of and curiosity about their own reactions to their patient's suffering.

Summarizing to this point, one key to the successful rehabilitation of the brain damaged patient is for staff to be as tolerant as possible of the patient's anxiety and confusion; to appreciate that the patient's deficits are often in three major spheres more or less simultaneously (neurological, neuro-orthopedic, and cognitive–psychological); to accept the patient's anxiety and emergency defenses as an understandable part of their process of working through feelings of helpless despair; and finally, to recognize that the price any competent staff pays for effective therapeutic engagement with catastrophically ill patients is to become periodically but temporarily emotionally distressed and impaired in their clinical effectiveness (Gunther, 1977, 1994).

Two final points about anger. The first phenomenon is the patient's anger for not being protected from catastrophe. Even competent staff will become the target of such anger, which, of course, is not personally directed against the individual care-giver, but can be vicious. Second, there is the anger felt between staff members themselves, especially around the inevitable disagreements over how best to proceed with any rehabilitation plan for a serious illness. Staff needs to expect both of these angers, and to learn to deal with them constructively rather than personally. Also, as noted above, the staff itself needs considerable emotional support and this should be expected and planned for.

Reaction patterns

In a nutshell, the major psychological target symptoms in the general patient population with neurological deficit can be seen as first and foremost a complex grief reaction for the mental function(s) that either were and are no more (the situation of loss), or for those functions which might have been but never occurred (in the case of developmental deficit). The resulting trauma to the sense of self includes the following to varying degrees: lowered self esteem, despair, depression, shame, frustration, anger (or rage), and massive anxiety or bewilderment. Of course, all of these affects may well be complicated by the expression of concurrent cognitive impairment. In our experience, these grief reactions do not occur in any fixed time sequence in spite of assertions to the contrary by some researchers (Elizabeth Kubler-Ross); rather they often occur more or less "all at once."

Two contrasting case examples will help. Many years ago one of us (FML) saw a middle-aged patient, whom we shall call Mr. Unknown, who came for psychotherapy complaining of anxiety and insomnia. During the history taking something about his hand movements invited us to ask about neurological illness. He explained that he had had a lobotomy about twenty years earlier. He became visibly shaken as he mentioned his life before and after the surgery. Specifically, he had noticed some changes in himself that were hard to describe but obviously frightening. After the session he promised to return for a second session the next day. However, he never came back!

Perhaps it was an error to ask this patient the question that elicited the history of lobotomy before Mr. Unknown felt sufficiently connected to his interlocutor to talk about such things. Possibly he did not feel comfortable enough but did seek out help with someone else. We hope so. But our guess would be that whatever private hell this patient went through he decided on his own that he was too terrified to deal with it in psychotherapy at the time he was seen by us. *Sometimes the changes in self are too much, the pain too great, and the personality or family resources insufficient for the task.* It is good that patients make their own decisions about whether and when to be involved in psychotherapy.

The second example, treated by MG, we shall call the case of the disabled poet, because some of his poems were published. This thirty-eight-year-old married construction worker with a high school education came to Chicago for rehabilitation from a small town out of state after a moderately serious head injury four years earlier. His initial rehabilitative and therapeutic services had been minimal. His family was devoted, though essentially uneducated, and their presence undoubtedly proved therapeutic.

Largely recovered physically, except for periodic head and limb pains, his memory was poor, as was his attention span (which was limited to ten minutes), his abstracting ability, and his ability to manage frustration without tantrums. He would not become dangerous to himself or others; but sometimes he just locked himself in the bathroom until the episode subsided.

In spite of this presentation, however, the poet was able to make use of once weekly psychotherapy. He learned to short-circuit his angry episodes; he developed intellectual controls and some structured withdrawal devices for his anxiety ridden disorganization (for example, by telling himself "soothing stories"), and was able to stop his desperate clinging to his wife, which greatly improved their relationship. How the psychotherapy achieved these accomplishments is debatable, but probably it involved some teaching, some practicing, and a measure of insight. It was also aided by the timely utilization of valium, lithium, and tegretol. Follow-up years later suggested these positive changes were permanent acquisitions.

One of the major problems psychotherapists face with neurological patients is that the alteration in the sense of self co-occurs with varying cognitive limitations in the ability to comprehend and emotionally work through the fact of damage. In other words, as Forrest (1994b) has lucidly summarized, at one extreme patients manifest denial or disavowal of damage as a more or less *mental* (meaning psychological) defense; or intermediately, they may neglect a body part or side as a *neuromental* defense (meaning both a neurological and psychological adaptation to injury); or at the other extreme they may present grosser loss of function, such as hemi-inattention for example, resulting from actual *diminished cortical representation (i.e., mostly a neurological manifestation)*. Yet the patient's ability to comprehend their loss necessarily influences the kind of psychological intervention.

Let us present a third case. Father Paul, a clergyman, was referred for psychoanalysis that began with his concern over a shyness that made it hard for him to deal with social relationships comfortably. He was also depressed and at times fearful of incipient suicidal impulses. Psychoanalysis was started, but five months into treatment he reported feelings of "grayness" that sounded like absence experiences, and a neurological workup was obtained which showed the presence of multifocal epilepsy involving especially the right temporal lobe. On antiepileptic medication the "grayness" disappeared, and now we understood more fully his habit of keeping detailed journals about his daily experiences. In effect Father Paul was using his journals to restore memories erased by epileptic seizures which had been occurring for many years without ever being understood or diagnosed. It is also interesting that there is a known correlation between seizures in the right temporal lobe, such as Father Paul had, and religiosity; his religious attitudes, however, were in no way altered by his epilepsy treatment. The psychoanalysis primarily dealt with the consequences of his having lived for many years with an undiagnosed medical/neurological condition that influenced his experience of himself and others. Over time he began to revise his views with many positive results.

We start brain injured patients in psychoanalytically oriented psychotherapy (or psychoanalysis) gradually, with short sessions and simple concrete compensational interactions, so as not to overload them, building upon whatever foundation of residual abilities each patient has at a given stage of their illness. The generalization here is not to generalize(!); each patient requires a unique plan fabricated for his personal profile of debits and assets—physical, social, cultural, linguistic, familial, economic, etc. Since abilities can and will fluctuate (i.e., during recovery the patient will move through regressive and progressive cycles), it is crucial that therapeutic plans remain flexible from day to day and over longer time frames, slowly moving into dealing with more complex and conflictual issues. Multiple resources may be necessary for working through the inevitable narcissistic injury associated with brain damage: emotional support from family, friends, and the entire rehabilitation team can serve as a kind of emotional "glue" for fragmentable parts of the patient's self. Psychotropic, neuroleptic, antidepressant and other medications may further assist dramatically in reducing emotional extremes and enhancing learning.

In the sections which follow we discuss three elements effecting psychoanalytical interventions with brain injured patients: (1) premorbid factors that effect outcome and technique, (2) general analytic treatment goals, and (3) specific analytic treatment approaches which can be tailored to the needs of particular patients.

Our general conclusion is that analytic treatment at times makes a decisive contribution to recovery, once the life-saving, acute phase medical, neuro-orthopedic, and neurological-neurosurgical efforts have begun. Naturally, there will also be situations in which analytic approaches may not be fruitful, or where it will be much less useful than other interventions. In this sense the utilization of the psychoanalytic component in rehabilitation is a judgment call for the entire team, to be decided without prejudice. Here a caveat seems in order, however: Calling the Fire Department after the entire house is ablaze is not a constructive use of resources. Psychoanalytic assistance is most useful *before* clinical situations reach the levels of crisis or stalemate.

Some of the premorbid factors that influence outcome

Premorbid personality provides decisive assets or debits to the recovery ledger sheet. Optimally one hopes for a patient with built-in effective coping strategies, solid self esteem, a sense of humor, wisdom, and a capacity to learn, including from the circumstance of illness (Kallert, 1993). With luck the patient will also be supported by a network of loving, caring family members and friends (Sandin, Cifu, & Noll, 1994; J. M. Stern, 1985). If present, the patients' prior experience in psychotherapy may further help prepare him or her for collaboration with the rehabilitation team, and for working through their illness emotionally. Unfortunately, these positive factors are frequently lacking in whole or in part and their absence complicates matters considerably.

When beneficial premorbid factors are missing the staff must in essence attempt to provide the missing functions on a temporary basis (i.e., as noted, they become the "glue" in the metaphor of fragmentation). But this implies a staff with adequate training in both technical knowledge and interpersonal skills, together with appropriate capacity for self-exploration, and for empathy. Besides routine acute care tasks, as well as special teaching activities, the staff members must serve as temporary "receptacles" helping to contain the patients' catastrophically intense, painful feelings (as noted earlier).

How to think of goals

The major goal of analytical treatment in the case of the brain injured is to assist optimal recovery of mind and brain, although there will always be significant honest differences among professionals about what this actually means. For example, some have suggested this means assisting the patients' acceptance that their innate goodness has not been destroyed, that is, not to give up hope of recovering significant components of their core sense of self (Block, 1987). This has been described by others as involving the incremental creation of a new self corresponding to the changed body and its altered capacities, but one with value and meaning for the patient (Gunther, 1977, 1994). Others write about "acceptance" as involving optimal contact between former and new identities, that is, maintaining personality consolidation in the face of obvious changes in the mind and brain (Geva & Stern, 1985; Scheidt & Schwind, 1992). Still others focus instead upon giving meaning to the patient's enduring object relationships (J. M. Stern, 1985). Clearly, there is a complex dynamic relationship between self states and object relationships (for example, the state of self and the human context are undoubtedly interrelated markers for episodic memories, which clearly both organize the self and map it onto space and time).

Summarizing, each of the apparently different therapeutic goals noted above can in itself be difficult to achieve, yet there will also be thresholds of achievement in these areas which might make a powerful difference in the patient's life. This stems from the fact that the goals noted each contribute to the larger aim of helping the patient confront a basic human dilemma: Who am I now and what am I worth?

Since the above goals are fairly general, however, we would like to discuss briefly somewhat more specific goals of analytic treatment.

Specific analytic treatment goals

Crisis intervention, careful diagnosis, attention to such things as the side effects of drugs, and gradual transition from support to insight-orientation is where the local therapeutic focus lies (Kallert, 1993; Sandin, Cifu, & Noll, 1994). Tailoring the approach to the specific patient requires detailed knowledge of the patient, his or her illness, culture, family, and particular therapeutic options (Forrest, 1994b; Persinger, 1993). Vocational rehabilitation and family therapy need to be considered where appropriate (Sandin, Cifu, & Noll, 1994). Therapeutically, the use of dream analysis can sometimes be of great help because, perhaps surprisingly, this usually does not require complex cognitive abilities (Geva & Stern, 1985).

Another issue relates to dealing with mortality. The possibility or actuality of impending death needs to be considered where this is on the mind of patient or his family. When the dying person wishes it, he and his family optimally should be supported in discussing this fact, saying good-bye, and finishing up unfinished business as much as this is possible or helpful to them. Sometimes, giving verbal permission to *let go* is most helpful. Alternatively, where the patient has no ability whatsoever to cope with his morbidity or mortality, these individuals still need our respect and support to discuss whatever they can. In other words, some families are not ready to face deficit in or the death of a loved one, and this situation requires the greatest of tact on the part of the medical staff. Remember, except where the patient is virtually unable to make life decisions and/or without family to assist (in which case we really do take over for him or her), our job is not to determine the patient's goals and to implement them whatever; rather, we are charged with helping the patient define and achieve his or her own chosen goals.

A final case example may help here. Ms. Sophie, a sixty-year-old patient developed a brain tumor during the fourth year of her psychoanalysis, shortly before she was about to end treatment. She received radiation therapy, and died about three months following the diagnosis. Incidentally, her diagnosis was made by her ophthalmologist after one of us (FML) sent her back for a repeat examination. What happened was that one day while on the analytic couch she complained that in conducting a routine eye examination her ophthalmologist had prescribed the "wrong" pair of glasses. It became obvious to her analyst that she was complaining about a visual field defect, not a visual acuity problem. She was advised to communicate this possibility to her eye doctor and get reexamined immediately.

Unfortunately, the speedy diagnosis of brain tumor and prompt treatment did not affect her fate and the remainder of her life included a stay in a hospital for radiation therapy. During this time her analyst visited her daily for abbreviated sessions. As death approached she eventually decided to move in with her brother and the brother's family in another city so as to be in a personal and supportive setting that was deeply meaningful to her.

Prior psychoanalytic treatment made it possible for this patient to deal openly with her impending death in a way that satisfied her greatly. Although previously fiercely independent and even some-what isolated, during her terminal illness she was able to let others take care of her and she easily gave and received love from the many friends and family who visited her, including her analyst. Because she was well aware of her impending death, she felt her resolve strengthened to share what life remained for her with others. Her candor opened the door to poignant discussions with all of us that in turn helped her have a sense of finishing up unfinished business. When we attended her funeral it was obvious how much she meant to all of us, and her analyst completed one stage of his own mourning for the dear friend that she had become to him over the years of their work together. It is impossible to forget Sophie, especially such things as her gentle admonitions whenever she noted her analyst making a mistake. She was ever meticulous and took great pride in managing many details in living and in dying.

Discussion

Obviously, much more could be said about the psychoanalytic treatment of neuropsychiatric patients, and what we can learn from it. Social, emotional, cognitive, and biological issues are interwoven in each story of human suffering. The psychoanalyst needs to be thoughtful about finding specific ways to help assuage the pain and promote healing. And of course, he will become quite frustrated along with everyone else when progress is impossible or modest. As John Gedo has put it "[the outcome of specific treatment] is necessarily the outcome of the simultaneous input of the CNS substrate, the social milieu, and so-called mental activities" (Gedo, 1995, p. 2). Or, as Hiroshi Utena (1996) has stated, analytic treatment aims at increasing the patient's freedom of choice, and freedom means maximizing brain function, social support, and the psychological–emotional ways in which we function. How we as psychoanalysts impart such skills and knowledge is, of course, only partially understood (Levin, 1995a,b; Levin & Kent, 1994, 1995; see also Chapter Four). Our detailed attention to all situations in which learning is facilitated, however, is gradually helping us understand how to better and more reliably create learning readiness (see especially Levin & Kent, 1995). We should also point out that at the same time that psychiatrists and analysts are helping neurological patients it is also a fact that neurological patients in analytic treatment are helping psychiatry and psychoanalysis learn about learning and rehabilitation particularly and generally.

Overview

Fred Levin

*M*apping the Mind began with the exploration of three basic correlations. Metaphorical transference interpretations were described, in which the analyst's affectivity was seen to open gates of memory and insight by priming (synchronously activating) the patient's primary cortical association zones for hearing, touch, and vision. Second, evidence was introduced showing that the psychological defenses of disavowal and repression can be defined in terms of right to left and left to right interhemispheric communication blocks, respectively. Third, learning was examined in terms of the brain's plasticity, and more specifically in terms of the cerebellum, which makes substantial contributions to learning. Extending from these discoveries eleven major principles appeared in the book's Overview chapter. These involved the following.

1. The brain's primary function is ordering experience. This involves some arbitrary, complex, yet eminently practical control mechanisms with feedback and feedforward qualities.
2. The brain's core organization involves learning modules that develop over time; these modules also form a hierarchical

structure of memory databases (associative networks) that double as communicative modes.

3. Syntactical language exposure primes the mind–brain, playing a critical role in neuropsychological development. This exposure taps built-in genetic potentials for abstract thinking, native language acquisition, advanced psychological development, and the ability to experience and contribute to one's culture. The primary sources for language exposure include parents, loved ones and friends.

4. Native language and the mind–brain's operating system share a grammar; possibly, what was first used in our species for communication within the brain itself was later adapted for communication with others (or vice versa!). In terms of the evolution of our species, syntactical language is likely built upon the foundation of signing (i.e., gestural, nonverbal) communication.

5. Human learning is a reflection of the capture of experience within the mind–brain's plasticity at various levels (individual neuron, neurons combined into localized networks, enlarged networks, hemisphere operations, whole brain, etc.), and appears to be genetically programmed and environmentally released (see point 3, above). The adequacy of this input is predictable in the species, but random for individuals.

6. Upon use, each mind–brain subsystem manifests its signature; this is potentially identifiable by therapists and researchers, and doing so may prove useful. It may help us gain insight into which anatomical structures are involved in various functional systems. For example, the cerebellum may express itself in awkwardness versus gracefulness, and in the experience of intuition.

7. Memory priming during psychoanalysis downloads procedural memories, activates transferences, and generally helps overcome repression and disavowal. The latter two defenses are likely related to interhemispheric communication blocks (in different directions) that prevent access to episodic memory and its associated affect, respectively. What gets isolated in the mind–brain requires integration into the whole for its activation, otherwise serious deficits can accrue.

8. Transferences accomplish a variety of effects: they bridge the hemispheres; stimulate and/or organize cerebellar-based

archaic memories; activate corticostriatal habit patterns acquired pre-Oedipally; tap lexical systems within the dominant hemisphere; identify gestural and/or prosodic systems bilaterally along with associated affects; and signify the particular "amusicality" that means neurocognitive deficit.

9. What we call abstracting may result from the integration of the experience of sensory input across various different modalities; this includes a mental function called metaphorical thinking based upon comparisons of differing experience. Such internal comparisons between systems are the mind–brain's method for adding depth and breadth to our knowledge bases, just as the creation of three-dimensional visual images is based upon a master image composed out of two slightly but significantly different visual perspectives of the same scene.

10. The prefrontal cortex, basal ganglia, and cerebellum are crucial learning-related mind–brain operating system elements. The operating instructions controlling the mind–brain also seem controllable, under at least some circumstances, by native language, which can specify such things as which hemisphere is used to listen to which sound categories.

11. Psychoanalysis is a method *par excellence* for decoding the various complex meanings of behavior, cognition, and affective patterning. In doing so psychoanalysts make use of language as a semiotic system, not limited to spoken or written syntactical language, that is, something that includes gestures and nonverbal communication (blended into a total communication).

12. In *Psyche and Brain*, the above insights have been reexamined along a number of additional dimensions. The work of Posner is introduced to complement and elaborate upon Ito's conception of the mind–brain operating system, described as an executive control network (ECN) with specifiable anatomy, physiology, and contents. This leads to a reconsideration of the relationship between learning and the various substructures of the ECN. The cerebellum and anterior cingulate clearly contribute decisively to working memory regulation, attentional shifts, the connectedness of conscious and unconscious systems, and general and specific anticipatory functions. But so do the basal ganglia, corpus callosum, hippocampal and amygdalar systems, etc.

Some final comments

Discussion of psychoanalysis and knowledge brought together earlier questions about learning, and dealt with our thinking about databases of mind–brain and their updating in real time. To this end it became necessary to downgrade dated ideas about so-called *internal representations*, along with aging computer analogies to mind–brain, and to upgrade the notion of *expert systems*. This highlights the importance of transfering knowledge between content domains in which experts are those with skill and familiarity in judging similarity or difference (between current and past problems) in specific knowledge areas. Out of such thinking we concluded that what analysts call transference, and neuroscientists call priming, is likely closely related to what psychologists call judging similarity. In this manner we were able to bring together the insights of psychologists, neuroscientists, and psychoanalysts to improve our appreciation of the psychoanalytic transference. Especially useful was Gabriel's work on aversive learning, Hadley's and Kent's on higher level information processing (including that of affect), and Gentner's work on similarity science.

Transference is such a critical area within psychoanalysis that it is likely that our attempt to adequately appreciate what it is doing, as a potentially adaptive pattern in our species, will take generations to unravel. However, a number of advances have been made towards this worthy goal. One, from the consideration of knowledge (versus learning) noted above, is that for transference to result in learning the experiencing subject must exist in a state where beliefs are not part of the mind–brain structure that provides for critical mental intellectual functions; more optimally, beliefs should constitute mere contents of the mind. Otherwise, the individual will not be sufficiently able to even temporarily suspend belief, and therefore, truly consider alternatives and update beliefs according to the best evidence.

A second major advance suggesting the advantages of transference for our species flowed from the considerations of how similarity/difference judgments might be accomplished cognitively with the highest level of efficiency. In this regard, it seemed that transferences might provide economy to decision making through its assumption that superficial matches between present and past persons might lead, upon further computational experience, to the discovery of deeper matches, and that the latter would then allow for successful reenactments and reworking of previous incompleted experiences. In other words, via transference we do not need to perform computationally costly searches for deep similarity; we only need to do so on those matches which already show superficial (transferential) similarity.

The examination of cerebellar and anterior cingulate mechanisms also lead indirectly to further reflection on the role of transference in activating special modalities of working memory, something which appeared likely to be a basic requirement or prestage for learning. In this sense it was suggested that psychoanalysis accomplishes the facilitation of learning (in specific content domains) by activating specific areas of working memory, primarily as a consequence of encouraging free association and spontaneous activity.

All of the above theoretical thinking led to some specific proposals about how best to conduct a clinical analysis in keeping with the apparent organizational features of the mind–brain under discussion. Most specifically, these included such approaches as the following: taking pains to avoid shame (which appears to drastically inactivate learning); dealing first and foremost with what is on the patient's mind (and therefore already activated in his or her working memory); proceeding always from what the patient knows to what is new (i.e., allowing the direction of learning to start from *within* zones of working memory activation rather than from outside of such zones); and learning how best to deal with and respect the patient's *novelty anxiety* (that form of anxiety which merely signals that the mind–brain is being asked to perform in areas of new functioning, ones not yet firmly enough established). Novelty anxiety is most often best dealt with by ignoring it in the sense of not bringing it specifically into the patient's awareness as something to examine.

Work around understanding our analytic patients brings us immediately into repeated contact with the dynamic unconscious (not often enough distinguished from what is merely nonconscious), and raises inevitable questions about how conscious and dynamically unconscious systems are related to each other. Based upon previous considerations raised primarily by Gedo, Ito,

Levin, Olds, Posner, Shevrin, Trevarthen and others, suggestions were made about what the conscious and unconscious systems are contributing individually and collectively. This story is naturally incomplete at present but certain key points were made which should be helpful to clinical work as well as theory construction.

First, consciousness is seen as an evolutionary development which allows us to modify data input at will and in real time when complex situations evolve that our mind–brain deems unlikely to be satisfactorily resolved by routine (contingency) planning. At these times, the mind–brain makes a critical shift, probably under anterior cingulate, basal ganglia, and/or cerebellar control, to a special mode that incorporates additional specific components of the ECN and increases versatility of planning and executing problem-solving functions. This shift brings certain elements of the situation into conscious awareness in a focused manner (i.e., it employs selective attention). One might speculate that the higher level, versatile functions which become potentially available under what the mind–brain deems special circumstances in normal individuals may also be the functions that are most compromised or missing in certain pathological conditions such as ADHD, LD, and autism where more limited or fixed problem solving strategies have become the norm.

Finally, chaos theory was employed to consider mind–brain from a mathematical perspective to better comprehend its awesome complexity. Using this unique perspective it seems that healthy minds are those that are sufficiently complex and/or flexible, so that old solutions are not applied in any routine fashion unless this makes sense. In other words, temporary failures should always result in intelligent shifts in methods of mind–brain operation. In this way the genetic loading that comes with mind–brain becomes optimally "installed" over time.

Last, in our discussion of the work of the late Jerry Sashin, we touched on the importance of the "container" function, which we generally know little about. This function refers to our ability to handle the intensity of affects without deteriorating in our adaptive ability, and this is what gets strengthened in most successful analyses.

Much more could be said about psychoanalysis and mind–brain. There is really no adequate way to briefly capture the essence of the journey traversed in a monograph such as this. I just hope the reader agrees that we have provided some useful ideas about mind–brain, and that focusing upon knowledge of these perspectives helps us form more sensitive and healing partnerships with our patients. And *Emotion and the Psychodynamics of the Cerebellum* (Levin, 2009) will provide still more integrations of the material presented herein. We invite your interest and feedback.

1. For example, the modern trend is to conceptualize mind–brain activity in terms of internal "representations", the nature of which is assumed to be self evident! My contention is that this is not helpful for the advancement of psychoanalytic science (see Chapter Thirteen for details). In its place I favor nonrepresentational, interdisciplinary theories of learning, such as those of Rapaport (1950, 1951a,b) and Gedo (1991a,b,c). Such learning theories reexamine how knowledge is acquired, an ancient epistemological question. Thus, a much more useful perspective is that of "expert systems" (covered in Chapter Four), which at least generates some novel perspectives on the concept of psychoanalytic transference. Regarding transference, I suggest that transference plays a decisive role in the reorganization and deepening of core knowledge systems. Chapter One is based upon such thinking and is elaborated upon in Chapters Four and Thirteen.

2. Gilmore (1994) takes me to task in my theorizing for not (systematically) addressing specific questions within philosophy of science, an approach that obviously appeals to her. Chapter One is a step towards addressing this gap. However, the reader should appreciate that the border between psychoanalysis and philosophy is no more

important than the borders with other disciplines, for example, with cognitive science or neuroscience. What is sophisticated from one perspective may well seem naïve from another, so we must be careful not to privilege one perspective for personal reasons. In fact, this has been my reason for favoring interdisciplinary approaches to psychoanalytic theory in general: it tends to minimize bias.

3. Creativity is such an exceedingly complex topic and as such requires a separate discussion. Let me note, however, Johnson-Laird's (1977) position, with which I agree, that creative thought contrasts with induction and deduction as a third variety of systematic thinking.

4. After coming to the conclusion that I do about the need for temporary suspension of belief for optimal learning to occur, I discovered the following quotation: "Hegel observed that the [person] . . . who is omnipotent cannot acquire knowledge from others. Psychoanalysis confirms that those individuals who cannot relinquish belief in their omnipotence cannot learn from the analyst" (Modell, 1993, p. 103). I also recall reading a book by Paul Reps (1961) called *Zen Flesh, Zen Bones* during my teenage years in which a story is told about a professor who visits a Zen master in Japan. The master pours the visitor tea, but does not stop when the cup is filled. The startled visitor asks why. The master responds that just as you cannot fill up a cup of tea that is already filled, so even a master cannot teach a visitor anything; the visitor must first empty himself. Obviously, my central thesis about one's willingness or ability to empty oneself has multiple roots.

5. Kant adds distinctions "between simple and compound propositions, between affirmative and negative propositions, between universal, particular, and singular propositions, and between [so-called] assertoric, apodictic and problematic propositions (Ryle, 1971, p. 68). Universal propositions, such as "All men are mortal," state something about every member of a class. Singular propositions are about one designated individual of a class, for example, "Socrates is mortal." Particular propositions are about at least one (or some) undesignated members of a class, for example, "Some men are mortal." Apodictic means incontestable or logically certain. Assertoric means "stating something as a fact rather than a mere possibility" (*Webster's Unabridged Dictionary*, s.v., 1958).

6. In fact, things were much worse for women, who ran the risk of being identified as heretics if their ideas and behavior did not conform. Recall the worst of the Inquisition; this continued in many forms for hundreds of years afterward, including within the New World as in the Salem Witch Trials.

7. The study of mind–brain often focuses upon neurons, rather than the glial cells (e.g., astrocytes) which support neurons. Recent imaging, however, is clarifying the stoichiometry (quantitative chemical relations) between neurotransmitter cycling (e.g., glutamate) and the ATP and glucose usage to which this cycling is coupled (Magistretti, Pellerin, Rothman, & Shulman, 1999).

8. Because of this, and the increased occurence of viral infections in the winter months, schizophrenics are more often born in the winter than one would expect by chance alone.

9. See also Schwartz, Stoess, Baxter, Martin, and Phelps (1996).

10. Of course, I am also arguing in general that the cerebellum likely plays a critical role in normal neurophysiology, such as that involved in learning in general (see Chapters Nine and Ten).

11. Modell's position on nature/nurture has actually become quite subtle. For example, although he has long argued the criticality of the holding environment, while seeking the details of exactly what such "holding" entails, he now holds that "the capacity to think metaphorically may have appeared in the evolution of our species before language itself" (Modell, 1997, p. 107; see also Levin, 1980, 1991). Metaphor, as he sees it, is no mere structure of speech; it is part of the developing mind and brain and thus the very means by which cognition itself occurs.

12. The locus coeruleus also plays a role akin to these other structures, for example in influencing the shifts between goal-directed versus exploratory behaviors (Usher, Cohen, Servan-Schreiber, Rajkowksi, & Aston-Jones, 1999).

13. Denial is also referred to as a "repudiation" of reality, which means that the experiencing subject regards some detail of reality as essentially non-existing or totally absent. This is significantly different, however, from two other defenses: disavowal and isolation of affect (see Basch, 1983).

14. For those interested in pursuing this area in more detail, the subject of brain asymmetry has been reviewed in general (Springer & Deutsch, 1981; Levy, 1974; Meyersberg & Post, 1979; Flor-Henry, 1983a,b, 1985) as well as with regard to psychoanalysis (Galin, 1974; Levin & Vuckovich, 1983).

15. Here I am referring to a novel explanation of psychological defense. I had previously considered this a novel definition of defense, but Burness Moore has correctly pointed out that "explanation" is more accurate than "definition." I am referring to types of conflict in which the basic mechanism is a communication block between the two

cerebral hemispheres. However, I do not claim that there might not be other explanations for conflict at a basic science level. Moreover, all conflict is not alleged to be the result of interhemispheric blockage, although some conflicting tendencies may well represent exactly this phenomenon.

16. Palombo (1998) considers the integration of unintegrated mind–brain components the central goal of psychoanalysis.

17. It is important that these new cells occur in the hippocampus, since this structure is responsible for the arrangement of databases of mind–brain (Palomobo, 1998); consequently, a disturbance in even a small number of cells in this supersenstive structure could have profound effects on mind–brain. As Palombo also notes, one of the key differences between us and other animals is our extensive ability to rearrange databases, under hippocampal control.

18. The research reported by Kempermann, by Gage and others from the Salk Institute, and from Goteborg, Sweden (P.S. Ericksson, E. Perlifieva, T. Bjork-Ericksson, and A.-M. Alborn) indicates that new cells have been identified in adult human brains, which has been a great surprise. This is very much different than the appearance of new glial cells, which is nothing special. In separate but related research Marshall (1998) and Gearhart (1998) have further demonstrated that stem cells can be grown in vitro which, under the right conditions, can differentiate into various specialized cells and tissues, including brain cells. In other words, these are multipotential stem cells, and their exploitation might eventually become the basis of replacing damaged brain cells, or grafting other organs (transplantation) far beyond what is possible now. We are living in exciting times!

19. Although it is beyond the scope of the present discussion, it is worth mentioning some experiments on so-called IEGs or immediate-early genes in spontaneous wakefulness and in sleep (Pompeiano, Cirelli, & Tononi, 1994), for what they contribute to understanding memory and other basic mind–brain processes. These studies show that IEGs can activate or inactivate various other genes such as c-fos, NGFI-A mRNA, and protein J. By carefully identifying which sleep-related genes are activated and which not, and then elucidating their functions, it becomes possible to accomplish such things as determining the true function of sleep once and for all. This is a very clever approach.

But there is another important reason for studying immediate-early gene activation, such as that of c-fos. We know that each of us has a biological clock located in our suprachiasmic nucleus, which is reset when light falls on our retinas. Morris, Viswanathan, Kuhlman, Davis, and Weltz (1998) have shown that the mechanism involved is that light ". . . induces . . . early response elements [such as] c-fos (and other IEG's, for example, nur77 and egr-3, a zinc finger transcription factor not previously identified in this part of the brain" (p. 1427). This means that some very basic processes in the brain involve gene activation. For example, Abel, Martin, Bartsch, and Kandel (1998) show that genes are activatable by neuronal activity itself. Thus, the molecular basis of memory may well hinge on the balance between chemical factors that *establish* and those which *inhibit* synaptic plasticity (*ibid.*, p. 338): this includes substances such as PKA and CREB (namely, cAMP-dependent protein kinase A, and cyclic adenosine monophosphate response element-binding protein).

20. A fascinating aspect of brain research deals with the narrower question of exactly how it is that environment and genetic loading interact. The key is appreciating the role of voluntary motion. Any voluntary action always simultaneously serves as a test of one's hypothesis about (a particular aspect of) the world (Jeannerod, 1985; see also Levin, 1993) and therefore leads ultimately to the defining and refinding of internal self-in-the-world models. Also, some maps of the world are literally etched into the brain, as can be seen from the work of Merzenich and colleagues (1984).

21. Later in this monograph I speculate that along with the cerebellum, the anterior cingulate and basal ganglia seem critically involved in such neural control.

22. Those interested in a more complete discussion of these models of Gedo and others will appreciate Wilson & Gedo, 1993, which gives a synopsis of their background, implications, and application.

23. The reader is also referred to other advances which are beyond the scope of this brief summary chapter, such as Levin & Kent, 1995; Levin, 1995a,b. These take up in considerable detail specific mind–brain integrations regarding such matters as the relationship between free association and learning, and the role of transference in expanding databases of mind and brain.

24. Note the identity between phase space in Chapter Five, and our expression system input space in the present chapter. We are really not attempting to confuse the reader, although sometimes we appear to have this intention! There are simply a number of expressions for describing a theoretical or virtual space in which variables interact.

25. I wish to thank Daniel Levin, Dennise Jarrard, John E. Gedo, Arnold Richards, David Forrest, and Meyer Gunther for their insightful suggestions. Versions of this paper have been presented to meetings of the American Psychoanalytic Association, May 19, 1994, the Psyche '94 International Conference at Osaka University Medical School, Osaka, Japan, October 6, 1994, the Houston Psychoanalytic Society, October 12, 1994, the Chicago Medical School, August 17, 1995, and the Chicago Institute for Psychoanalysis, October 30, 1996.

26. I am in no way asserting that transference is some variety of regression in the service of the ego. The analysis of the function of transference is far too complex to be characterized in such a reductionistic way.

27. The arguments expressed here are subject to quite a number of logical objections. For example, insects choosing webs could also be seen as selecting for the discovery of new varieties of flowers where the cost in death of some insects is tolerable from the viewpoint of species adaptation. So-called perceptual errors are extensively discussed in the psychological literature on top-down processing, object representation (including prototype theory), and learning theory. An in-depth foray into these topics, however, is beyond the conceptual boundaries of this chapter.

28. Assuming *a priori* that there is an intrinsic contradiction between the adaptive and the conflictual view of transference would be similar to assuming that there must be an intrinsic contradiction between the adaptive and the structural psychoanalytical points of view. Yet as Hartmann (1939) suggests, the adaptive perspective is merely a complementary framework to the perspective emphasizing dynamics (drive) and structure (defense) (see also Rapaport & Gill, 1967).

29. The regression occurs not in ego functions (i.e., it is not to be thought of as involving cognition), but instead involves such variables as false vs. true self attributes. In general, however, Freud referred to three kinds of regression, indicating, respectively, a move toward what is older (in time), more primitive (in form), or closer to sensory experience (so-called "formal regression") (Freud, 1900a, p. 548).

30. The early work of Freud shows interesting connections to some of these ideas. Freud (1900a) wrote of associations that he called the linkage of perceptions in memory that they were based on two factors, simultaneity and similarity. In the Freudian system of chapter seven there are two subsystems—one linked to perception but lacking memory; the other possessing memory but no perceptual capability.

The subsystem Freud (1900a) called "pcpt" in his picket fence reflex-arc model (pp. 537–538) is linked to consciousness and might well correspond with what is currently known as working memory, really a variety of short-term memory. The reader will appreciate that working memory is one crucial aspect of the transference phenomenon as highlighted in this paper. Freud's second system (in the same picket fence model) relates to long-term memories and the psychoanalytic unconscious.

Freud also discusses judgments of similarity both in *Psychopathology of Everyday Life* (1901b) and in *Jokes and Their Relationship to the Unconscious* (1905a). In each of these texts it is clear that Freud is postulating a topographic model in which interconnected but independent systems of representation contribute to mind–brain function. Seen retrospectively, Freud's model resembles a neural network of specialized nodes. Sirigu and Grafman (1996) demonstrate that episodic (personal) memory is, as Freud surmised, a product of the integration of various interconnected specialized nodal subsystems of memory. The independence of nodal centers is proven by the dissociability of the specific mental functions they subserve. For example, in episodic memory impairment the "who," "when," "where," and "what" of experience can be independently eliminated.

31. Wilson and Weinstein (1996) believe that transferences allow the opportunity for better resolution of "early disregulating experiences"; they state that optimally, for analytic treatment to work, "the analyst strives . . . to be inside the ZPD yet outside the transference" (p. 167). By "outside the transference" they mean that the analyst does not enter into the reliving, except to a minor degree; by "inside the ZPD" they mean that the analyst operates in ways that optimize learning by means of co-constructing with the analysand the "ZPD setting" (pp. 189–190). By "ZPD" and "ZPD setting", the authors are referring to a modified view of the original Vygotsky concept as follows: "processes that beget the differences between an analysand's ability to advantageously make use of the dyadic nature of the clinical situation as contrasted with solitary introspection or self-analysis, in order to acquire insight and capacities that promote self-knowledge and ultimately self-regulation" (p. 171). To Wilson and Weinstein, psychoanalysis requires a transference object, and all insight occurs within the mental world of object relationships. This internal world of related self and objects is "the ZPD setting" (p. 171).

32. According to Stern, people with developmental deficits also tend to have night terrors, contact with the structuralizing other person can

be seen as the key to what is clearly adaptive. In this way Stern reached a point (of understanding structuralization through self–self-object interaction) similar to that reached by Kohut, but from a neuro-physiological starting point.

33. The similarity of the three domains—psychoanalysis, cognitive science, and neuroscience—is supported by at least three levels of evidence. The first involves comparing subprocesses and properties. From this perspective the defining characteristics of transference (displacement of feelings/behavior from old to new figures), judging similarity (comparing patterns on the basis of superficial or deep structural similarity), and priming memory (stimulus-evoked responses in which the new reads out the old pattern) are noted to very closely resemble each other. The second level of evidence comes from work such as that of Gabriel, Vogt, Kubota, Poremba, and Kang (1991) on avoidance learning in rabbits, which shows that their reac-tions to predictive clues elicits established responses in the limbic thalamus and posterior cingulate cortex. Most interesting, Gabriel and colleagues have been able to identify the electroencephalic signa-ture of particular learned responses and to track it from one brain area to another, thus demonstrating that similarity matching and learning responses are connected concretely (and not just abstractly) in mind–brain. A third line of evidence comes from Hadley's conceptual work on the organization of the limbic system. According to Hadley (1992), two basic organizing principles are involved in any system of goal selection or motivation: (1) the maintaining of familiar (i.e., simi-lar) neural firing patterns and (2) the use of pleasure–pain steering signals in a matching–mismatching process. Examination of the particular hierarchical organization of the limbic system shows strong circumstantial evidence that the kind of learning that we call trans-ferential most likely involves making comparisons and integrations at multiple sites within memory, In other words, the limbic circuit seems uniquely poised to capitalize on judgments of similarity and differ-ence at various levels of abstraction (for an amplification of these ideas, see Levin and Kent, 1995, pp. 120–127).

34. By *working memory* I mean that stage in the processing of information that actively maintains short-term memory (Ungerleider, 1995). In this stage, approximately 7±2 chunks of information are handled during a brief period (about half a minute), after which they either begin fixation into long-term memory and become retrievable (Siegel, 1995) or are discarded. Cells that maintain cues and thus support

working memory "have been found in the inferior temporal cortex (visual patterns or color cues), the premotor cortex (cues for particular responses), and the prefrontal cortex (all types of cues)" (Ungerleider, 1995, p. 774). The functional significance of working memory is that it provides a mechanism for delayed responses and for adjusting the data stored.

35. The implication is that transference is its own motivator in the sense that transference refers to a built-in pattern that impels us to engage in a particular type of similarity judging, memory priming pattern of behavior.

36. What Lassen means by this is that when we are thinking spontaneously, each area devoted to a particular sensory modality aspect of our experience activates only what is necessary for the manipulation of the data in the memory involved (in other words, so-called working memory). But there is no corresponding activation of connected areas that are responsible for creating the memory in the first place. Thus, certain kinds of recollection (as against perception) are better suited for the rearrangement of data than for its recording.

37. Regarding points P-1 and P-2, perhaps a better way to explain the situation would be to say that when we attempt to make a transference interpretation from point P-2 we are outside the zone of activated working memory and that clinically such efforts are therefore more likely to result in anxiety and nonrecognition. This will make integration of the new knowledge difficult or impossible. By contrast, if we attempt a transference interpretation from point P-1, we are inside a zone of activated working memory and learning will tend to proceed naturally and easily.

38. Forrest (personal communication) points out that working memory may also involve a component of planning, assembling, and higher-order thinking (in this he is supported by the research of Patricia Goldman Rakic). Essentially, the ability to think of seven or so items at once facilitates thought but probably does not account entirely for the contribution of working memory. Forrest adds, for example, that creative thinking must have much of the brain percolating with hovering elements of thought, whereas working memory includes some kind of critical gating function. My own sense of the matter is that working memory is critically tied to consciousness, a subject I discuss in some detail in Levin (1997b).

39. Forrest (1996b) reviews King and Pribram's 1995 book on consciousness mechanisms, a topic different from that of this essay. In his

review, Forrest notes Searle's position that the following features of consciousness need to be accounted for: "subjectivity, unity, intentionality, attention, gestalt, familiarity, mood, and situatedness" (p. 1495).

40. Rapaport (1951a) summarizes Freud's views on consciousness as follows: (a) "it is the sense organ for the perception of psychic qualities, the objects of which are excitations of the extero- and interoceptors"; (b) it can be aroused but has no memory function; (c) it is the effect of attention cathexis (that is, it uses energy at the disposal of the ego); (d) attention cathexis is regulated early in development by the pleasure principle and later by the reality principle; (e) attention cathexis can serve repression (i.e., defense) or (as a hypercathexis) raise ideas into consciousness (p. 335, n. 14).

41. There is no space for a detailed elaboration and support of my general assertion about hypercomplexity, so let me use two clinical examples as an illustration of the kind of subtle complexity I am describing, and attempt to illustrate how conscious mechanisms invariably play a role in hypercomplex variables. Balint (1987) describes a patient who looked to the world and himself as though he was there (i.e., alert and involved consciously) when he really was only very partially conscious of his activities, mental and other. She points out how this was discovered clinically, and notes that Freud indicated that consciousness requires a specification of its level, which can vary from coma to vigilance. A patient of mine and I discovered in him a mental state to which he was habituated and in which his consciousness was significantly diminished, although he looked quite normal otherwise. Only he and I understood how, during these periods, he retreated from conscious awareness of feelings, and also from consciousness of the fact of his retreat. And it took a lot of analytic work to piece together what these defensive maneuvers protected him from. I would contend that experience such as this is not uncommon, but that discussions of such phenomena are unlikely to be studied by any discipline other than psychoanalysis.

42. Those familiar with the ECN extensions as reviewed in Chapter Six may wish to jump to the following section.

43. Levin and Vuckovich (1983) have speculated that psychoanalysis is perfectly designed to accomplish such a task, as, for example, when we overcome so-called horizontal and vertical splits in the ego (conditions which they conceptualize as disavowal, i.e., right-to-left, and repression, i.e., left-to-right interhemispheric communication blocks).

44. Our idea coincides with a paper of Opatow (1998) cited by Shevrin (1998a). Opatow begins with imagining the situation of the infant that Freud discusses, hallucinating wish fulfillment. Assume the infant has fed at mother's breast, and is now imagining doing so again, that is, hallucinating (imagining) the breast. He or she is feeling hungry, yet associating to the source of food, softness, and comfort in the arms of mother. However, the pleasure in the imagery of being at mother's breast does not satisfy, that is, it is not the same as really being there, and it also does not last. After a period of time frustration ensues, and the familiar distress signals begin which signal the mother to the infant's need to have an actual feeding. However, if these cycles are repeated sufficiently, Opatow argues, at some point a momentous decision is made by the infant developmentally: "*it negates the entire mental mode of hallucinating (imagining) wish fulfillment, not simply individual instances of doing so . . .*" and, as Opatow puts it (cited by Shevrin) "*at this juncture both consciousness and the unconscious are born*" (Shevrin, 1998a, p. 11). The unconscious thus begins as a mental set associated with the negation of the mode of hallucinated wish fulfillment, yet still guided by what Freud called the pleasure principle. In contrast, consciousness continues under what Freud called the reality principle. Opatow states clearly, however, and this seems correct clinically, that these two mental domains are not clearly demarcated, and thus remain mixed to partial degrees forever, with unconscious elements continually influencing behavior via transference, especially when wishes are at variance with reality "and the ability to obtain current appropriate satisfaction is impaired" (Shevrin, 1998a) and where conscious events or subliminally perceived events influence the unconscious.

From the perspective of Posner, and especially Shallice, in our opinion, the developing young mind operates with a hovering attention, and so long as ordinary wishes become satisfied without difficult delays, it operates using fairly low level reflex type attentional mechanisms. However, as a consequence of significant (excessive) frustration, there begins to occur a decisive shift: the infant becomes capable of shifting the attentional system from low level contingency planning to high level executive control, something it accomplishes by briefly expanding the executive control network. At this moment, what comes into existence is the distinction between consciousness and the unconscious, because the infant's problems of matching inner needs with outer realities requires consciousness for its capacity to take reality into account, and the unconscious to properly reflect and protect wishes and needs. Clearly, conflicts of all sorts are a continuing possibility, and require an adaptive repertoire fulfilled by all subsequent personality development.

45. Recent research by Usher, Cohen, Servan-Schreiber, Rajkowski, and Aston-Jones (1999) indicates that the locus coeruleus (LC) may also play a role in attentional shifts ". . . in exploratory behavior and responsiveness to novelty . . ." (p. 554, fn. 27). By this means the LC "may mediate shifts between [these modes] . . ." (*ibid.*). It is difficult to know, however, if such shifts (in novelty) are really comparable to the kind of shifts discussed above (in relation to difficulty and novelty). It appears, nevertheless, that considerable redundancy is built in to the mind–brain, so the multiple structures noted may be performing essentially the same function or at least complementing each other in the operation of the ECN.

46. See Tranel and Damasio (1985).

47. Thanks to Michael I. Posner for his comments on this and the subsequent chapter.

48. The second part of this paper is called "The conundrum of conscious–unconscious relations: Part 2—The tagging of memory, the dynamic unconscious, and the executive control network".

49. The first concerns Shevrin and colleagues' work (Shevrin, 1997a; Shevrin, Bond, Brakel, Hertel, & Williams, 1996) identifying an EEG signature of unconscious processing, and what functions the unconscious and conscious systems appear to contribute to the overall neural network. The second concerns research by Posner (Posner, 1994; Posner & Raichle, 1994) on the executive control network (ECN). The third identifies research by Gedo (1991a,b, 1993a,b, 1996a,b, especially Chapters Five and the Epilogue, 1997; also see Schore, 1997), and by Levin (1991, 1997a,b,c) in search of a psychoanalytic theory of learning. The fourth highlights Trevarthen's research on consciousness (1975, 1979, 1984, 1985, 1989, 1990, 1993, 1995, 1997), including the idea of consciousness as the awareness of the motivations of others. Trevarthen's approach is based upon the premise that self-organizing principles of brain underlie caretaker–infant engagement (Barry, 1987, 1998, 2000, p. 297; see also Roose, 1994; Shevrin, 1997b).

50. An example of this complexity is seen in the multiplicity of criticisms Allen (1998) raises against the work of Baars (1988), another recognized expert in the field of consciousness research.

51. (1) Arousal is the level of alertness (varying from coma to hyperalertness), usually described as controlled by the reticular activating system (but also influenced by the executive control network (ECN) as described by Posner (1994); (2) vigilance we believe refers to maintaining the state of alertness, a function related to the locus coeruleus release of norepinephrine (NE) and the effect of this messenger particularly on the right frontal lobe (see Posner & Raichle, 1994); (3), orienting, as concerns the visual system, involves moving the eyes to a location in response to some cue, and this results from enhanced activity in the superior colliculus, the pulvinar (thalamus), and parietal lobe (Posner & Raichle, 1994, pp. 166–167); selection refers to picking an object to foveate from among a number of choices, which Posner & Raichle (p. 49) describe as the product of series of steps involving cueing, alerting, interrupting, localizing, disengaging, moving to a new target, and inhibition; (4) shifting, refers to shifting gaze from one target to another, involving a disengage, move, engage sequence, under the influence of the same neural structures noted above under the heading of orienting.

52. Since signals compete for our attention in consciousness, only some elements of perception could possibly win out; from a psychoanalytic perspective, these are no doubt chosen based upon deeper goals, often totally unconscious (see Levin, 1997d; Sandler, 1996). In other words, our interest at any given time is selectively expressive of our deep unconscious motivational state. For example, a mother will selectively hear her own child, even while sleeping. And if our brain decides that the time to eat is approaching, instructions are relayed to various sense organs and we begin to investigate the availability of food. Similarly, if we are sexually aroused, as a current priority, our superficial behavior will subtly reflect this desire.

53. One of us (JEG) had a clinical experience with a patient (who would have been classified in the past as a "bad" hysteric) who avoided the awareness of threats by literal flight, syncope, or sleep. She enacted this out on occasion by falling asleep on her analyst's couch, which felt breast-like to her, and these enactments were not unconscious because at such times she always dreamt of these events and was very much aware of her self-state.

54. Modern psychoanalysis has also developed a complex view of affects, including their role as motivators (Roose, 1994). But as we stated at the outset of our paper, sorting out the role of consciousness, motivation, and affect, all clearly closely related, is beyond the scope of any brief discussion.

55. The best example of inner-directed focus would be that desirable distribution of attention which we use in the process of associating in psychoanalysis.

56. Gerald Edelman (1998; see also Levin, 2000a), working some of the same ground, focuses upon what he calls re-entry, by which he means complexity in the form of some concentration of connectedness, based upon the linkage between internal mental/brain models, or, we would speculate, on the basis of two other potential mechanisms: the feedback provided by the whole brain inputting the output of part of itself, or, the connection with other brains, so that each brain's output becomes input for otherwise unconnected parts of the both brains. This latter mechanism underscores the importance we are placing generally in consciousness as awareness of the consciousness of others.

57. An example of convergence might be the following, as regards the function of consciousness. When we are re-presenting information to ourselves as a stage in information processing, there is good reason to believe that we are receiving critical information from a number of divergent sources, which in essence provide what in psychology are called associations, namely input from various association cortex including the following: the corpus callosum (which connects parallel architechtonic units in the different hemispheres), the prefrontal and various other related areas of cortex (so-called working memory), the cerebellum (where various models of the self-in-the-world are stored and related to each other), and the anterior cingulate, described by Posner as having a critical role in orchestrating various kinds of complexity.

58. The amygdalas are quite complex: they contain testosterone receptors and play a role in both sexes regarding the expression of sexuality. In addition, they mediate stress; not only is a major output from the amygdala directed to the hypothalamus, but studies of brain receptors for substance P and its antagonists have identified that "... the amygdala in particular ... [is] a potential site for the action of established antidepressant drugs" (Kramer et al., 1998, p. 1643). Levin (1997f) has also reviewed some additional cognitive aspects of the amygdala of interest to psychoanalysis.

59. The concept of "creativity" has this same characteristic of a portmanteau!

60. In the meantime, however, it is possible to construct proto-neurophysiological models (Rubinstein, 1997) to accommodate the clinical data of psychoanalysis.

61. Later in this essay we will elaborate on our idea that the conscious system helps the unconscious system make necessary changes in memory that constitute learning. This contribution of consciousness to the interpretation of nonsymbolic self-organization might also be conceptualized as a two-step process, more or less following Ito's suggestions for learning within the skeletomuscular system.

62. Here Ito is referring to his "self-in-the-world model" without using this terminology, to keep it more general (see Levin, 1991 for many citations of Ito's pioneering work).

63. We wish to note that Allen, Buxton, Wong, and Courchesne (1997) have determined that the cerebellum also functions to anticipate what will happen next, and is alerted whenever this computation fails to guess correctly. It would be interesting if this implies that the learning of the cerebellum grows out of anticipation that may also express a wish, and not only a probability judgment.

64. As an aside, philosophically "will" was introduced by Aristotle; however, recent work denies the cogency of such a category (Toulmin, 1975). Gazzaniga has made clear his belief that the sense that we direct our actions is largely a fiction and the result of the interpreter function of our left hemisphere. Libet (1993, cited in Brakel & Snodgrass, 1998) has evidence that all events begin non-consciously in that the timing of events which become conscious is consistently antedated 500 ms, the time required from initiation (or stimulation) until the recognition in consciousness. ". . . The time between the awareness of a conscious wish to act and the action allows time for psychological modification, including conscious vetoing, repression, and various transformations and distortions" (Brakel & Snodgrass, 1988, p. 908).

65. At first, it would seem that the problem of locating *will* might be addressed by respecting that *will* is a network property of the entire brain itself. This position, however, avoids committing oneself to what subsystem is determinative. It should be clear that this question is one of the more difficult issues facing us. The reader can decide if he believes our efforts to delineate *will* as *motivation* brings us any closer to a real solution.

66. Posner's work (Posner 1994; Posner & Raichle, 1994), as most readers are well aware, has centered around the anterior cingulate as the leading element in the system controlling attention, especially visual attention.

67. Gerald Edelman has particularly focused upon this area of large scale neural systems, but also apparently without conclusive results, at least to this point (Levin, 2000a).

68. Our gratitude for the input of Michael Posner is sincerely acknowledged.

69. One of Shevrin's areas of research over the years has been subliminal perception, a most popular area in psychology. Space, however, does not allow us to pursue many interesting questions concerning the research on this most important and interesting subject.

70. It is most important to note that the statement that consciousness confers a reality sense should not be taken to mean that perception can invariably be easily differentiated from memory (of internal events); for example, anyone involved with clinical psychiatry or psychoanalysis knows full well that individuals often cannot make such a distinction when they are waking up from dreams, or even during waking life, for example, whenever the actualities of some situation are directly contrary to that person's assumptions about the nature of things. In fact, this is one reason people are easily brainwashed.

71. In an earlier note we have suggested a possible mechanism for the way such consciousness-assisted changes in memory (learning) might occur, based upon Ito's insightful remarks about a possible two-step process for learning in the skeletomuscular system.

72. Let us make an analogy. The computer software that constructs a document is often required for a particular computer to open and utilize that very document; in an analogous manner, consciousness, through its particular formatting, may be the critical element which enables us to record, organize, modify, and retrieve particular information. The word "modify" in the last sentence is particularly important, since it is the modification of memory that we associate with learning. As we argue in our discussion, in part, consciousness relates to the outside world; but it also can focus on inner life, in which case consciousness can serve the function of modifying unconscious memories or their assigned meaning.

73. The problem with all this is that there is no actual evidence that infants can summon such RIGs (Slap & Slap-Shelton, 1991) on the basis of "wishes". The problem thus becomes how much one cares to conjecture.

74. One could ask, however: What if the mode of wish fulfillment is a later achievement, connected with the appearance of symbolic thought? Obviously, the ordering of developmental steps cannot be ignored as an empirical question that remains to be determined.

75. Posner describes, as an expansion of the executive control network (ECN), the inclusion of the following additional structures: various

association cortex and sensory cortex, thalamus, cerebellum, and basal ganglia. All of these can then function, together with anterior and posterior subsystems, in an overarching system that subserves attention. It should be noted that there is some significant overlap between the work of Ito and the thinking of Posner. For example, Ito himself refers to the importance of the anterior cingulate gyrus. It appears that there is a general interest in the complex contribution of the anterior cingulate (Devinsky, Morrell, & Vogt, 1995).

76. A recent review by P. W. Gold (1998) of a book on attention deficit hyperactivity disorder (ADHD) by R. A. Barkley (1997) makes clear the enormous complexity of the contributions of the prefrontal cortex to the following: the general hierarchical mobilization and to control "of simpler units of behavior into more complex ones (Gold, 1998, p. 1149); to maintaining the pursuit of current goals over discontinuous periods of time, while avoiding distractions; bringing behavior "under control of internal information—that is, under the control of the self . . ." (*ibid.*); to regulation of affect; to internalization of speech; and to reconstitution, meaning being able to decompose sequences of events or messages "into their component parts or [to] . . . resynthesize [them] into entirely new messages or behaviors" creatively (*ibid.*).

77. The cerebellar anticipatory function is reported upon by Allen, Buxton, Wong, and Courchesne (1997). It makes sense that if the cerebellum is indeed associated with learning, it should be sensitive in this manner. In other words, since each motor act makes assumptions about the universe in which the act is to occur, the errors that are discovered in such interactions with the world necessarily lead to changes in our internal databases about how the world is structured. This conclusion about the critical nature of cerebellar prediction and feedback for learning is further supported by the research of T. Sejnowski of the Salk Institute (as reported in Wickelgren, 1998, p. 224). Sejnowski has shown that human cerebellar modeling software greatly enhances learning in robots by allowing short-term predictions of, for example, where things are likely to be, given a particular trajectory. These predictions then become further modified by the robot's real world learning experience.

78. "Over-all, the anterior cingulate cortex appears to play a crucial role in initiation, motivation, and goal-directed behaviors. The anterior cingulate cortex is part of a larger matrix of structures that are engaged in similar functions. These structures form the rostral limbic system and include the amygdala, periaqueductal gray, ventral striatum, orbitofrontal and anterior insular cortices. The system formed by

these interconnected areas assesses the motivational content of internal and external stimuli and regulates context-dependent behaviors" (Devinsky, Morrell, & Vogt, 1995, p. 279).

79. Giulio Tononi argues, based upon his understanding of Edelman's work (on salience and re-entry), and Gestalt Psychology Principles, that a conjunction is required, a synchronization of a large ensemble of cells ("the dynamic core") within the brain, for integration to occur (Tononi & Edelman, 1998). Here integration has two meanings: the first refers to the coming together into a single image of the various sensory qualities involved in the visual system (cf. the binding problem). The second refers to the more general creation of a higher quality ordering of the brain based upon the high degree of connectedness (as, for example, between the various maps of sensory qualities in the system under examination). Tononi and Edelman's argument is that consciousness requires this dynamic core which would include posterior corticothalamic regions involving perceptual categorization and anterior regions involving "concept formation, value-related memory, and planning" (p. 1850). In our discussion we believe essentially the same hypothesis is already covered by stated hypotheses of Posner and colleagues on the ECN.

80. Protecting privacy accomplishes a number of related goals, including minimizing the effects of external coercion, and allowing time for working through feelings without distractions.

81. By changes, we mean the preferred size and complexity of the neural networks they strategically employ in special vs. routine circumstances.

82. The dynamic unconscious is likely implicated at this point.

83. Once tagged, mind–brain databases become updatable.

84. In an interesting paper Slap and Brown (1998) point out the limitations of Freud's structural theory, especially in relationship to the findings of neuroscience regarding perception. In short, there are pathways into memory which do not involve consciousness (e.g., subliminal perception), as noted in our discussion of the work of Shevrin. In contrast, Slap's proposed schema model does not suffer from any such limitations. We would also point out that Levin and Trevarthen's suggestions about how the conscious system comes to assist the unconscious system through well-timed shifts in the complexity of the problem-solving strategy (and the neural network assigned to difficult cognitive/emotional tasks), is entirely consistent with Slap's schema theory.

85. Shifts to the conscious system are likely to increase cognitive efficiency because of the availability of symbolic codes, just as Freud suggested when he referred to "word presentations".

86. These results are relatively unappreciated because they are hidden in a superb article in *The Annual of Psychoanalysis* (1990) and require some mathematical knowledge to fully digest. I will attempt to correct this situation.

87. Utilizing Stuart Kauffman's ideas about self-organization, Palombo has written brilliantly (1998) on applying evolutionary theory to the mind–brain to understand what happens in ego development or a psychoanalysis.

88. Matte Blanco's work is much less known in the United States than in South America. It is, of course, impossible to correct this situation without writing a treatise on his work, which would require a separate paper. However, the reader will appreciate an attempt later in this essay to explicate that part of Matte Blanco's work most relevant to chaos theory.

89. In his concept of "Neural Darwinism", Edelman (1987) sees development as a stochastic process that involves complex interactions and communications between migrating and functioning brain cells, surviving and dying brain cells, and the very processes which these cells subserve. Through massive connectedness (what Edelman calls re-entry) mind–brain systems create "values". Ultimately, the process is adaptive, warm blooded and biological, not cold and machine-like.

90. Some problems in mathematics, especially differential calculus, according to Galatzer-Levy, were once solved only by approximation, or not solved at all because of the difficulty factor. After chaos theory was invented and applied to calculus, however, it became possible for the first time to find real solutions to some of these intractable problems. In the process of using computers to model such solutions, amazing pictures also emerged highly suggestive of phenomena that underlie complex behavior within mathematical systems. These phenomena are the subject of the latter parts of this essay.

91. In other words, values of x are computed using the above formula. Each value is computed by subtracting the previous value of x from the number 1 and multiplying that number by the number "a" (and also by the previous value of x). In the series, the calculations of x start with x=0 and continue for a extremely large number of iterations. The Feigenbaum diagram graphs these values on the vertical axis, with sequential values of the variable "a" moving from left to right along the x or horizontal axis. As this happens, a most remarkable pattern

appears that no one anticipated before computers made these calculations and graphs with exquisite precision.

92. This means as we move to the right in the Feigenbaum diagram, once chaotic or rapid doubling has started, that each doubling occurs more than four times faster than the previous doubling required. This is what produces the sensational cascading pattern.

93. One commonly known fractal is the snowflake, which has the shape of a six-pointed star when looked at grossly. Under the microscope, however, the six-pointed shape appears to be a fundamental unit from which the entire snowflake is made. That is, no matter how many magnifications, we continue to see six-pointed shapes as the essential components from which larger elements of the snowflake are composed.

94. This containment parameter may be decisive for the outcome of successful development, since the ability to contain (i.e., manage affect or self soothe) is a requirement for successful adaptation generally. Further comments are made on this container function at the end of this essay, where Sashin and Callahan's 1990 work is elaborated upon.

95. In other words, that such changes are too quick to indicate real or significant psychological development.

96. The so-called *butterfly effect* suggests that the added presence of a single butterfly somewhere in the world, say Japan, can be shown to have ramifying effects on the weather in a place completely around the globe, say Chicago!

97. The Mandelbrot set, a fascinatingly beautiful diagram of chaos, is a close relative of the Fiegenbaum diagram, and it is named after Bernard Mandelbrot, who did so much to establish the mathematics of fractals and their computer applications.

98. This is accomplished by means of something called Lyaplonov coefficients.

99. Phase space simply refers to the space illustrated by the mathematical diagrams. These are usually two dimensional drawings which depict events that can be considered to be of three or more dimensions. The word trajectory implies that if you watched the diagram draw itself, say on a computer, you would see the picture start at a single point, and then move across the two dimensions of the screen in a complex pattern, leaving behind it a line which represents a picture that in essence is the attractor. This pathway could be simple, or complex, but it is a clever way of showing development.

100. Japanese sword makers discovered how to make the strongest swords over 1000 years ago by folding the forged steel upon itself repeatedly, forming what can now be recognized as an inner fractal geometry (similar to that in French bread).

101. This is a mathematical way of saying that the trajectories we label as chaos are predetermined by exact specifiable mathematical equations that we can discover.

102. I regret that I am introducing so many novelties in such a short chapter! If the reader will bear with me, however, I will momentarily attempt to sort out what symmetry breaking means. Arthur Springer of the University of California (Davis) has been of great help in this matter.

103. The late David N. Schramm, of the University of Chicago, made his major contribution in the area of connecting the cosmology of the so-called Big Bang and particle physics, primarily through his idea that there are only three families of subatomic particles. Schramm based his assessment of the nature of the Big Bang, I assume, at least partially on considerations of symmetry-breaking.

104. For someone trained in Chicago, where Kohut lived and worked, one cannot help but consider Kohut's so-called twinship (self-object) transference as another way of thinking of Matte Blanco's phase of symmetry.

105. In Kohut's self-psychology this separateness would indicate a shift out of a self-object transference and into a self-libidinal object transference.

106. Shevrin's paper, while superficially describing why we need consciousness, is really a paper that brilliantly describes how conscious mechanisms are the critical requirement for learning which changes the vast non- and un-conscious parts of the mind and brain. Without such learning human progress would be impossible. This essay on chaos theory is partly an attempt to get more precise about how such learning might occur. My other essay, written with Colwyn Trevarthen (Chapter Thirteen), makes a further attempt to tie together loose ends towards making a synthesis about mechanisms of change (whether developmental or learning-related), but this time in terms of bridging neurological and psychological perspectives. I know the density of my arguments can be hard on the reader, but I hope that the reader also appreciates the sincere effort I am making to explain things on the frontier of our knowledge without oversimplifying.

107. A ten dimensional space merely means that the model involves ten variables, each considered to represent a important spatial dimension.

Current "string theory" and its derivative theories in physics employ the same kind of idea of n-dimensionality, often imagining a world composed of the four usual dimensions (three spatial and one for time) plus added dimensions of a seemingly fanciful sort (i.e., as a mental construct), which are, of course, not "visible" to humans, but which are imaginable and have a theoretical validity nevertheless.

108. A recent note from Howard Shevrin observes the following: "I presented a panel on subliminal evoked response potentials (ERPs) at the Society for Psychophysiological Research meetings. Now subliminal ERPs look like noise to the naked eye, and ERP researchers like to see what ERPs look like. In order to show that subliminal ERPs have the same structure as supraliminal ERPs, something that our statistical findings amply bore out, we multiplied the subliminal ERP plots by a factor, thus 'blowing up' the subliminal ERPs and bringing them into the same amplitude range as the supraliminal ERPs. The factor was four." In other words, the correlation of Giannitripani's rule to Feigenbaum's point cannot yet be ruled out, although it is still very far from certain. I include my speculations, as well as Howard Shevrin's remark, in this essay to indicate the primitive state we are in regarding the application of chaos theory to psychoanalysis and sister sciences studying mind–brain.

109. The author wishes to thank Drs. Robert Galatzer-Levy, Charles Jaffe, and George Klumpner for their input to this work. The earliest version of this paper was presented October 12, 1994, to the Houston Psychoanalytic Society, Houston, Texas, and was later published as Levin, 1995c, which appeared with two companion essays. The first companion essay is Chapter Four in this book, which deals with the special relationship between the psychoanalytic transference, the judging of similarity and transfer of knowledge, and the priming of memory. The second companion essays, Chapters One and Three in this book, first examine some complex philosophical questions that enter into our psychoanalytic theories and affect the analyst's neutrality and interventions, and then consider the function of beliefs.

110. Bucci (1985) describes four models of representations: (1) verbal mediation, in which memories are coded verbally, (2) a common code mode, in which all inputs into long-term memory are coded in a single abstract code (whether the data coded is verbal or nonverbal, (3) perceptual dominance, in which coding is a function of the perceptual–sensory modality involved, and (4) dual coding, where two distinctly different codes each participate, one for verbal and the

other for nonverbal experience. Bucci favors the last system, claiming the support of experimental psychology research, pointing out the ready application of this dual coding model to psychoanalysis. Interpretations are understood to facilitate a "referential" system that bridges verbal and nonverbal worlds. I personally find Bucci's referential system the most attractive, but we do not yet know which system of coding is actually employed by the mind–brain. Readers interested in this particular debate may wish to consult Levin (1991, especially, pp. 1–42, 145–164, 193, and 201–218).

111. The artificial network structures (artificial intelligence) created by interdisciplinary teams are interesting and important models, but they do not answer the question as to how our mind–brain accomplishes its specific tasks, that is, identify what subprocesses are involved and which pathways of the brain support these activities. In this regard, some experts have proposed that "representation" best refers to "patterns of activation" that comprise a particular neural network's response to a particular stimulus (Cohen & Servan-Schreiber, 1992). In such computer models nodes may represent concepts (ideas), directional arrows between nodes stand for such things as computer diagnosis of complex problems. These ideas are interesting, but they are only half of the work: the remainder involves the more difficult project of making psychological-neurological correlations.

112. One might say that the idea of "representation is a bit like the natural sciences themselves: fallible, not indubitable . . . and never entirely free of ambiguity or the possibility of error or oversight" (Davis & Hersh, 1981, p. 347).

113. Gentner as quoted above describes how judging similarity at a deep level seems to be innate in humans and primates. This implies that the subcortical structures noted are probably critical parts not only for neural control but also for the judging of similarity and knowledge transfer.

114. For example, Balaban's experiments transplanting embryonic brain tissues between various bird species result in the alteration of expected adult behavior of these birds. Their conclusion is that certain behavior is clearly preprogrammed or hardwired into the parts exchanged. But Balaban's (1990) research is best categorized as an ingenious effort to specify the constraints and organizational principles underlying mind–brain; as such it will be extremely important for what it can eventually clarify about the control mechanisms of such phenomena as learning "windows", whether in birdbrains or

humans! The zone of interaction between nurture and nature is finally getting exactly the attention it deserves, from biologically sophisticated analysts, and from analytically attentive biologists.

115. "Remodeling" might describe this step well, since final modifications are probably involved to make what is internalized apt for the rest of self organization. Once again, judgments and tolerances regarding "same/different" would seem to be involved.

116. Pamela McCorduck in *Machines Who Think* (1979) and Ernest W. Kent in *The Brains of Men and Machines* (1981) help clarify that problem-solving systems exist which are neither human nor alive. Robots and computers are knowledgeable; that is, they share with virtually every form of life on earth the capacity to transduce input into complex output. This is true as much of DNA molecules, bacteria, viruses, mycobacteria, and simple unicellular creatures as it is of all of us eukaryotes. Therefore, we should not be so arrogant as to believe that we are the only "intelligent" creatures, since humans are just one more form of life on earth. Moreover, even the lowly fly and cockroach are smart enough to outwit us most of the time! And there is hardly any debate about the vast intelligence of whales, porpoises, and the great apes. Humans, of course, give themselves special credit for inventing such things as syntactical language and empathy, believing that this proves our superiority. But of course, we also invented the bomb! One can only conclude that we have a lot to learn from other specialists about knowledge in nonhuman or even nonliving systems, just as experts in other fields involving inorganic knowledge need to compare what they discover with what is understood about the varieties of organic knowledge bases.

    Incidentally, if it is difficult to define knowledge, it is no less easy to delineate intelligence. For example, there is a story told about a researcher who uses mice to study intelligence. What he finds interesting is that the mice who are most successful in getting through complex mazes quickly are also the easiest to induce to put their heads into a guillotine, so they can sacrificed and their brains examined. On the other hand, the so-called stupid or dull mice fight intensively to avoid having their heads chopped off!

117. Writing this essay has been an arduous task, during which I observed the following that led me to the above conclusion. I noted that I was able to effectively make use of my word processor only during the initial phase of writing. Once the writing advanced to the stage of a final draft, however, I found that I needed to have a periodic printout

of the manuscript, which I then would hold in my hand while reading it and making final corrections. That is, I needed to make the final corrections with real pen on real paper, not on the word processor. I believe this is because I needed the particular kinesthetic, tactile, and visual experience to optimally retrieve my knowledge of editing. I would further speculate that this might be necessary because this comes closer to the original sensory experience involved in my learning how to edit. In this manner it became obvious to me that even adults require subtle forms of sensory priming to facilitate thinking within specific problem domains.

118. The nature of this activity by the anterior cingulate is under active investigation by a number of groups. One (Bush et al., 1998) notes that in general there is agreement that the "anterior cingulate cortex . . . allocates attentional resources when faced with competing information-processing streams or to mediate response selection . . ." (p. 276). This subject is taken up in more detail in Chapters Fourteen and Fifteen.

119. MENDAC is an acronym for mental health needs of deaf adults and children. It was begun at Michael Reese Hospital in 1973 to provide outpatient psychiatric services for indigent deaf patients. Eugene Mindel, Laszlo Stein, and Fred Levin were its founders.

REFERENCES

Abel, T., Martin, K. C., Bartsch, D., & Kandel, E. R. (1998). Memory suppresser genes: Inhibitory constraints on the storage of long-term memory. *Science, 279*: 338–341.

Albus, S. (1971). A theory of cerebellar function. *Mathematical Bioscience, 10*: 25–61.

Albus, S. (1981). *Brain, Behavior, and Robotics*. Peterborough, NH: BYTE Books/McGraw-Hill.

Alkon, D. L. (1985). Calcium-mediated reduction of ionic currents. *Science, 30*: 1037–1045.

Allen, G., Buxton, R. B., Wong, E. C., & Courchesne, E. (1997). Attentional activation of the cerebellum independent of motor involvement. *Science, 275*: 1940–1943.

Allen, J. A. (1998). Delineating conscious and unconscious processes: Commentary on Baars on contrastive analysis. *PSYCHE: An Interdisciplinary Journal of Research on Consciousness, 1*(9), August 1994 (Filename: psyche-1–9-allen), http://psyche.cs.monash.edu.au/v1/psyche-1-09-allen.html.

Anderson, J. A., & Rosenfeld, E. (Eds.) (1989). *Neurocomputing: Foundations of Research*. Cambridge, MA: MIT Press.

Andreasen, N. C., Arndt, S., Swayze II, V., Cizadlo, T., Flaum, M., O'Leary, D., Ehrhardt, J. C., & Yuh, W. T. C. (1994). Thalamic abnormalities in schizophrenia visualized through magnetic resonance image averaging. *Science, 266*: 294–298.

Annett, M. (1985). *Left, Right Hand and Brain*. Hillsdale, NJ: Erlbaum.

Antrobus, J., Ehrlichman, H., Werner, M., & Wollman, M. (1982). The REM report and the EEG: Cognitive processes associated with the cerebral hemispheres. In: W. P. Koella (Ed.), *Sleep* (pp. 119–151). Basel: Karger.

Aronowitz, B. R., Decaria, C., Allen, A., Weiss, N., Saunders, A., Margolin, L., Moscovich, S., Bauma, M., & Hollander, E. (1997). The neuropsychiatry of autism and Asperger's disorder: Review of the literature and case reports. *CNS Spectrums: The International Journal of Neuropsychiatric Medicine, 2*(5): 43–60.

Awerbuch, B., Cowen, L., & Smith, M. (1994). Efficient synchronous distributed symmetry breaking. Proceedings of the 26th Annual Symposium on the Theory of Computation, Montréal, Canada. http://theory.Ics.mit.edu/~mass/stoc94.html

Baars, B. J. (1988). *A Cognitive Theory of Consciousness*. Cambridge: Cambridge University Press.

Baars, B. J. (1994). A thoroughly empirical approach to consciousness. *PSYCHE, 1*(6) (Filename: psyche-94–1–6-contrastive-1-baars), http://psyche.cs.monash.edu.au/v1/psyche-94–1–6-contrastive-1-baars.html

Baars, B. J. (1997). Commentary on paper by Mark Solms. *Journal of the American Psychoanalytic Association, 45*(3): 707–714.

Bachrach, H. M., Galatzer-Levy, R., Skolnikoff, A., & Waldron, S. (1991). On the efficacy of psychoanalysis. *Journal of the American Psychoanalytic Association, 39*(4): 871–916.

Bachtereva, N. P., Abdullaev, Y. G., & Medvedev, S. V. (1992). Neuronal correlates of the higher-order semantic code in humans. *Electroencephalography and Clinical Neurophysiology, 82*(4): 296–301.

Baddeley, A. (1986). *Working Memory*. Oxford: Clarendon Press.

Baer, D. M. (1989). Neurobiological aspects of anger/rage. Paper read to the American Psychoanalytic Association.

Baker, B. (1996). OCD, tics follow strep throat in some children. *Clinical Psychiatry News*, March issue, p. 16.

Balaban, E. (1990). Avian brain chimeras as a tool for studying species behavioral differences. In: N. Dldourin, F. Dieterien-Lievre & J. Smith (Eds.), *The Avian Model in Developmental Biology* (pp. 105–484). Paris: CNRS Press.

Balint, E. (1987). Memory and consciousness. *International Journal of Psychoanalysis, 68*(4): 475–484.

Barinaga, M. (1997). Consciousness research: Visual system provides clues to how the brain perceives. *Science, 275*: 1583–1585.

Barkley, R. A. (1997). *Attention-deficit Hyperactivity Disorder: A Handbook for Diagnosis and Treatment*. New York: Guilford Press.

Barnes, J. (1982). *Aristotle*. Oxford: Oxford University Press, 1989.

Barry, V. C. (1987). Maturation, integration, and psychic reality. *The Annual of Psychoanalysis, 15*: 3–21, Hillsdale, NJ: Analytic Press.

Barry, V. C. (1998). Review of *Cognitive Science and the Unconscious* (1997), D. J. Stein (Ed.), Washington, DC: American Psychiatric Press. *The Bulletin of the Institute for Psychoanalysis, Chicago, 7*(1): 9–10.

Barry, V. C. (2000). Reflections on interactive and self-organizing aspects of learning in psychoanalysis. *The Annual of Psychoanalysis, 28*: 7–20.

Bartlett, F. C. (1932). *Remembering: A Study in Experimental and Social Psychology*. Cambridge: Cambridge University Press.

Basch, M. F. (1975). Perception, consciousness, and Freud's "Project". *The Annual of Psychoanalysis, 3*: 3–20.

Basch, M. F. (1976). Psychoanalysis and communication science. *The Annual of Psychoanalysis, 4*: 385–421.

Basch, M. F. (1983). The perception of reality and the disavowal of meaning, *The Annual of Psychoanalysis, 11*: 125–154.

Baxter, L. R. Jr. (1990). Brain imaging as a tool in establishing a theory of brain pathology in obsessive compulsive disorder, *Journal of Clinical Psychiatry, 51*: 22–25.

Baxter, L. R. Jr. (1994). Positron emission tomography studies of cerebral glucose metabolism in obsessive compulsive disorder. *Journal of Clinical Psychiatry, 55*(Suppl): 54–59.

Bechara, A., Tranel, H., Damasio, H., Adolphs, R., Rockland, C., & Damasio, A. R. (1995). Double dissociation of conditioning and declarative knowledge relative to the amygdala and hippocampus in humans. *Science, 269*: 1115–1118.

Biziere, K. (1994). Modulation of immune response by the C.N.S. Paper read to the International Symposium on Mind–Body Problems, Osaka University Medical School, Osaka, Japan.

Blakeslee, S. (1994). Brain study examines a rare woman: She cannot discern fear, or even feel it. *New York Times*, 18 December 1994.

Block, S. H. (1987). Psychotherapy of the individual with brain injury. *Brain Injury, 1*(2): 203–206.

Bogen, J. E. (1990). Partial hemispheric independence with the neocommissures intact. In: C. Trevarthen (Ed.), *Brain Circuits and Functions of the Mind: Essays in Honor of R. W. Sperry* (pp. 215–230). New York: Cambridge University Press.

Bornstein, R. F., & Pittman, T. S. (1992). *Perception Without Awareness.* New York: Guilford Press.

Brakel, L. A. W., & Snodgrass, M. (1998). From the brain, the cognitive laboratory, and the couch. *Journal of the American Psychoanalytic Association, 46*(3): 897–920.

Brenner, C. (1982). *The Mind in Conflict.* New York: International Universities Press.

Brenner, I. (1996). Trauma, perversion, and 'multiple personality'. *Journal of the American Psychoanalytic Association, 44*(3): 785–814.

Breuer, J., & Freud, S. (1895d). *Studies on Hysteria. S.E., 2.* London: Hogarth Press.

Bridgeman, B. (1996). What we really know about consciousness: Review of a cognitive theory of consciousness by Bernard J. Baars, *Psyche: An interdisciplinary [electronic] journal of research on consciousness,* http://psyche.cs.monash.edu.au/

Bucci, W. (1985). Dual coding: A cognitive model for psychoanalytic research. *Journal of the American Psychoanalytic Association, 53:* 571–608.

Bucci, W. (1993). The development of emotional meaning in free association: A multiple code theory. In: A. Wilson & J. E. Gedo (Eds.), *Hierarchical Concepts in Psychoanalysis: Theory, Research, and Clinical Practice* (pp. 3–47). New York: Guilford Press.

Bush, G., Whalen, P. J., Rosen, B. R., Jenike, M. A., McInerney, S. C., & Rauch, S. L. (1998). The counting stroop: An interference task specialized for functional neuroimaging-validation study with functional MRI. *Human Brain Mapping, 6:* 270–282.

Çambel, A. B. (1993). *Applied Chaos Theory: A Paradigm for Complexity.* Boston, MA: Academic Press.

Cannon, W. (1942). Voodoo death. *American Anthropologist, 44:* 169–181.

Carbonnell, J. (1981). *Subjective Understanding of Belief Systems.* Ann Arbor, MI: University of Michigan Press.

Cavell, M. (1988). Interpretation, psychoanalysis, and the philosophy of mind. *Journal of the American Psychoanalytic Association, 36*(4): 859–880.

Channel, D. F. (1991). Special kinds of knowledge. *Science, 253:* 573–574.

Chivukula, R. S., Cohen, A., Lane, K., & Simmons, E. (1997). High-energy particle physics and cosmology: Electroweak symmetry breaking. http://buphy.du.edu/bu/PartPhy.html

Christensen, A. L. (1992). Outpatient management and outcome in relation to work in traumatic brain injury patients. *Scandinavian Journal of Rehabilitation Medicine Supplement, 26*: 34–42.

Chugani, H. I., & Phelps, M. E. (1986). Maturational changes in cerebral function in infants determined by FDG positron emission tomography. *Science, 231*: 840–843.

Cloninger, C. R. (1991). Brain networks underlying personality development. In: B. J. Carroll & J. E. Barrett (Eds.), *Psychopathology and the Brain* (pp. 183–204). New York: Raven Press.

Cohen, J., & Servan-Schreiber, D. (1992). Introduction to neural network models. *Psychiatric Annals, 22*: 3.

Collins, A. W. (1985). *Thought and Nature*. Notre Dame, IN: University of Notre Dame Press.

Crane, T. (1995). Intentionality. In: T. Honderich (Ed.), *The Oxford Companion to Philosophy* (pp. 412–413). Oxford: Oxford University Press.

Crick, F., & Koch, C. (1992). The problem of consciousness. *Scientific American, 267*:125–136.

Crook, J. H. (1988). The experiential context of intellect. In: R. W. Byrne & A. Whiten (Eds.), *Machiavellian Intelligence: Social Expertise and the Evolution of Intellect in Monkeys, Apes, and Humans* (pp. 347–362). Oxford: Clarendon Press.

Crow, T. J. (1982). The biology of schizophrenia. *Experientia, 38*: 1275–1282.

Crow, T. J. (1986a). The continuum of psychosis and its implication for the structure of the gene. *British Journal of Psychiatry, 149*: 419–429.

Crow, T. J. (1986b). Left-brain, retrotransposons, and schizophrenia. *British Medical Journal, 293*: 3–4.

Crow, T. J. (1986c). Secular changes in affective disorder and variations in the psychosis gene. *Archives of General Psychiatry, 43*(1): 1013–1014.

Czikzentmihalyi, M. (1975). *Beyond Boredom and Anxiety: The Experience of Play in Work and Games*. San Francisco, CA: Jossey-Bank.

Damasio, H., Grabowski, T., Frank, R., Galaburda, A. M., & Damasio, A. R. (1994). The return of Phineas Gage: Clues about the brain from the skull of a famous patient. *Science, 264*: 1102–1105.

Davis, P. J., & Hersh, R. (1981). *The Mathematical Experience*. Boston: Houghton Mifflin.

Dawson, J. (1993). "Memory cells spin an ever-changing tale, states scientist." *Minneapolis Star-Tribune*, 14 May 1996, p. 5B.

Decety, J., Sjohlm, H., Ryding, E., Stenberg, G., & Ingvar, D. H. (1990). The cerebellum participates in mental activity: Tomographic measurements of regional cerebral blood flow. *Brain Research, 535*(2): 313–317.

Deeke, L., Scheid, P., & Kornhuber, H. H. (1969). Distribution of readiness potential, pre-motion positivity, and motor potential of the human cerebral cortex preceding voluntary finger movement. *Experimental Brain Research, 7*: 158–168.

Dehaene, S., Posner, M. I., & Tucker, D. M. (1994). Localization of a neuronal system for error detection and compensation. *Psychological Science, 5*(5): 303–305.

Demos, E. V. (1985). The revolution in infancy research. Presented to the American Society of Adolescence, Dallas, Texas.

Denman, C. (1994). Strange attractors and dangerous liaisons: A response to Priel and Schreiber. *British Journal of Medical Psychology, 67*(3): 219–222.

Devaney, R. L. (1989). *An Introduction to Chaotic Dynamical Systems* (2nd edn). Reading, MA: Addison-Wesley.

Devaney, R. L. (1990). *Chaos, Fractals and Dynamics: Computer Experiments in Mathematics.* Reading, MA: Addison-Wesley.

Devinsky, O., Morrell, M. J., & Vogt, B. A. (1995). Contributions of anterior cingulate cortex to behavior. *Brain, 118*: 279–306.

Donald, M. (1991). *Origins of the Modern Mind.* Cambridge, MA: Harvard University Press.

Dong, D. W. (1997). Symmetry breaking columns. In: *Essay on Computational Neuroscience*, Rockerfeller University, dawei@hope.caltech. edu http://www.cs.utexas.edu/users/nn/web-pubs/htmlbook 96/dong/node8.html

Dudai, Y. (1987). On neuronal assemblies and memories (reporter of Dahlem Conference). In: J. P. Changeux & M. Konishi (Eds.), *The Neural and Molecular Bases of Learning* (pp. 339–410). New York: John Wiley.

Eccles, J. (1973). *The Understanding of the Brain.* New York: McGraw-Hill.

Eccles, J., Szentágothai, J., & Ito, M. (1967). *The Neural Machine.* New York: Springer.

Edelman, G. (1987). *Neural Darwinism: The Theory of Neuronal Group Selection.* New York: Basic Books.

Edelman, G. (1989). *The Remembered Present: A Biological Theory of Consciousness.* New York: Basic Books.

Edelman, G. (1998). Discussion of consciousness. Chicago Institute of Psychoanalysis, 65th Anniversary Symposium.

Edelson, M. (1988). *Psychoanalysis: A Theory in Crisis.* Chicago, IL: University of Chicago Press.

Eickelman, D. F. (1985). *Knowledge and Power in Morocco.* Princeton, NJ: Princeton University Press.

Eisley, L. C. (1971). *Enclycopedia Britannica,* vol. 7, 200th Anniversary Edition. Chicago, IL: William Benton, p. 86.

Eisley, L. C. (1975). *All the Strange Hours: The Excavation of a Life.* New York: Charles Scribner's Sons.

Ekeberg, Ö. (1995). Studies of Artificial Neural Systems (SANS) Home Page, section of "Computational Neuroscience", www@eeb.ele. tue.nl [Department of Numerical Analysis and Computing Science, Royal Institute of Technology, Stockholm, Sweden].

Emde, R. (1988). Development terminable and interminable: I. and II. Innate and motivational factors from infancy. *International Journal of Psychoanalysis, 69*(1): 23–42, 283–296.

Estevez-Gonzalez, A., Garcia-Sanchez, C., & Junque, C. (1997). Attention: A complex cerebral function. *Revista de Neurologia, 25*(148): 1989–1997 [Spanish].

Flor-Henry, P. (1983a). *The Cerebral Basis of Psychopathology.* Littleton, MA: Wright-PSG.

Flor-Henry, P. (1983b). Neuropsychological studies in patients with psychiatric disorders. In: K. M. Hilman & P. Satz (Eds.), *Neuropsychology of Human Emotion* (pp. 193–220). New York: Guilford Press.

Flor-Henry, P. (1985). Psychiatric aspects of cerebral lateralization. *Psychiatric Annals, 15*: 429–434.

Fónagy, I. (1971). Double coding in speech, *Semiotica,* 3: 189–222.

Fónagy, I. (1987). Vocal expressions of emotions and attitudes. *VS: Quaderni di studi semiotici,* 47–48: 65–85.

Forrest, D. V. (1987). Dream of the rarebit fiend: Neuromedical synthesis of unconscious meaning. *Journal of the Academy of Psychoanalysis,* 15: 331–363.

Forrest, D. V. (1991a). Mind, brain, and machine: Action and creation. *Journal of the American Academy of Psychoanalysis, 22*(1): 29–56.

Forrest, D. V. (1991b). Mind, brain, and machine: Object recognition. *Journal of the American Academy of Psychoanalysis,* 19: 555–577.

Forrest, D. V. (1994a). Interdisciplinary perspectives on psychoanalysis. Paper presented to Psyche '94, International Symposium on Mind, Body, and Brain, Osaka, October 7.

Forrest, D. V. (1994b). Psychotherapy of patients with neuropsychiatric disorders. In: S. C. Yodofsky & R. E. Hales (Eds.), *The American Psychiatric Press Textbook of Neuropsychiatry* (pp. 533–560). Washington, DC: American Psychiatric Press.

Forrest, D. V. (1995). Artificial mind: The promise of neural networks. *Samiksa: Journal of the Indian Psychoanalytical Society, 49*: 45–72.

Forrest, D. V. (1996a). Epilogue. In: D. Stein (Ed.), *Neural Networks and Psychopathology*. Cambridge: Cambridge University Press.

Forrest, D. V. (1996b). Book review of *Scale in Conscious Experience: Is the Brain Too Important to Be Left to Specialists to Study?* J. King & K. H. Pribram (Eds.), Mahwah, NJ: Lawrence Erlbaum.

Forrest, D. V. (1997). Psychotherapy of neuropsychiatric disorders. In: S. Yadofsky & R. Hales (Ed.), *The American Psychiatric Press Textbook of Neuropsychiatry*. Washington, DC: APPI.

Fosshage, J. L. (1997). Listening/experiencing perspectives and the quest for a facilitating responsiveness. In: A. Goldberg (Ed.), *Conversations in Self Psychology: Progress in Self Psychology, Vol. 13* (pp. 33–55). Hillsdale, NJ: Analytic Press.

Frank, A. (1969). The unrememberable and the unforgettable: Passive primal repression. *Psychoanalytic Study of the Child, 24*: 48–77.

Freud, A. (1965). *Normality and Pathology of Childhood*. New York: International Universities Press.

Freud, S. (1891). On the interpretation of aphasias. *S.E., 3*: 240–241. London: Hogarth Press.

Freud, S. (1895). Project for a scientific psychology, *S.E., 1*: 295–397. London: Hogarth Press.

Freud, S. (1900a). *The Interpretation of Dreams. S.E., 4–5*. London: Hogarth Press.

Freud, S. (1901b). *The Psychopathology of Everyday Life. S.E., 6*: 1–279. London: Hogarth Press.

Freud, S. (1905a). *Jokes and Their Relation to the Unconscious. S.E., 8*: 3–258. London: Hogarth Press.

Freud, S. (1905e). *Fragment of an Analysis of a Case of Hysteria. S.E., 7*: 3–122. London: Hogarth Press.

Freud, S. (1910a). Five lectures on psychoanalysis. *S.E., 11*: 9–55. London: Hogarth Press.

Freud, S. (1910e). The antithetical meaning of primal words. *S.E., 11*: 153–162. London: Hogarth Press.

Freud, S. (1911b). Formulations on the two principles of mental functioning. *S.E., 12*: 213–226. London: Hogarth Press.

Freud, S. (1912b). The dynamics of transference. *S.E.*, *12*: 99–108. London: Hogarth Press.

Freud, S. (1912–1913). *Totem and Taboo. S.E.*, *13*: 1–161. London: Hogarth Press.

Freud, S. (1914c). On narcissism: An introduction. *S.E.*, *14*: 73–102. London: Hogarth Press.

Freud, S. (1914g). Remembering, repeating and working through. *S.E.*, *12*: 147–156. London: Hogarth Press.

Freud, S. (1915a). Observations on transference-love. *S.E.*, *12*: 157–171. London: Hogarth Press.

Freud, S. (1915e). The unconscious. *S.E.*, *14*: 159–216. London: Hogarth Press.

Freud, S. (1916–1917). *Introductory Lectures on Psycho-analysis. S.E.*, *15–16*. London: Hogarth Press.

Freud, S. (1920g). *Beyond the Pleasure Principle. S.E.*, *18*: 7–64. London: Hogarth Press.

Freud, S. (1923b). *The Ego and the Id. S.E.*, *19*: 12–66. London: Hogarth Press.

Freud, S. (1924a). Neurosis and psychosis, *S.E.*, *19*:12–65. London: Hogarth Press.

Freud, S. (1924e). The loss of reality in neurosis and psychosis. *S.E.*, *19*: 183–190. London: Hogarth Press.

Freud, S. (1953) [1891]. *On Aphasia*, E. Stengel (Trans.). New York: International Universities Press. [German Original: *Zur Auffassung der Aphasien. Eine kritische Studie*. Leipzig: Franz Deutike.]

Friberg, L., & Roland, P. E. (1987). Functional activation and inhibition of regional cerebral blood flow and metabolism. In: J. Olesen & L. Edvinsson (Eds.), *Basic Mechanisms of Headache* (pp. 2–30). Amsterdam: Elsevier.

Frick, R. B. (1982). The ego and the vestibulocerebellar system. *Psychoanalytic Quarterly, 51*(1): 95–122.

Fried, D., Crits-Christoph, P., & Luborsky, L. (1992). The first empirical demonstration of transference in psychology. *Journal of Nervous and Mental Disease, 180*: 326–331.

Gabriel, M. (1991). Brain dynamic circuit interactions and learning, research perspective. *Newsletter, Beckman Institute, University of Illinois, 3*(2): 2, 10–11.

Gabriel, M., Vogt, B. A., Kubota, Y., Poremba, A., & Kang, E. (1991). Training-stage related neuronal plasticity in limbic thalamus and cingulate cortex during learning: A possible key to mnemonic retrieval. *Behavioral Brain Research, 46*: 175–185.

Galaburda, A. M., LeMay, M., Kemper, T., & Geschwind, N. (1978). Right–left asymmetries in the brain. *Science, 199*: 852–856.

Galatzer-Levy, R. (1978). Qualitative change from quantitative change: mathematical catastrophe theory in relation to psychoanalysis, *Journal of the American Psychoanalytic Association, 26*: 921–935.

Galatzer-Levy, R. (1988). On working through: A model from artificial intelligence. *Journal of the American Psychoanalytic Association, 36*: 125–151.

Galatzer-Levy, R. (1995). Dynamical systems theory: Prediction and self similarity. *Journal of the American Psychoanalytic Association, 43–44*: 1085–1113.

Galatzer-Levy, R. (1997). Chaotic possibilities: Towards a new model of development. Presented to the Chicago Psychoanalytic Society October 27.

Galin, D. (1974). Implications for psychiatry of left-right cerebral specialization. *Archives of General Psychiatry, 31*: 572–583.

Gallup, G. G. Jr. (1985). Do minds exist in species other than our own? *Neuroscience and Biobehavioral Reviews, 9*: 631–641.

Gardner, M. R. (1989). *Self Inquiry*. Hillsdale, NJ: Analytic Press.

Gardner, S. (1994). Commentary of Priel and Schreiber 'On Psychoanalysis and non-liner dynamics'. *British Journal of Medical Psychology, 67*(3): 223–225.

Garfinkel, A., Spano, M., Ditto, W., & Weiss, J. (1992). Controlling cardiac chaos. *Science, 257*: 1230–1235.

Gearhart, J. (1998). New potential for human embryonic stem cells. *Science, 282*: 1061–1062.

Gedo, J. E. (1978). The analyst's affectivity and the management of transference. Paper read to the Chicago Psychoanalytic Society.

Gedo, J. E. (1979). *Beyond Interpretation*. New York: International Universities Press.

Gedo, J. E. (1981). *Advances in Clinical Psychoanalysis*. New York: International Universities Press.

Gedo, J. E. (1984). *Psychoanalysis and Its Discontents*. New York: Guildford Press.

Gedo, J. E. (1986). *Conceptual Issues in Psychoanalysis*, Hillsdale, NJ: Analytic Press.

Gedo, J. E. (1988). *The Mind in Disorder*, Hillsdale, NJ: Analytic Press.

Gedo, J. E. (1989a). Psychoanalytic theory and Occam's razor. Paper read at the Chicago Psychoanalytic Society.

Gedo, J. E. (1989b). Self psychology: A post Kohutian view. In: D. Detrick & S. Detrick (Eds.), *Self Psychology: Impressions and Contrasts* (pp. 415–428). Hillsdale, NJ: Analytic Press,

Gedo, J. E. (1991a). The biology of mind. In: F. M. Levin *Mapping the Mind* (Foreword). Hillsdale, NJ: Analytic Press.

Gedo, J. E. (1991b). *The Biology of Clinical Encounters.* Hillsdale, NJ: Analytic Press: pp. xi–xx.

Gedo, J. E. (1991c). Between prolixity and reductionism: Psychoanalytic theory and Occam's Razor, *Journal of the American Psychoanalytic Association, 39*(1): 71–86.

Gedo, J. E. (1993a). The hierarchical model of mental functioning: Sources and implications. In: A. Wilson & J. Gedo (Eds.), *Hierarchical Concepts in Psychoanalysis: Theory, Research, and Clinical Practice.* New York: Guilford Press.

Gedo, J. E. (1993b). *Beyond Interpretation* (revised edn), Hillsdale, NJ: Analytic Press

Gedo, J. E. (1994). Analytic interventions: the question of form. In: A. K. Richards & A. D. Richards (Eds.), *The Spectrum of Psychoanalysis.* Madison, CT: International Universities Press.

Gedo, J. E. (1995). Working through as a metaphor and as a modality of treatment. *Journal of the American Psychoanalytic Association, 43*(2): 335–356.

Gedo, J. E. (1996a). Epigenesis, regression, and the problem of consciousness. *The Annual of Psychoanalysis, 24*: 93–102.

Gedo, J. E. (1996b). *The Languages of Psychoanalysis.* Hillsdale, NJ: Analytic Press.

Gedo, J. E. (1997). Reflections on metapsychology, theoretical coherence, hermeneutics, and biology. *Journal of the American Psychoanalytic Association, 45*(3): 779–807.

Gedo, J. E., & Goldberg, A. (1973). *Models of the Mind.* New York: Basic Books.

Gentner, D., & Ratterman, J. J. (1991a). Language and the career of similarity. In: S. A. Gelman & J. P. Byrnes (Eds.), *Perspectives on Language and Thought: Interrelations in Development* (pp. 225–284). London: Cambridge University Press.

Gentner, D., & Ratterman, J. J. (1991b). The roles of similarity in transfer: Determinants of similarity based reminding and mapping. Cognitive Science Technical Report CS-9112. Beckman Institute, University of Illinois.

Geschwind, N., & Galaburda, A. M. (1985). Cerebral lateralization: III. *Archives of Neurology, 42*: 634–654.

Geva, N., & Stern, J. M. (1985). The use of dreams as a psychotherapeutic technique with brain injured patients. *Scandinavian Journal of Rehabilitation Medicine Supplement, 12*: 47–49.

Gill, M. (1976). Metapsychology is not psychology. *Psychological Issues,* Monograph 36. New York: International Universities Press, pp. 71–105.

Gill, M. (1994). *Psychoanalysis in Transition.* Hillsdale, NJ: Analytic Press.

Gillett, E. (1996). Learning theory and intrapsychic conflict. *International Journal of Psychoanalysis, 77*: 689–707.

Gilmore, K. (1994). Book review: Mapping the Mind: The Intersection of Psychoanalysis and Neuroscience, by Fred M. Levin, Hillsdale, NJ: The Analytic Press, 1991. *Psychoanalytic Quarterly, 63*(4): 781–783.

Gleick, J. (1987). *Chaos: Making a New Science.* New York: Viking Press [reprinted New York: Penguin, 1988].

Gold, P. W. (1998). Lack of attention from loss of time: review of "ADHD and the Nature of Self Control" by R. A. Barkley. Guilford Press: New York, 1997. *Science, 281*: 1149–1150.

Gray, R. M., & Davisson, L. D. (2004). *Introduction to Statistical Signal Processing.* Cambridge University Press.

Graybiel, A. M. (1984). Neurochemically specified subsystems in the basal ganglia. In: D. Evered & M. O. O'Connor (Eds.), *Functions of the Basal Ganglia* (pp. 114–149). London: Pitman Press.

Grene, M. (1979). *A Portrait of Aristotle.* Chicago, IL: University of Chicago Press.

Grinker, R. R. Sr. (1940). Sigmund Freud: A few reminiscences of a personal contact. *Journal of Orthopsychiatry, 10*: 850.

Grünbaum, A. (1984). *The Foundations of Psychoanalysis.* Berkeley, CA: University of California Press.

Guckenheimer, J. (1994). University of Maryland Home Page "Chaos at Maryland", www.enee.umd.edu (also reachable via http://www.cs.tcd.ie/www/kellyfj/kellyfj.html).

Guckenheimer, J., & Holmes, P. (1983). *Nonlinear Oscillations, Dynamical Systems, and Bifurcations of Vector Fields.* New York: Springer-Verlag.

Gulick, D. (1992). *Encounters with Chaos.* McGraw-Hill.

Gunther, M. S. (1977). The threatened staff; a psychoanalytic contribution to medical psychology. *Comprehensive Psychiatry, 18*: 385–397.

Gunther, M. S. (1994). Countertransference issues in staff caregivers who work to rehabilitate catastrophic-injury survivors. *American Journal of Psychotherapy, 48*(2): 209–220.

Hadley, J. L. (1985). Attention, affect, and attachment. *Psychoanalytic and Contemporary Thought, 8*: 529–550.

Hadley, J. L. (1987). Discussion of "Psychological development and the changing organization of the brain," by Fred M. Levin. Read to the Chicago Psychoanalytic Society.

Hadley, J. L. (1989). The neurobiology of motivational systems. In: J. Lichtenberg (Ed.), *Psychoanalysis and Motivation* (pp. 337–372). Hillsdale, NJ: Analytic Press.

Hadley, J. L. (1992). The instincts revisited. *Psychoanalytic Inquiry, 12*: 396–418.

Hadley, J. L. (2000). The self organization and the autonomy system. *Annual of Psychoanalysis, 28*: 67–84.

Hale, J., & Kocak, H. (1991). *Dynamics and Bifurcations*. New York: Springer-Verlag.

Harrow, M. (1994). What factors are involved in the vulnerability of schizophrenics to delusions and thought disorder? Paper presented to the International Symposium on Mind–Body Problems, Osaka University Medical School, Osaka, Japan.

Hartmann, H. (1939). Ego psychology and the problem of adaptation. In: D. Rapaport (Ed.), *Organization and Pathology of Thought: Selected Sources* (pp. 362–396). New York: Columbia University Press, 1951.

Hartmann, H. (1960). *Psychoanalysis and Moral Values*. New York: International Universities Press.

Hartmann, H. (1964). *Essays on Ego Psychology*. New York: International Universities Press.

Hawking, S. W. (1988). *A Brief History of Time*. New York: Bantam Books.

Heisenberg, W. (1971). *Physics and Beyond*. New York: Harper and Row.

Holt, E. (1967). Beyond vitalism and mechanism: Freud's concept of psychic energy. In: J. Masserman (Ed.), *Science and Psychoanalysis* (Vol. 11) (pp. 1–41). New York: Grune & Stratton.

Holt, R. (1989). *Freud Reappraised: A Fresh Look at Psychoanalytic Theory*. Guildford: New York.

Horowitz, M. (1988). *Introduction to Psychodynamics*. New York: Basic Books.

Ingvar, D. (1979). Brain activation patterns revealed in measurements of regional cerebral blood flow. In: J. E. Desmedt (Ed.), *Progress in Clinical Neurophysiology* (Volume 6) (pp. 200–215). London: S. Karger.

Ingvar, D. (1994). Motor memory—a memory of the future. *Behavioral and Brain Sciences, 17*: 210–211.

Ito, M. (1981). *Blueprints of the Brain.* Tokyo: Shizen. [Japanese]

Ito, M. (1982). Questions in modeling the cerebellum, *Journal of Theoretical Biology, 99*: 81–86.

Ito, M. (1984a). The modifiable neural network of the cerebellum. *Japanese Journal of Physiology, 34*: 781–792.

Ito, M. (1984b). Cerebellar plasticity and motor learning. *Experimental Brain Research, 9*: 165–169.

Ito, M. (1985a). Synaptic plasticity in the cerebellar cortex that may underlie the vestibulo-ocular adaptation. In: A. Berthoz & M. Jones (Ed.), *Adaptive Mechanisms in Gaze Control* (pp. 213–221). Amsterdam: Elsevier.

Ito, M. (1985b). Memory system in the cerebellum. In: Y. Tsukada (Ed.), *Perspectives on Neuroscience: From Molecule to Mind* (pp. 214–235). Tokyo: University of Tokyo Press.

Ito, M. (1986). *The Cerebellum and Neural Control.* New York: Raven Press.

Ito, M. (1988). Neural control as a major aspect of higher-order brain function. Presented to the Pontifical Academy Symposium on Principles of Design and Operation of the Brain, Rome, Italy.

Ito, M. (1993). How does the cerebellum facilitate thought? In: T. Ono, L. R. Squire, M. B. Raichle, D. A. Perret, & M. Fukuda (Eds.), *Brain Mechanisms of Perception and Memory* (pp. 651–658). Oxford: Oxford University Press.

Ito, M. (1998). Consciousness from the viewpoint of the structural–functional relationships of the brain. *International Journal of Psychology, 33*(3): 191–197.

Iverson, S. D. (1984). Behavioral effects of manipulation of basal ganglia neurotransmitters. In: D. Evered & M. O. O'Connor (Eds.), *Functions of the Basal Ganglia* (pp. 183–200). London: Pitman Press.

Iwata, M. (1996). Creativity in modern painting and the cerebral mechanism of vision. *The Annual of Psychoanalysis, 24*: 113–130.

Jackson, E. A. (1989). *Perspectives of Nonlinear Dynamics.* Oxford: Oxford University Press.

Jeannerod, M. (1985). *The Brain Machine.* Cambridge, MA: Harvard University Press.

Jeannerod, M. (1994). The representing brain: Neural correlates of motor intention and imagery. *Behavioral and Brain Sciences, 17*: 187–202.

Johnson-Laird, P. (1977). *Human and Machine Thinking*. Hillsdale, NJ: Lawrence Erlbaum.

Just, M. A., Carpenter, P. A., Keller, T. A., Eddy, W. F., & Thulborn, K. R. (1996). Brain activation modulated by sentence comprehension. *Science, 274*: 114–116.

Kallert, T. W. (1993). Selected aspects of coping with illness and psychotherapeutic treatment of stroke patients, *Rehabilitation (Stuttg.), 32*(2): 99–106 [German].

Kandel, E. R. (1976). *The Cellular Basis of Behavior*. New York: Freeman.

Kandel, E. R. (1998). A new intellectual framework for psychiatry. *American Journal of Psychiatry, 155*: 457–469.

Kandel, E. R., & Spencer, W. A. (1968). Cellular neurophysiological approaches to the study of learning. *Physiological Reviews, 48*: 65–135.

Kaplan-DeNour, A., & Bauman, A. (1980). Psychiatric treatment in severe brain injury: a case report. *General Hospital Psychiatry, 2*(1): 23–34.

Kempermann, G., & Gage, F. H. (1998). Closer to neurogenesis in adult humans. *Nature Medicine, 4*(5): 555–157.

Kempermann, G., Brandan, E. P., & Gage, F. H. (1998). Environmental stimulation of 129/SvJ mice causes increased cell proliferation and neurogenesis in the adult dentate gyrus. *Current Biology, 8*(16): 939–942.

Kent, E. W. (1981). *The Brains of Men and Machines*. Peterborough, NH: BYTE/McGraw-Hill.

Kesner, R. P. (1984). The neurobiology of memory: Implicit and explicit assumptions. In: G. Lynch, J. L. McGaugh, & N. M. Weinberger (Eds.), *Neurobiology of Learning and Memory* (pp. 111–118). New York: Guilford Press.

Kety, S. (1982). The evolution of concepts of memory. In: A. L. Beckman (Ed.), *The Neural Basis of Behavior* (pp. 95–101). Jamaica, NY: Spectrum.

Kiell, N. (1988). *Freud Without Hindsight: Reviews of His Work (1893–1938)*. Madison, CT: International Universities Press.

Kim, S.-G., Ugurbil, K., & Strick, P. L. (1994). Activation of a cerebellar output nucleus during cognitive processing, *Science, 265*: 949–951.

Klein, G. (1968). *Psychoanalytic Theory: An Exploration of Essentials*. New York: International Universities Press.

Klein, G. (1976). *Psychoanalytic Theory*. New York: International Universities Press.

Kohut, H. (1971). *The Analysis of the Self*. New York: International Universities Press.

Kohut, H., & Seitz, P. F. (1963). Concepts and theories of psychoanalysis. In: J. M. Wepman & R. Heine (Eds.), *Concepts of Personality* (pp. 113–141). Chicago, IL: Aldine.

Kramer, M. S., Cutler, N., Feighner, J., Shrivastava, R., Carman, J., Sramek, J. J., Reines, S. A., Liu, G., Snavely, D., Wyatt-Knowles, E., Hale, J. J., Mills, S. G., MacCoss, M., Swain, C. J., Harrison, T., Hill, R. G., Hefti, F., Scolnick, E. M., Cascieri, M. A., Chicchi, G. G., Sadowski, S., Williams, A. R., Hewson, L., Smith, D., Carlson, E. J., Hargreaves, R. J., & Rupniak, N. M. J. (1998). Distinct mechanism for antidepressant activity by blockade of central substance P receptors. *Science, 281*: 1640–1644.

Langer, S. K. (1967). *Mind: An Essay on Human Feeling, Volume 1*. Baltimore, MD: Johns Hopkins University Press.

Lashley, K. S. (1950). In search of the engram, *Symposium Soc. Exp. Biol., 4*: 454–482.

Lassen, N. A. (1987). Cerebral blood flow measured by Xenon-133. *Nuclear Medicine Communications, 8*: 535–548.

Lassen, N. A. (1994a). [Where do thoughts occur?] *Ugeskrift for Laeger, 156*(27), 4004–4005 [Dutch].

Lassen, N. A. (1994b). Where do thoughts occur? Paper presented to Psyche '94, International Symposium on Mind, Brain, and Body, Osaka.

Lassen, N. A., & Ingvar, D. H. (1961). The blood flow of the cerebral cortex determined by radioactive krypton-85. *Experientia, 17*: 42–43.

Lassen, N. A., Ingvar, D. H., & Skinhøj, E. (1978). Brain function and blood flow. *Scientific American, 239*: 62–71.

Leavy, D. E. (1992). William James and the art of human understanding. *The American Psychologist, 47*:152–160.

LeDoux, J. (1996). Remembering the past: Two facets of episodic memory explored with PET. Presented to the American College of Psychoanalysts, New York, 3 May.

Levenson, E. A. (1994). The uses of disorder—chaos theory and psychoanalysis. *Contemporary Psychoanalysis, 30*: 5–27.

Levey, M. (1984–1985). The concept of structure in psychoanalysis. *Annals of Psychoanalysis, 8*: 321–348.

Levin, F. M. (1980). Metaphor, affect, and arousal: How interpretations might work. *The Annual of Psychoanalysis, 8*: 231–248.

Levin, F. M. (1987). Brain plasticity, learning, and psychoanalysis, *The Annual of Psychoanalysis, 15*: 49–96.

Levin, F. M. (1988a). Introduction. In: Max M. Stern, *Repetition and Trauma* (pp. 2–38). Hillsdale, NJ: Analytic Press.

Levin, F. M. (1988b). Psychological development and the changing organization of the brain. Paper read at the American Psychoanalysis Association, New York.

Levin, F. M. (1989). Discussion of "Psychoanalytic theory and Occam's razor" by J. E. Gedo. Paper read at to the Chicago Psychoanalytic Society.

Levin, F. M. (1991). *Mapping the Mind: The Intersection of Psychoanalysis and Neuroscience.* Hillsdale, NJ: Analytic Press.

Levin, F. M. (1993). The developmental, hierarchical model: neural control, natural language, and the recurrent organization of the brain. In: A. Wilson & J. Gedo (Eds.), *The Hierarchical-Developmental Model* (pp. 153–169). New Haven, CT: Yale University Press.

Levin, F. M. (1994). The relationship between Freud's free associative method, the creation of "windows" (learning readiness), and the self-induced priming of memory. Paper presented to the Houston Psychoanalytic Society, Houston, Texas.

Levin, F. M. (1995a). Notes: Oct. 6–7, 1994, Psyche '94, International Symposium on Mind–Body Problems, Osaka, Japan, *Psychoanalytic Quarterly*, LXIV(2): 429–432.

Levin, F. M. (1995b). Psychoanalysis and interdisciplinary research: The integration of neuroscience and the psychoanalytic theory of learning. *Samiksa: Journal of the Indian Psychoanalytical Society*, 49:1–12.

Levin, F. M. (1995c). Psychoanalysis and knowledge, Part 1: The problem of representation and alternative approaches to learning. *The Annual of Psychoanalysis*, 23: 95–114.

Levin, F. M. (1995d). Psychoanalysis and knowledge, Part 3: Some thoughts on a line of development of a philosophy of mind. *The Annual of Psychoanalysis*, 23: 131–151.

Levin, F. M. (1995e). Psychoanalysis and the brain. In: B. Moore & B. Fine (Eds.), *Psychoanalysis: The Major Concepts* (pp. 537–552). New Haven, CT: Yale University Press.

Levin, F. M. (1995f). Psychoanalysis and knowledge, Part II—The special relationship between psychoanalytic transference, similarity judgment, and the priming of memory. *The Annual of Psychoanalysis*, 23: 117–130.

Levin, F. M. (1996a). Neuroscience reports: Review of Priel and Schrieber on transference and chaos theory. *Psychoanalytic Quarterly*, 65(4): 843–846.

Levin, F. M. (1996b). Review of Priel and Schrieber's work bridging bifurcation theory and psychoanalysis. *Psychoanalytic Inquiry*, *LXV*(4): 843–846.

Levin, F. M. (1997a). Discussion of Mark Solms' "Why consciousness?" *Journal of the American Psychoanalytic Association*, 45(3): 732–739.

Levin, F. M. (1997b). Integrating some mind and brain views of transference: The phenomena. *Journal of the American Psychoanalytic Association*, 45(4):1121–1152.

Levin, F. M. (1997c). Review of Shevrin et al. (1996). In: *General Hospital Psychiatry*. New York: Elsevier Science, Inc.

Levin, F. M. (1997d). Discussion of Galatzer-Levy's paper: Towards a new model of development, presented to the Chicago Psychoanalytic Society, October 28.

Levin, F. M. (1997e). Discussion of paper by Michael I. Posner on the Executive Control Network, at the meeting of the American College of Psychoanalysts, San Diego, CA, May 19.

Levin, F. M. (1997f). Neuroscience Section. The amygdala, hippocampus, and psychoanalysis. *Psychoanalytic Quarterly*, *LXVI*(3): 555–568.

Levin, F. M. (1997g). Some thoughts on attention. *Samiksa: Journal of the Indian Psychoanalytic Society*, 51: 23–30.

Levin, F. M. (1998). The Freudian unconsciousness: Its function as seen from the perspective of recent developments in psychoanalysis, cognitive psychology, and neuroscience, Presentation to the Washington Psychoanalytic Foundation, Feb. 7, Arlington, VA.

Levin, F. M. (2000a). Review of papers presented to the 65th Anniversary Symposium of the Chicago Institute for Psychoanalysis. *The Annual of Psychoanalysis*, 28: 3–5.

Levin, F. M. (2000b). Learning, development, and psychopathology: applying chaos theory to psychoanalysis. *The Annual of Psychoanalysis*, 28: 85–104.

Levin, F. M. (2009). *Emotion and the Psychodynamics of the Cerebellum*. London: Karnac.

Levin, F. M., & Gunther, M. (1996). The psychoanalytic treatment of neuropsychiatric patients. *Samiksa: Journal of the Indian Psychoanalytical Society*, 50: 21–29.

Levin, F. M., & Kent, E. W. (1994). Psychoanalytic transference, judging similarity, and the priming of memory: One phenomenon, three perspectives. Paper presented to Psyche '94, International Symposium on Mind, Brain, and Body, Osaka.

Levin, F. M., & Kent, E. W. (1995). Psychoanalysis and knowledge: Part 2. The special relationship between psychoanalytic transference, similarity judgment, and the priming of memory. *Annual of Psychoanalysis, 50*: 117–130.

Levin, F. M., & Trevarthen, C. (1997). Subtle is the Lord: the relationship between consciousness, the unconscious, and the executive control network (ECN) of the brain, presented to the Gedo Festschrift Symposium, October 18, Chicago, Illinois.

Levin, F. M., & Trevarthen, C. (2000). Subtle is the Lord: the relationship between consciousness, the unconscious, and the executive control network (ECN) of the brain. *The Annual of Psychoanalysis, 28*: 105–125.

Levin, F. M., & Vuckovich, D. M. (1983). Psychoanalysis and the two cerebral hemispheres. *Annual of Psychoanalysis, 11*: 171–199.

Levin, F. M., & Vuckovich, D. M. (1987). Brain plasticity, learning and psychoanalysis. *Annual of Psychoanalysis, 15*: 19–96.

Levy, J. (1974). Psychobiological implications of bilateral symmetry. In: S. Dimond & G. Beaumont (Eds.), *Hemispheric Functions in the Human Brain* (pp. 121–183). New York: Halsted Press.

Levy, J., & Trevarthen, C. (1976). Metacontrol of hemispheric function in human split-brain patients. *Journal of Experimental Psychology: Human Perception and Performance, 2*(3): 299–312.

Libet, B. (1993). The neural time factor in conscious and unconscious events. In: T. Nagel (Ed.), *Experimental and Theoretical Studies of Consciousness* (pp. 123–146). CIBA Foundation Symposium 174. New York: Wiley.

Lichtenberg, J. D. (1983). *Psychoanalysis and Infant Research.* Hillsdale, NJ: Analytic Press.

Lichtenberg, J. D. (1989a). *Psychoanalysis and Motivation.* Hillsdale, NJ: Analytic Press.

Lichtenberg, J. D. (1989b). A theory of motivational–functional systems as psychic structure. *Journal of the American Psychoanalytic Association, 3*: 57–72.

Luborsky, L., Bachrach, H., Graff, H., Pulver, S., & Christoph, P. (1979). Preconditions and consequences of transference interpretations: a clinical investigation. *Journal of Nervous Mental Diseases, 167*: 391–401.

Lynch, G., McGough, J. L., & Weinberger, N. M. (Eds.) (1984). *Neurobiology of Learning and Memory.* New York: Guilford Press.

MacLean, P. (1985). Stepwise brain evolution with respect to socialization and speech. Paper read at the American Academy of Adolescence, Dallas, Texas.

Magistretti, P. J., Pellerin, L., Rothman, D. L., & Shulman, R. G. (1999). Energy on demand. *Science, 283*: 496–497.

Makara, G. B., Palkovits, M., & Szentágothai, J. (1980). The endocrine hypothalamus and the hormonal response to stress. In: H. Selye (Ed.), *Selye's Guide to Stress Research* (pp. 280–337) New York: Van Nostrand Reinhold.

Margolis, H. (1987). *Patterns, Thinking, and Cognition.* Chicago, IL: University of Chicago Press.

Marshall, E. (1998). Use of stem cells still legally murky, but hearing offers hope. *Science, 282*: 1962–1963.

Matte Blanco, I. (1986). Understanding Matte Blanco. *International Journal of Psychoanalysis, 67*: 251–273.

Matte Blanco, I. (1989). Comments on "From Symmetry to Asymmetry" by Klaus Fink. *International Journal of Psychoanalysis, 78*: 491–496.

Mattingly, J. B., Davis, G., & Driver, J. (1997). Preattentive filling-in of visual surfaces in parietal extinction. *Science, 275*: 671–674.

McCorduck, P. (1979). *Machines Who Think.* San Francisco, CA: W. H. Freeman.

Medin, D. L., Goldstone, R. L., & Gentner, D. (1993). Respects for similarity. *Psychology Review, 100*(2): 254–278.

Merzenich, M. M., Randall, J. N., Stryker, M. P., Cynander, M. S., Schoppmann, A., & Zook, J. M. (1984). Somatosensory cortical maps change following digit amputation in adult monkeys. *Journal of Comparative Neurology, 224*: 591–605.

Meyersberg, H. A., & Post, R. M. (1979). A holistic developmental view of neural and psychological process, *British Journal of Psychiatry, 135*: 139–155.

Minshew, N. J. (1992). Neurological localization in autism. In: E. Schopler & G. B. Mesibov (Eds.), *High-Functioning Individuals with Autism* (pp. 65–90). New York: Plenum Press.

Modell, A. (1978). The nature of psychoanalytic knowledge. *Journal of the American Psychoanalytic Association, 26*: 641–658.

Modell, A. (1993). *The Private Self.* Cambridge, MA: Harvard University Press.

Modell, A. (1997). The synergy of memory, affects and metaphor. *Journal of Analytical Psychology, 42*:105–117.

Moore, B. E. (1988). On affects. In: H. Blum, Y. Kramer, A. D. Richards, & A. Richards (Eds.), *Fantasy, Myth, and Reality* (pp. 401–419). New York: International Universities Press.

Moore, B. E., & Fine, B. (1968). *A Glossary of Psychoanalytic Terms and Concepts*. New York: American Psychoanalytic Association.

Moraitis, G. (1988). Exploration of the phobias as the fear of the unknown. *Annual of Psychoanalysis, 16*: 231–250.

Moraitis, G. (1991). Phobias and the pursuit of novelty. *Psychoanalytic Inquiry, 11*: 296–315.

Moran, M. G. (1991). Chaos theory and psychoanalysis: The fluidic nature of the mind. *International Journal of Psychoanalysis, 18*: 211–221.

Morell, V. (1996). Research news: Setting a biological stopwatch. *Science, 271*: 905–906.

Morozov, A. M. (1989a). Psychotherapy of post-traumatic borderline neuropsychiatric disorders. *Vrach. Delo., 2*: 88–90. [Russian]

Morozov, A. M. (1989b). Psychotherapy of patients with a history of craniocerebral trauma. *Zh. Vopr. Neirokhir., 5*: 41–43. [Russian]

Morris, M. E., Viswanathan, N., Kuhlman, S., Davis, F. C., & Weltz, C. J. (1998). A screen for genes induced in the suprachiasmic nucleus by light. *Science, 279*: 1544 [This week in Science, p. 1427].

Nagy, E., & Molnar, P. (1994). Homo imitans or Homo provocans? Abstract. *International Journal of Psychophysiology, 18*(2): 128.

Newell, A., & Simon, H. A. (1985). Computer science as empirical inquiry: Symbols and search. In: J. Haugeland (Ed.), *Mind Design: Philosophy, Psychology, and Artificial Intelligence* (pp. 35–66). Cambridge, MA: MIT Press.

Nicolis, G., & Prigonine, I. (1981). Symmetry breaking and pattern selection in far from equilibrium systems. *Proceedings of the National Academy of Science of the U.S.A., 78*: 659–663.

Nicolis, G., & Prigonine, I. (1989). Dynamical systems and complexity. In: *Exploring Complexity*. New York: Freeman.

Nielsen, J. R. (Ed.) (1977). *The Collected Works of Niels Bohr, Volume 10, Complementarity Beyond Physics (1928–1962)*. Amsterdam: North Holland Publishing.

Niwa, S.-I. (1989). Schizophrenic symptoms, pathogenic cognition, and behavioral features: Discussion of the 'language' of the brain and of 'mind'. In: M. Namba & H. Kaiya (Eds.), *Main Currents of Schizophrenia Research*. Tokyo: Hesco International [Japanese].

Nottebohm, F. (1985). Neuronal replacement in adulthood, *Annals of the New York Academy of Science, 457*: 143–162.

Nunberg, H., & Federn, E. (Eds.) (1975). *Minutes of the Vienna Psychoanalytic Society*, vol. 4. New York: International Universities Press.

Olds, D. D. (1992). Consciousness: A brain-centered informational approach. *Psychoanalytic Inquiry, 12*(3): 419–444.

Olds, D. D. (1994). Connectionism and psychoanalysis. *Journal of the American Psychoanalytic Association, 42*: 581–612.

Olds, D. D. (1997). Introduction (Commentary on paper by Mark Solms). *Journal of the American Psychoanalytic Association, 45*(3): 704–706.

Opatow, B. (1998). The distinctiveness of the psychoanalytic unconscious. *Journal of the American Psychoanalytic Association, 45*(3): 865–890.

Orenstein, M. (1992). Imprisoned intelligence. Unpublished doctoral dissertation, The Institute for Clinical Social Work (Chicago).

Orenstein, M. (1999). *Smart But Stuck*. New York: Haworth Press.

Pally, R. (1997). Developments in neuroscience, I: How brain development is shaped by genetic and environmental factors. *International Journal of Psychoanalysis, 78*: 587–594.

Palombo, J. (1985). The treatment of borderline neurocognitively impaired children. *Clinical Social Work Journal, 13*: 117–128.

Palombo, J. (1987). Selfobject transferences in the treatment of borderline neurocognitively impaired children. *Child and Adolescent Social Work Journal, 1*: 18–33.

Palombo, S. R. (1992). Connectivity and condensation in dreaming. *Journal of the American Psychoanalytic Association, 40*: 1139–1159.

Palombo, S. R. (1998). *The Emergent Ego: Complexity and Coevolution in the Psychoanalytic Process*. Madison, CT: International Universities Press.

Peitgen, H.-O., Jürgens, H., & Saupe, D. (1992). *Chaos and Fractals: New Frontiers of Science*. New York: Springer-Verlag.

Persinger, M. A. (1993). Personality changes following brain injury as a grief response to the loss of the sense of self: phenomenological themes as indices of local liability and neurocognitive structuring as psychotherapy. *Psychological Reports, 72*(3): 1059–1068.

Peterfreund, E. (1971). Information systems and psychoanalysis, *Psychological Issues*, Monograph, 25–26. New York: International Universities Press.

Pfeffer, A. (1961). Follow-up study of a satisfactory analysis. *Journal of the American Psychoanalytic Association, 9*: 698–718.

Pfeffer, A. (1963). The meaning of the analyst after analysis: A contribution to the theory of therapeutic results. *Journal of the American Psychoanalytic Association, 11*: 229–244.

Poincaré, H. (1916–1954). *Oeuvres de Henri Poincaré, 10 volumes.* Paris: Académie des Sciences de Paris.

Polanyi, M., & Prosch, H. (1975). *Meaning.* Chicago, IL: University of Chicago Press.

Pompeiano, M., Cirelli, C., & Tononi, G. (1994). Immediate-early genes in spontaneous wakefulness and sleep: Expression of c-fos, NGFI-A mRNA, and protein J. *Sleep Research, 3*: 80–96.

Pompian, N. W., & Thum, D. P. (1988). Dyslexic/learning disabled students at Dartmouth. *Annals of Dyslexia, 38*: 278–286.

Posner, M. I. (1988). Structures and functions of selective attention. In: T. Boll & B. Bryant (Eds.), *Master Lectures in Clinical Neuropsychology and Brain Function: Research, Measurement, and Practice* (pp. 171–202). Washington, DC: American Psychological Association.

Posner, M. I. (1994). Attention: The mechanisms of consciousness. *Proceedings of the National Academy of Science* (USA), *91*: 7398–7403.

Posner, M. I. (1995). Seeing the mind. *Science, 262*: 673–674.

Posner, M. I. (1996). New images of mind. *The General Psychologist, 32*(3): 79–84.

Posner, M. I., & DiGirolamo, G. J. (1996). Conflict, target detection and cognitive control. Technical Report No. 96-02, Institute of Cognitive and Decision Sciences, University of Oregon.

Posner, M. I., & Raichle, M. (1994). *Images of Mind.* New York: Scientific American Library.

Posner, M. I., & Rothbart, M. K. (1994a). Attentional regulation: From mechanism to culture. In: P. Bertelson, P. Elen, and G. d'Ydewalle (Eds.), *International Perspectives on Psychological Science, Vol. 1, Leading Themes* (pp. 41–55). Hillsdale, NJ: Lawrence Erlbaum.

Posner, M. I., & Rothbart, M. K. (1994b). Constructing neuronal theories of mind. In: C. Koch & J. L. Davis (Eds.), *Large-Scale Neuronal theories of the Brain* (pp. 183–199). Cambridge, MA: MIT Press.

Posner, M. I., & Rothbart, M. K. (1995). Attentional regulation: From mechanism to culture. In: P. Bertelson, P. Eelen, & G. D'Ydavalle (Eds.) *Current Advances in Psychological Science* (pp. 41–55). London: Erlbaum.

Posner, M. I., & Rothbart, M. K. (1997). Attention, self regulation, and consciousness. Presented to the Association for Research on Nervous and Mental Diseases, New York, Dec. 5–6, 1997.

Posner, M. I., Abdullaev, Y. G., McCandliss, B. D., & Sereno, S. C. (1992). Anatomy, circuitry and plasticity of word reading. Technical Report No. 96-04, University of Oregon, Institute of Cognitive and Decision Sciences. (Also appears in: *Normal Reading and Dyslexia*, J. Everatt (Ed.), London: Routledge).

Pribram, K. H. (1962). The neuropsychology of Sigmund Freud. In: A. J. Bachrach (Ed.), *Experimental Foundations of Clinical Psychology* (pp. 442–468). New York: Basic Books.

Pribram, K. H., & Gill, M. M. (1976). *Freud's Project Reassessed*. New York: Basic Books.

Priel, B., & Schreiber, G. (1994). On psychoanalysis and non-linear dynamics: The paradigm of bifurcation. *British Journal of Medical Psychology, 67*)(3): 209–218.

Provence, S., & Lipton, R. (1962). *Infants in Institutions*. New York: International Universities Press.

Quinodoz, J.-M. (1997). Transitions in psychic structures in the light of deterministic chaos theory. *International Journal of Psychoanalysis, 78*(4): 699–718.

Rakik, P. (1985). Limits of neurogenesis. *Science, 227*: 1054–1056.

Random House College Dictionary, Revised Edition (1988). New York: Random House.

Rao, S. C., Rainer, G., & Miller, E. K. (1997). Integration of what and where in the primate prefrontal cortex. *Science, 276*: 821–824.

Rapaport, D. (1950). *Emotions and Memory* (2nd edn). New York: International Universities Press.

Rapaport, D. (Ed. and Trans.) (1951a). *Organization and Pathology of Thought: Selected Sources*. Austen Riggs Foundation Monograph No. 1. New York: Columbia University Press.

Rapaport, D. (1951b). Conclusion: Towards a theory of thinking. In: D. Rapaport (Ed. and Trans.), *Organization and Pathology of Thought: Selected Sources* (pp. 689–730). Austin Riggs Foundation Monograph No. 1. New York: Columbia University Press.

Rapaport, D. (1974). *The History of the Concept of Association of Ideas*. New York: International Universities Press.

Rapaport, D., & Gill, M. M. (1967). The point of view and assumptions of metapsychology. In: M. M. Gill (Ed.), *Collected Papers of David Rapaport* (pp. 795–811). New York: Basic Books.

Rees, G., Frackowiak, R., & Firth, C. (1997). Two modulatory effects of attention that mediate object categorization in human cortex. *Science, 275*: 835–838.

Reiser, M. F. (1984). *Mind, Brain, Body*. New York: Basic Books.

Reiser, M. F. (1990). *Memory in Mind and Brain*. New York: Basic Books.

Relkin, N., Plum, F., Mattis, S., Eidelberg, D., & Tranel, D. (1996). Impulsive homicide associated with an arachnoid cyst and unilateral frontotemporal cerebral dysfunction. *Seminars in Neuropsychiatry, 1*(3): 172–183.

Reps, P. (1961). *Zen Flesh, Zen Bones*. Rutland, VT: Charles E. Tuttle.

Retterstol, N. (1983). Course of paranoid psychosis in relation to diagnostic group. *Psychiatric Clinics of North America*, 16:198–206.

Rettersol, N. (1985). The course of paranoid psychoses in relation to diagnostic grouping. In: P. Pichot, P. Berner, R. Wolf, & K. Thau (Eds.), *Psychiatry* (pp. 551–556). New York: Plenum.

Reynolds, G. P. (1987). Dopamine receptor asymmetry in schizophrenia. *Lancet*, 25: 979.

Ricoeur, P. (1981). The metaphorical process as cognition, imagination, and feeling. In: M. Johnson (Ed.), *Philosophical Perspectives on Metaphor* (pp. 228–247). Minneapolis: University of Minnesota Press.

Rizzuto, A. M. (1990). The origins of Freud's concept of object representation ("Objektvorstellung") in his monograph "On Aphasia: its theoretical and technical importance." *International Journal of Psychoanalysis, 71*(2): 241–248.

Roland, E. J. (1981). Somatotopical tuning of post-central gyrus during focal attention in man. A regional cerebral blood flow study. *Journal of Neurophysiology, 46*: 744–754.

Roland, E. J., & Friberg, L. (1985). Localization of cortical area activated by thinking. *Journal of Neurophysiology, 53*: 1219–1243.

Roose, S. P. (1994). Depression as illness, depression as psychic state: Conflicts in theory and treatment. Presented to Psyche '94, Symposium on Mind–Body Problems, Osaka, Japan, Oct 6.

Rosenblatt, A. D., & Thickstun, J. T. (1977). *Modern Psychoanalytic Concepts in a General Psychology, Psychological Issues, Monograph 11*. New York: International Universities Press.

Rosenblatt, A. D., & Thickstun, J. T. (1994). Intuition and consciousness. *Psychoanalytic Quarterly, 63*(4): 696–714.

Rosenzweig, M. R., & Bennett, E. L. (Eds.) (1976). *Neural Mechanisms of Learning and Memory*. Cambridge, MA: MIT Press.

Ross, W. D. (Ed.) (1955–1962). *The Works of Aristotle*, Vols. 1–12. Oxford: Clarendon Press.

Rubinstein, B. B. (1974). On the role of classificatory processes in mental functioning: Aspects of a psychoanalytic theoretical method. *Psychoanalysis and Contemporary Science, 3*: 101–185.

Rubinstein, B. B. (1976). Hope, fear, wish, expectation, and fantasy. *Psychoanalysis and Contemporary Science, 5* P3–60.

Rubinstein, B. B. (1997). *Psychoanalysis and the Philosophy of Science,* R. Holt (Ed.). *Psychological Issues Monograph, 62/63,* Madison, CT: International Universities Press.

Ryle, G. (1949). *The Concept of Mind.* London: Hutchison's University Library.

Ryle, G. (1971). Category, s.v. *Encyclopedia Britannica.* Chicago, IL: William Benton.

Sacks, O. (1984). *A Leg to Stand On.* New York: Summit Books.

Saitoh, O., Niwa, S., Hiramatsu, K., Kameyama, T., Rymer, K., & Ito, K. (1984a). Abnormalities in late positive components of event-related potentials may reflect a genetic predisposition to schizophrenia. *Biological Psychiatry, 19*: 293–303.

Saitoh, O., Niwa, S., Hiramatsu, K., Kameyama, T., Rymer, K., & Ito, K. (1984b). P-300 in siblings of schizophrenic probands. In: J. Mendelwicz & H. M. van Praag (Eds.), *Advances in Biological Psychiatry* (pp. 46–59. New York: Karger.

Salton, G. (1991). Developments in automated text retrieval. *Science, 253*: 974–980.

Sameroff, A. (1983). Developmental systems. In: P. Mussen (Ed.), *Handbook of Child Psychology* (pp. 237–294). New York: Wiley.

Sandin, K. J., Cifu, D. X., & Noll, S. F. (1994). Stroke rehabilitation: Part 4—Psychologic and social implications. *Archives of Physical and Medical Rehabilitation, 5*(Spec. No): S52–55.

Sandler, J. (1996). The unconscious and the representational world. *Samiksa, 50*: 1–10.

Sandler, J., & Rosenblatt, B. (1962). The concept of the representational world. *Psychoanalytic Study of the Child, 17*: 128–145.

Sasaki, K., Tsujimoto, T., Nambu, A., Matsuzaki, R., & Kyuhou, S. (1994). Dynamic activities of the frontal cortex in calculating and thinking. *Neuroscience Research, 19*: 229–233.

Sashin, J. (1985). Affect tolerance: A model of affect-response using catastrophe theory. *Journal of Social and Biological Structures, 8*: 175–202.

Sashin, J., & Callahan, J. (1990). A model of affect using dynamical system. *The Annual of Psychoanalysis, 18*: 213–231.

Schafer, R. (1976). *A New Language for Psychoanalysis*. New Haven, CT: Yale University Press.

Scheidt, D. E., & Schwind, A. (1992). Psychodynamic aspects of coping with illness in stroke: experiences with a psychotherapy group, ["Abteilung Psychotherapie und Psychosomatik"] *Psychotherapy, Psychosomatik, Midizinische Psychologie, 42*(2): 54–59. [German]

Schiff, S. J., Jerger, K., Duong, D. H., Chang, T., Spano, M. L., & Ditto, W. L. (1994). Controlling chaos in the brain. *Nature, 370*(6491): 615–620.

Schildkraut, J. J., & Kety, S. (1967). Biogenic amines and emotion. *Science*, 156: 21–30.

Schlessinger, N., & Robbins, F. B. (1983). *A Developmental View of Psychoanalysis*. New York: International Universities Press.

Schlessinger, N., Gedo, J., Miller, J., Pollock, G., Sabshin, M., & Sadow, L. (1967). *The Scientific Styles of Breuer and Freud and the Origins of Psychoanalysis*. *Psychological Issues Monograph 34/35* (pp. 187–207). New York: International Universities Press, 1976.

Schore, A. (1994). *Affect Regulation and the Organization of the Self*. Hillsdale, NJ: Lawrence Erlbaum.

Schore, A. (1997). A century after Freud's Project: Is a rapprochement between psychoanalysis and neurobiology at hand? *Journal of the American Psychoanalytic Association, 45*(3): 807–840.

Schwaber, E. (1983). A particular perspective on analytic listening. *The Psychoanalytic Study of the Child*, 38: 519–546.

Schwartz, A. (1987a). Drives, affects, behavior, and learning: Approaches to a psychobiology of emotion and to an integration of psychoanalytic and neurobiologic thought. *Journal of the American Psychoanalytic Association*, 35: 467–506.

Schwartz, A. (1987b). Reification revistited. Unpublished manuscript.

Schwartz, J. M., Stoessl, P. W., Baxter, L. R. Jr., Martin, K. M., & Phelps, M. E. (1996). Systematic changes in cerebral glucose metabolic rate after successful behavior modification treatment of obsessive compulsive disorder. *Archives of General Psychiatry, 53*(2): 109–113.

Searle, J. (1995a). The mystery of consciousness, Part I. *New York Review of Books, 42*(17): 60.

Searle, J. (1995b). The mystery of consciousness, Part II. *New York Review of Books, 42*(18): 54.

Searle, J. (1995c). Consciousness, its irreducibility. In: T. Honderich (Ed.), *The Oxford Companion to Philosophy* (p. 153). Oxford: Oxford University Press.

Sereno, A. (1996). Parsing cognitive processes: psychopathological and neurophysiological constraints. In: S. Matthysse, F. M. Benes, D. L. Levy & J. Kagan (Eds.), *Psychopathology: An Evolving Science of Mental Disorder* (pp. 407–432). Cambridge: Cambridge University Press.

Shallice, T. (1988). *From Neuropsychology to Mental Structure.* Cambridge: Cambridge University Press.

Shevrin, H. (1973). Brain wave correlates of subliminal stimulation, unconscious attention, primary- and second-process thinking and repressiveness. *Psychological Issues Monograph No. 30, 8*(2): 56–87.

Shevrin, H. (1992). Subliminal perception, memory, and consciousness: cognitive and dynamic aspects. In: R. F. Bornstein & T. S. Pittman (Eds.), *Perception Without Awareness: Cognitive, Clinical, and Social Perspectives* (pp. 123–142). New York: Guilford Press.

Shevrin, H. (1997a). Commentary on Solms' paper. *Journal of the American Psychoanalytical Association, 45*(3): 746–752.

Shevrin, H. (1997b). Psychoanalysis as the patient: High in feeling, low in energy. *Journal of the American Psychoanalytical Association, 45*(3): 746–752

Shevrin, H. (1998a). Why do we need to be conscious? A psychoanalytic answer. In: D. F. Barone, M. Hersen, & V. B. VanHasselt (Eds.), *Advanced Personality* (pp. 1–23). New York: Plenum Press.

Shevrin, H. (1998b). The Freud–Rapaport theory of consciousness. In: R. F. Bornstein & J. M. Masling (Eds.), *Empirical Perspectives on the Psychoanalytic Unconscious, Empirical Studies of Psychoanalytic Theories, Vol. 7* (pp. 45–70). Washington, DC: American Psychological Association.

Shevrin, H., Bond, J., Brakel, L. A. W., Hertel, R. K., & Williams, W. J. (1996). *Conscious and Unconscious Processes: Psychodynamic, Cognitive, and Neurophysiological Convergences.* New York: Guilford Press.

Shin, L. M., Kosslyn, S. M., McNally, R. J., Alpert, N. M., Thompson, W. L., Rauch, S. L., Macklin, M. L., & Pitman, R. K. (1997). Visual imagery and perception in post traumatic stress disorder. *Archives of General Psychiatry, 54*: 233–241.

Siegel, D. J. (1995). Memory, trauma, and psychotherapy. *Journal of Psychotherapy Practice and Research, 4*: 93–122.

Sirigu, A., & Grafman, J. (1996). Selective impairments within episodic memories. *Cortex, 32*: 83–95.

Slap, J. W., & Brown, J. H. (1998). Congruence of the neuroscience of perception and memory with a model of the mind, unpublished manuscript.

Slap, J. W., & Saykin, A. J. (1983). The schema: Basic concepts in a nonmetapsychological model of the mind. *Psychoanalysis and Contemporary Thought*, 6: 305–325.

Slap, J. W., & Slap-Shelton, L. (1991). *The Schema In Clinical Psychoanalysis*. Hillsdale, NJ: Analytic Press.

Smaller, M. (1993). Louis Shapiro: Dean of Chicago analysts. *American Psychoanalyst*, 27(1): 26–67.

Smith, H. F. (1997). Creative misreading: Why we talk past each other. *Journal of the American Psychoanalytic Association*, 45(2): 335–357.

Snyder, S. H. (1984). Neurosciences. *Science*, 225: 1255–1257.

Soderstrom, S., Fogelsjoo, A., Fujl-Meyer, K. S., & Stensson, S. (1988). A program for crisis-intervention after traumatic brain injury. *Scandinavian Journal of Rehabilitation Supplement*, 17: 47–49.

Solms, M. (1997). What is consciousness. *Journal of the American Psychoanalytic Association*, 45(3): 681–703.

Sperry, R. W. (1950). Neural basis of the spontaneous optokinetic response produced by visual inversion. *Journal of Comparative and Physiogical Psychology*, 43: 482–489.

Sperry, R. W. (1952). Neurology and the mind-brain problem. *American Scientist*, 40: 291–312.

Sperry, R. W. (1968). Hemisphere disconnection and unity of consciousness. *American Psychologist*, 23: 723–733.

Sperry, R. W. (1983). Consciousness, personal identity, and the divided brain. *Neuropsychologia*, 22(6): 661–673.

Sperry, R. W., & Zaidel, D. (1977). Some long-term motor effects on cerebral commissurotomy in man. *Neuropsychologia*, 15(2): 193–204.

Spitz, R. A. (1945). Hospitalism, *Psychoanalytic Study of the Child*, 1: 53–74.

Spitz, R. A. (1965). *The First Year of Life*. New York: International Universities Press.

Springer, S. P., & Deutsch, G. (1981). *Left Brain, Right Brain*. San Francisco, CA: Freeman.

Spruiell, V. (1993). Deterministic chaos and the sciences of complexity: Psychoanalysis in the midst of a general scientific revolution. *Journal of the American Psychoanalytic Association*, 41(1): 3–44.

Squire, L. R., & Zola-Morgan, S. (1991). The medial temporal memory system. *Science*, 253: 1380–1385.

Stablum, F., Leonardi, G., Mazzoldi, M., Umiltà, C., & Morra, S. (1994). Attention and control deficits following closed head injury. *Cortex*, XXX(4): 603–618.

Stablum, F., Mogentale, C., & Umiltà, C. (1996). Executive functioning following mild closed head injury. *Cortex, 32*: 261–278.

Stern, D. N. (1985). *The Interpersonal World of the Infant*. New York: Basic Books.

Stern, D. N. (1997). *Unformulated Experience*. Hillsdale, NJ: Analytic Press.

Stern, J. M. (1985). The quality of the psychotherapeutic process in brain-injured patients. *Scandinavian Journal of Rehabilitation Medicine Supplement, 12*: 42–43.

Stern, M. M. (1988). *Repetition and Trauma: Toward a Teleonomic Theory of Psychoanalysis*. Hillsdale, NJ: Analytic Press.

Stone, L. (1995). Transference. In: B. E. Moore & B. D. Fine (Eds.), *Psychoanalysis: The Major Concepts* (pp. 110–120). New Haven, CT: Yale University Press.

Strachey, J. (1950). Editor's introduction to Freud's Project. *S.E., 1*: 292–293. London: Hogarth Press.

Strenger, C. (1991). *Between Hermeutics and Science: Psychological Issues Monograph 59*. New York: International Universities Press.

Stuss, D. T., Picton, T. W., & Alexander, M. P. (2001). Consciousness, self-awareness and the frontal lobes. In: S. Salloway, P. Malloy, & J. Duffy (Eds.), *The Frontal Lobes and Neuropsychiatric Illness*. Washington, DC: American Psychiatric Press.

Thom, R. (1975). *Structural Stability and Morphogenesis: An Outline of a General Theory of Models*. Reading, PA: Benjamin.

Thomas, A. W. (1995). *Confronting the Infinite*. Singapore: World Scientific.

Thompson, R. F. (1986). The neurobiology of learning and memory. *Science, 233*: 941–947.

Thompson, R. F. (1987). Activity-dependence of network properties. In: J.-P. Changeux & M. Konishi (Ed.), *The Neural and Molecular Basis of Learning* (pp. 473–550). Chichester, NY: Wiley.

Tononi, G., & Edelman, G. M. (1998). Consciousness and complexity. *Science, 282*: 1846–1851.

Toulmin, S. (1975). Self-knowledge and knowledge of the "self". Presented to the Center for Psychosocial Studies, Chicago.

Tranel, E., & Damasio, A. R. (1985). Knowledge without awareness: An autonomic index of facial recognition by prosopagnosics. *Science, 228*: 1453–1454.

Trevarthen, C. (1975). Psychological activities after forebrain commissurotomy in man: concepts, and methodological hurdles in testing. In: F. Michel & B. Schott (Eds.), *Les Syndromes de Disconnxion*

Calleuse Chez L'Homme, Actes du Colloque interntional de LYON 1974 (pp. 181–210). Lyon: Hôpital Neurologique.

Trevarthen, C. (1979). The tasks of consciousness: How could the brain do them? *CIBA Foundation Series 69, Excerpta Medica* (pp. 187–252). Amsterdam: Elsevier.

Trevarthen, C. (1984). Hemispheric specialization. In: S. R. Gieger et al. (Eds.), *Handbook of Physiology* (Volume 2) (pp. 1129–1190). Washington, DC: American Physiological Society.

Trevarthen, C. (1985). Facial expressions of emotion in mother–infant interaction. *Human Neurobiology, 9*: 21–32.

Trevarthen, C. (1989). Development of early social interactions and the affective regulation of brain growth. In: C. von Euler, H. Forssberg, & Hugo Lagercrantz (with V. Landin) (Eds.), *Neurobiology of Early Infant Behaviour: Proceedings of an International Wallenberg Symposium at the Wenner-Gren Center, Stockholm, August 28-September 1, 1988* (pp. 191–216). Basingstoke, Hampshire: Macmillan.

Trevarthen, C. (1990). Integrative functions of the cerebral commissures. In: F. Boller & J. Grafman (Eds.), *Handbook of Neuropsychology, Vol. 4* (pp. 49–83). New York: Elsevier (Biomedical Division).

Trevarthen, C. (1993). Brain science and the human spirit. In: J. B. Ashbrook (Ed.), *Brain, Culture, and the Human Spirit: Essays from an Emergent Evolutionary Perspective* (pp. 129–181). Lanham, New York: University of America.

Trevarthen, C. (1995). Contracts of mutual understanding: Negotiating meanings and moral sentiments with infants. *Journal of Contemporary Legal Issues, 6*: 373–405.

Trevarthen, C. (1997). Macmurray's 'mother and child': Defining the infant's natural place in the field of the personal. In: H. A. Carson (Ed.), *The Primacy of Persons as Agents in Relationships: Essays on the Post Modern Philosophy of John Mcmurray* (pp. 1–24). Atlantic Heights, NJ: Humanities Press International.

Tucker, D. M., Watson, R. T., & Heilman, K. M. (1977). Discrimination and evocation of affectively intoned speech in patients with right parietal disease. *Neurology, 27*: 947–950.

Ungerleider, L. G. (1995). Functional brain imaging studies of cortical mechanisms for memory. *Science, 270*: 769–775.

Urade, Y., Kitahama, K., Ohishi, H., Haneko, T., Mizuno, N., & Hayashi, O. (1993). Dominant expression of mRNA for prostaglandin D synthase in leptomeninges, choroid plexus, and oligodendrocytes of the adult rat brain, *Proceedings of the National Academy of Science USA, 90*: 9070–9074.

Usher, M., Cohen, J. D., Servan-Schreiber, D., Rajkowski, J., & Aston-Jones, G. (1999). The role of the locus coeruleus in the regulation of cognitive performance. *Science, 283*: 549–554.

Utena, H. (1996). Loss of freedom in mental disorders: A biopsychosocial conception. *The Annual of Psychoanalysis, 24*: 131–140.

Van der Kolk, B. A. (1997). The psychobiology of post traumatic stress disorder. *The Journal of Clinical Psychiatry, 58*(Suppl. 9): 16–24.

Vargha-Khadem, F., Gadian, D. G., Watkins, K. E., Connelly, A., Paesschen, W. Van, & Mishkin, M. (1997). Differential effects of early hippocampal pathology on episodic and semantic memory. *Science, 277*: 376–380.

Vygotsky, L. S. (1956). *Selected Psychological Investigations.* Moscow: Izdatel'stve Academii Pegagogischeskikh Nauk.

Waelder, R. (1962). Psychoanalysis, scientific method, and philosophy, *Journal of the American Psychoanalytic Association, 10*: 617–637.

Walsh, W. H. (1971). Kant, s.v. *Encyclopedia Britannica* (pp. 217–223). Chicago, IL: William Benton.

Webster's New International Dictionary, 2nd edn, Unabridged (1958). W. A. Neilson (Ed.). Springfield, MA: G. & C. Merriam.

Weinberger, J., & Weiss, J. (1997). The psychoanalytic versus cognitive conception of the unconscious. In: D. J. Stein (Ed.), *Cognitive Science and the Unconscious.* Washington, DC: American Psychoanalytic Press.

White, A. R. (1982). *The Nature of Knowledge.* Totowa, NJ: Rowman and Littlefield.

Whitehead, A. N. (1929). *Process and Reality: An Essay is Cosmology,* D. R. Griffin & D. Sherborne (Eds.). Free Press, 1979.

Wickelgren, I. (1998). New clues to movement control and vision. *Science, 282*: 224–225.

Wilson, A. (1995). Mapping the minds of relational psychoanalysis: Some critiques, questions, and conjectures. *Psychoanalytic Psychology, 12*: 9–29.

Wilson, A., & Gedo, J. E. (Eds.) (1993a). *Hierarchical Concepts in Psychoanalysis: Theory, Research, and Clinical Practice.* New York: Guilford Press.

Wilson, A., & Gedo, J. E. (1993b). Hierarchical concepts in psychoanalysis. In: A. Wilson & J. E. Gedo (Eds.), *Hierarchical Concepts in Psychoanalysis: Theory, Research, and Clinical Practice* (pp. 311–324). New York: Guilford Press.

Wilson, A., & Weinstein, L. (1996). The transference and the zone of proximal development. *Journal of the American Psychoanalytic Association, 44*: 167–200.

Wilson, A., Passik, S. D., & Faude, J. P. (1990). Self-regulation and its failures. In: J. Masling (Ed.), *Empirical Studies of Psychoanalytic Theories* (Volume 3) (pp. 149–213). Hillsdale, NJ: Analytic Press.

Winnicott, D. W. (1960). Ego distortion in terms of true and false self. In: *Maturational Processes and the Facilitory Environment* (pp. 140–152). New York: International Universities Press, 1965.

Winnicott, D. W. (1969). *The Child, the Family, and the Outside World.* Baltimore, MD: Penguin Books.

Winson, J. (1985). *Brain and Psyche: The Biology of the Unconscious.* Garden City, New York: Anchor Press/Doubleday.

Wittgenstein, L. (1953). *Philosophical Investigations.* Oxford: Basil Blackwell.

Wolf, E. (1990). Clinical responsiveness: corrective or empathic? *Psychoanalytic Inquiry, 10*(3): 420–432.

Wong, P. S., Shevrin, H., & Williams, W. (1994). Conscious and nonconscious processes: An ERP index of an anticipatory response in a conditioning paradigm using visually masked stimuli. *Psychophysiology, 1*: 87–101.

Yamawaki, S., Uchitomi, Y., Kugaya, A., Hayashi, T., Okamoto, Y., Takebayashi, M., & Motohashi, N. (1994). Depressive symptoms induced by IFN therapy. Paper read to the International Symposium of Mind–Body Problems, Osaka University Medical School, Osaka, Japan.

Young, J. Z. (1978). *Programs of the Brain.* New York: Oxford University Press.

Zeki, S. (1992). The visual image in mind and brain. *Scientific American, 267*(3): 68–76.

Zeman, A. Z. J., Grayling, A. C., & Lowey, A. (1997). Editorial: Contemporary theories of consciousness. *Journal of Neurology, Neurosurgery, and Psychiatry, 62*: 549–552.

INDEX